"This is the most informed, perceptive, and sensible book I've seen on the subject of evaluating online teaching. It should be required reading for both professors who teach online and those who evaluate their performance."
—Peter Seldin, Distinguished Professor of Management, Pace University and author, *The Teaching Portfolio: A Practical Guide to Improved Performance and Promotion/Tenure Decisions*

"ONLINE EDUCATORS' ALERT! *Evaluating Online Teaching* is a 'best practices handbook' designed expressly for faculty, administrators, and ITs. If you need solid evidence to evaluate the quality of your online teaching or MOOCs, *Evaluating Online Teaching* is the only comprehensive guide to take you through the step-by-step process. It's a must read."
—Ronald A. Berk, professor emeritus, The Johns Hopkins University

"Providing practical, easy-to-follow models and templates grounded in best pedagogical practices, *Evaluating Online Teaching* is an essential resource for educators and administrators committed to ensuring high-quality online courses and programs."
—Steven G. Jones, associate professor of political science, and director, Center for Faculty Development, Georgia College and State University

"Since Higher Ed institutions can no longer run away from the messy business of online teaching evaluation, it is a blessing to have a book like this to offer us not only a solid reason to open the can, but also the practical methods to handle the worms! This is a thorough and ground-breaking resource for administrators, faculty, and support staff to conquer the messiness of online teaching evaluation."
—Sharon Guan, director, Faculty Instructional Technology Services (FITS), DePaul University

"I found the focus on formative approaches especially helpful, as well as the consistent focus on learning outcomes and student engagement rather than a one-size-fits static teaching method for online learning and evaluation. This book provides faculty and administrators a comprehensive guide to assessing online teaching performance without losing sight of the ultimate course goal of enhancing learning."
—Ken Ryalls, president, The IDEA Center

"As an online instructor, I went years without student ratings and had only one administrative review using an instrument designed for face-to-face classes. *Evaluating Online Teaching* offers valuable tools and processes at a critical time, as more instructors teach online every year. This book emphasizes everything important for anyone involved in evaluating online teaching, starting with the premise that online teachers can be as effective as classroom colleagues. The authors advocate a holistic approach and provide the best tools and processes to make that happen."
—Kevin Kelly, online instructor, and former manager of online teaching and learning, San Francisco State University

"As someone who has been teaching online for over 10 years, including teaching courses designed by others and designing and teaching online courses of my own, I found this book to be invaluable to those just starting to teach online or those teaching for years. I thought the book was well organized and did a great job of capturing the interest of the reader with research to back up the content and practical applications making it a useful tool for those teaching online courses."
—Joseph "Mick" La Lopa, associate professor, School of Hospitality and Tourism Management, Purdue University

"Compelled by the demands of teaching across distance, educators at all levels are paying unprecedented attention to instructional design issues. Foremost among these is the question: What should our students know after each phase of instruction, how will we ascertain that each individual has achieved that knowledge, and what changes, if any, are indicated, in the teaching system? Every teacher, student teacher, and administrator who recognizes the importance of this key question will benefit from Tobin, Mandernach, and Taylor's text, with its 'practical guidelines for developing programs, measurement instruments, and campus policies for evaluating online teaching.'"

—Michael Grahame Moore, Distinguished Professor Emeritus of Education, The Pennsylvania State University, and editor, *The American Journal of Distance Education*

"Evaluating online teaching is an increasingly important task. This book provides comprehensive coverage of the context, issues, practices, and strategies for assessing teaching both formatively and summatively. Copiously illustrated with examples and practical tips, this book is a useful resource for those who find themselves faced with the task of examining the quality of instruction in a networked environment."

—Clark Quinn, executive director, Quinnovation, and author, *The Mobile Academy*

"This book is an essential resource for online instructors, department heads, and administrators for whom the evaluation of online teaching has become an increasingly important issue for both policy and practice. The authors emphasize "teaching as teaching" and give practical, research-based guidance on how to design evaluation instruments that respond to the realities of the online teaching environment. They include illustrations from several major online programs and opportunities for readers to reflect on their own practices."

—Gary E. Miller, executive director emeritus, Penn State World Campus

"The authors provide invaluable insights into evaluation as a critical element in the continuing evolution of online learning. With many practical examples, it is a fine read for faculty, administrators, and researchers."

—Anthony G. Picciano, professor and executive officer, PhD Program in Urban Education, The Graduate Center, City University of New York

"This book is a much-needed, comprehensive resource for evaluating online teaching. It offers well-researched, practical advice on applying teaching evaluation techniques common to all forms of teaching with an emphasis on practices that are unique to the online learning environment."

—Rob Kelly, editor, *Online Classroom*

"This book will help you systematically review the way you evaluate online teaching. Thought questions at the end of each chapter help to contextualize the principles for your campus."

—Francine Glazer, assistant provost and director, Center for Teaching and Learning, New York Institute of Technology

EVALUATING ONLINE TEACHING

EVALUATING ONLINE TEACHING

Implementing Best Practices

Thomas J. Tobin
B. Jean Mandernach
Ann H. Taylor

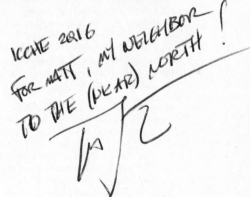

ICCHE 2016
FOR MATT, MY NEIGHBOR
TO THE (DEAR) NORTH!

JB JOSSEY-BASS™
A Wiley Brand

Published by Jossey-Bass
A Wiley Brand
One Montgomery Street, Suite 1000, San Francisco, CA 94104-4594—www.josseybass.com

Jossey-Bass books and products are available through most bookstores. To contact Jossey-Bass directly call our Customer Care Department within the U.S. at 800-956-7739, outside the U.S. at 317-572-3986, or fax 317-572-4002.

Wiley publishes in a variety of print and electronic formats and by print-on-demand. Some material included with standard print versions of this book may not be included in e-books or in print-on-demand. If this book refers to media such as a CD or DVD that is not included in the version you purchased, you may download this material at http://booksupport.wiley.com. For more information about Wiley products, visit www.wiley.com.

Library of Congress Cataloging-in-Publication Data is on file.

9781118910368 (Pbk.)
9781118910344 (Ebk.)
9781118910382 (Ebk.)

Printed in the United States of America
FIRST EDITION
PB Printing   10 9 8 7 6 5 4 3 2 1

CONTENTS

ACKNOWLEDGMENTS

The authors are especially grateful to Academic Impressions for bringing us together in order to host a three-day conference called "Evaluating Online Teaching" in Phoenix, Arizona, between July 31 and August 3, 2013. In preparing for the conference, this book's three authors compared their areas of expertise against the existing scholarship about evaluating online teaching and discovered an opportunity to help to establish standards and best practices. Toward that end, this book presents practical guidelines for developing programs, measurement instruments, and campus policies for evaluating online teaching.

The authors wish to thank the following people and institutions for their willingness to share their ideas, stories, and best practices:

- April Bellafiore, Bristol Community College
- Ron Berk, Johns Hopkins University, Emeritus
- Dee Fabry and Colin Marlaire, National University
- Keith Keppley, Limestone College
- Steven McGahan, Christina Jackson, and Karen Premer, University of Nebraska at Kearney
- Anthony Piña, Sullivan University
- Hank Radda, Kelly Sanderson, Monte McKay, and John Kemper, Grand Canyon University
- Glenn Johnson, Jim Rosenberger, and Mosuk Chow, The Pennsylvania State University

The authors also wish to thank the many colleagues and students whose ideas and questions have helped to shape our research and practices in assessment and online-course development, delivery, and evaluation since the mid 1990s. Members of the Professional and Organizational Development (POD) Listserv and attendees of the Sloan-C, Distance Learning Administration, and University of Wisconsin-Madison Distance Teaching and Learning annual conferences deserve special mention and gratitude.

ABOUT THE AUTHORS

Thomas J. Tobin is the coordinator of learning technologies in the Center for Teaching and Learning (CTL) at Northeastern Illinois University in Chicago, Illinois. In the field of online-teaching evaluation, he is best known for his work on administrative-evaluation practices and policy development; his article on "Best Practices for Administrative Evaluation of Online Faculty" (2004) is considered a seminal work in the field and has been cited in more than 150 publications. Since the advent of online courses in higher education in the late 1990s, Tom's work has focused on using technology to extend the reach of higher education beyond its traditional audience. He advocates for the educational rights of people with disabilities and people from disadvantaged backgrounds. Tom serves on the editorial boards of the *Online Journal of Distance Learning Administration* and the *Journal of Interactive Online Learning*, and he speaks and publishes in many areas related to distance education, including copyright, evaluation of teaching practice, academic integrity, and universal design for learning.

B. Jean Mandernach is a research professor and the director of the Center for Innovation in Research and Teaching (CIRT) at Grand Canyon University in Phoenix, Arizona. Jean created a standard format for student evaluation of online teaching practices, starting with her time at Park University in Parkville, Missouri. Jean's research focuses on enhancing student learning through innovative online instructional strategies, integration of emergent technology, and evaluation of online teaching. As the director of the teaching and learning center, Jean's scholarly and professional work is dedicated to fostering effective, innovative, scholarly teaching. In addition to her mentoring activities, Jean publishes research examining online assessment, perception of online degrees, integration of emerging technologies in the online classroom, and the development of effective faculty evaluation models.

Ann H. Taylor is the director of the John A. Dutton e-Education Institute at the Pennsylvania State University and is a leader in the development of faculty peer evaluations for online teaching. Annie has worked in the field of distance education since 1991, focusing on learning design and faculty development. As the director of an institute that is focused on learning design for distance education, Annie guides her college's strategic vision and planning for online learning. She works with a variety of stakeholders to plan and implement online degree and certificate programs tailored to the needs of working adult professionals. Annie serves on numerous Penn State committees focused on strategic planning, policies, and procedures related to the university's distance learning initiatives, and she has been an active member of the university faculty senate since 2007. While serving as a university administrator, Annie still likes to have a hands-on aspect to her work. She regularly works with university colleagues to create resources for faculty members who teach online and shares her work as a writer and public speaker. She serves on the editorial board for *eLearn Magazine,* an online publication of the Association for Computing Machinery (ACM), and is an active reviewer for several distance-learning journals.

EVALUATING ONLINE TEACHING

PART ONE

PLANNING

CHAPTER ONE

CHALLENGES IN EVALUATION OF ONLINE TEACHING

The growth of online learning has created an opportunity to reexamine teaching practices through a scholarly lens. The review and evaluation of teaching practices in general are sometimes performed in a pro forma fashion or only for summative reasons such as promotion and tenure decisions. Donna Ellis at the University of Waterloo in Waterloo, Ontario, sees teaching evaluation as a holistic enterprise: "teaching and its assessment should ... be seen as scholarly activities. The review of teaching is an intentional process—one that is carefully designed, situated in context, and leads to interpreting teaching effectiveness based on multiple sources and types of evidence" (2012). Online courses offer us a rich variety of information sources from which to study and improve our teaching practices.

Evaluating Online Teaching is an attempt to bring together the disparate strands of research and best practices for evaluating online teaching practices in higher education. This book targets three key audiences in the higher-education community:

- Administrators who wish to create and adopt consistent standards for evaluating the teaching practices in online courses
- Faculty members who wish to know what criteria are evaluated as best practices in online teaching

- Support staff and teaching center personnel who work closely with faculty members and administrators to implement effective pedagogical skills across campus

The instructors, technologists, and administrators who read this book will walk away with a clearer understanding of four phases of the evaluation process for online teaching:

1. Developing evaluation skill sets
2. Creating and applying evaluation methods for administrative, peer, student, and self-reviews
3. Preparing faculty members for the evaluation process
4. Sustaining the online-teaching-evaluation life cycle

A Theoretical Foundation

Our approach in this book relies on the theoretical frameworks seen in Chickering and Gamson (1987) and, later, Chickering and Ehrmann (1996), in which best practices for teaching with technology are outlined in seven core principles:

- Encourage student-faculty contact.
- Develop reciprocity and cooperation among students.
- Use active learning techniques.
- Give prompt feedback.
- Emphasize time on task.
- Communicate high expectations.
- Respect diverse talents and ways of learning.

There are also several best-practice guidelines for online instructors that rely on large-scale studies performed during the 2000s and early 2010s, especially Savery (2005) and McCullom (2010), in which the best online teaching relies on several areas of focus:

- Make learning goals and paths clear to students.
- Use deliberate practice and mastery learning strategies.
- Provide prompt, constructive feedback.
- Provide a balance of challenge and support.
- Elicit active, critical reflection.
- Link inquiries to genuine issues of high interest to the learners.

- Develop learners' effectiveness as learners.
- Create an institutional environment that supports and encourages inquiry.

Two studies in particular help to undergird the strategies advocated in this book. The Hanover Research Council (2009) established three categories of online instructional behavior: planning and development, teaching in action, and student assessment and data evaluation. The work of the Penn State Online Faculty Engagement Subcommittee (2011) established measurable faculty competencies for online teaching:

- Attend to unique challenges of distance learning.
- Be familiar with unique learning needs.
- Achieve mastery of course content, structure, and organization.
- Respond to student inquiries.
- Provide detailed feedback.
- Communicate effectively.
- Promote a safe learning environment.
- Monitor student progress.
- Communicate course goals.
- Provide evidence of teaching presence.

Based on all of these studies and approaches, this book presents a variety of real-world case studies to support various configurations of assessment techniques, including variables such as institution type, size, and union status. In order to set the stage for what readers will encounter in the book, it is useful to think back, for a moment, to the early days of online teaching.

The same core attributes go into good online teaching as go into good teaching in other modalities. All good faculty members teach their courses using clear expectations for themselves and for their students. Good teaching relies on a theoretical and logical framework. Best practices for teaching in any medium include the following:

- Making interactions challenging yet supportive for students
- Asking learners to be active participants in the learning process
- Acknowledging variety in the ways that students learn best
- Providing timely and constructive feedback

Online and face-to-face teaching share core teaching behaviors. Throughout this book, we will show that the differences between online and face-to-face teaching have to do with the specific techniques employed to demonstrate those behaviors. Our emphasis will be to showcase ways of evaluating online teaching that serve two distinct ends: first, comparing the performance of online instructors against themselves and their peers, regardless of the modality in which they teach, and second, identifying practices unique to online teaching.

The evaluation of teaching in general has undergone several similar cycles between a single dominant teaching method and a plurality of teaching methods. Some examples highlight how the growth of online teaching can be seen as the latest iteration of that cycle.

In the 1970s and 1980s, the model for evaluating teaching was its contribution to "faculty vitality." The dominant mode of teaching in higher education was the synchronous, classroom-based course. Faculty members were judged on how well their students were able to perform on examinations and in the workplace. In a 1978 issue of *New Directions for Institutional Research* called "Evaluating Faculty Performance and Vitality," Bogen upholds the "vigor" of faculty members' interactions with students—the "fit" between students' expectations and faculty members' interests—as the key predictor of their teaching effectiveness. He says that "we could learn much from the coach, who in large measure owes his career not to his technical competence but to the success of his securing a match between the student-athlete's needs and the institution's ability to satisfy those needs" (Bogen, p. 62). Similar to the climate today, in 1978 Bogen saw higher education as "entering an era of declining enrollments and relatively reduced public expenditures" (p. 64). The best teachers were seen as those who could hold and keep the interests of their students through the process of "fitting" the goals of the classroom to align best with the students' expectations.

The evaluation principles outlined in Seldin's *Successful Faculty Evaluation Programs: A Practical Guide to Improve Faculty Performance and Promotion/Tenure* (1980) are focused exclusively on face-to-face teaching, yet, despite language about voice volume and eye contact, the principles themselves are robust and can be applied to online teaching with only slight modification.

- **Instructor knowledge.** Does the instructor exhibit content mastery, breadth, depth? Has he or she religiously kept abreast of the discipline? Is his or her subject expertise appropriately demonstrated in the classroom? Is his material appropriate to the level of the course? And appropriate to the level of student preparation?

- **Method of instruction.** Does the classroom presentation exhibit clear signs of planning and organization? Is the material clearly presented? Is class time used efficiently? Does the instructor adapt methods to meet new situations? Is special or supplementary material (e.g., handouts) effectively handled by the instructor? How much critical thinking and analysis by students in the class does he or she elicit?

- **Instructor-student rapport.** Does the instructor demonstrate fair and equitable treatment of the students in the class? Are questions answered in a direct and understandable manner? Does the instructor betray any sarcasm in dealing with students? Does he or she encourage student involvement when relevant? In dealing with student viewpoints contrary to his or her own, does the instructor encourage full and fair class discussion? Does he or she appear receptive to student suggestions? What is the best description of the instructor-student relationship as exhibited in the classroom?

- **Teaching behaviors.** Is the instructor's oral delivery too rapid, too slow? Can he or she be heard easily? Is his or her choice of language understandable to the students? Is the classroom activity level too high, too low? Does the instructor at times express himself or herself nonverbally? Does he or she exhibit any distracting mannerisms? Does he or she maintain eye contact with students? Is he or she blind to any part of the classroom and fail to call on students in that area?

- **Enthusiastic teaching.** Does the instructor exude enthusiasm for the subject? Does he or she show signs that he or she enjoys teaching? How hard does he or she try to stimulate students to master the subject? Does he or she encourage informal discussions with students before or after class?

- **Concern for teaching.** Does the instructor show interest in improving his or her teaching by an analysis of classroom performance and by innovating new teaching techniques? Does the instructor make the subject relevant to students and tie it to recent developments? Does the instructor seek out colleagues for discussions on teaching improvement?

- **Overall.** What parts of the teaching seemed particularly to enhance the learning process? What suggestions are needed to improve the teaching performance? Does the instructor merit recommendation to the students you advise? Was the classroom observation under circumstances that permitted accurate judgment on the efficacy of the teaching-learning process? How would you rate this instructor against others in the department? In the institution?

By the early 1990s, the personal computer was hailed as a means of advancing knowledge and decried as a source of extra work for already-busy faculty members. Computers were seen as adding to existing faculty-member workloads, especially with the advent of e-mail systems, which created a new and demanding communication stream outside of the traditional classroom-and-office-hours scenario. Several theorists began to discriminate among the categories of teaching behaviors and the *technē* (τεχνη) of the specific methods used to achieve those broader results, methods that were in flux with the advent of new time-shifting technologies.

Braskamp and Ory's seminal work, *Assessing Faculty Work* (1994), defines "assessment" in light of its etymological roots as a process of "sitting beside," with the evaluator "judging and providing feedback about the other's performance," in a "dialogue and discourse, with one person trying to understand the other's perspective before giving value judgments" (p. 13). This squares well with their examination of what goes into "the work of teaching," which is rooted in the precomputer practices prevalent up until the late 1980s. Although the authors include items such as "developing computer exercises" (p. 41) in their catalog of faculty teaching work, the assumption is that computers are stand-alone machines that can be used like other development tools to supplement face-to-face instructional methods. It is also worth noting that Braskamp and Ory advocate the holistic evaluation of teaching—all faculty-produced teaching tasks should be assessed via methods as diverse as written appraisals, rating scales, interviews, observations, videotaping, external indicators (e.g., teaching awards), achievement measures, and teaching portfolios (pp. 165–236). All of these methods continue to be best practices for incorporating teaching evaluation into a larger institution-wide scheme of evaluation and planning.

The American Association for Higher Education's (AAHE) "9 Principles of Good Practice for Assessing Student Learning" from 1996 hold equally in the face-to-face and online environments:

1. The assessment of student learning begins with educational values.
2. Assessment is most effective when it reflects an understanding of learning as multidimensional, integrated, and revealed in performance over time.
3. Assessment works best when the programs it seeks to improve have clear, explicitly stated purposes.
4. Assessment requires attention to outcomes but also and equally to the experiences that lead to those outcomes.

5. Assessment works best when it is ongoing, not episodic.
6. Assessment fosters wider improvement when representatives from across the educational community are involved.
7. Assessment makes a difference when it begins with issues of use and illuminates questions that people really care about.
8. Assessment is most likely to lead to improvement when it is part of a larger set of conditions that promote change.
9. Through assessment, educators meet responsibilities to students and to the public. (Astin et al., 1996, pp. 1–3)

Indeed, AAHE's principles help online teachers to avoid the common mistake of facilitating online courses as "read and respond" analogs to postal correspondence courses (albeit at a faster pace). These values preface the current focus areas in online teaching on authentic assessment (getting learners involved in real-world problems and issues) and engaged discovery (in which teaching happens within a sense of shared inquiry).

The pendulum is now swinging back toward seeing "teaching as teaching" regardless of the delivery medium. Although indications that students are learning, such as those advocated by the New Leadership Alliance for Student Learning and Accountability (2012), remain fairly constant, faculty members who teach online and the administrators who evaluate them are today able to take advantage of deeper and more detailed records of their teaching. Gardiner, Corbitt, and Adams (2010) advocate folding online teaching into institutions' overall program assessment model, and several recent theorists have called for "crosswalks" to map online teaching methods against cognate face-to-face techniques.

For example, we find that most of the online teaching evaluation instruments in use today are created to evaluate content design rather than teaching practices—or, at best, include the evaluation of teaching practices alongside the evaluation of design concerns. The assumption that the instructor of an online course is also its designer is a common belief that must be challenged in these times of master-course development, in which one person designs the content and environment and many others teach from it. Arreola (2007) echoes this assumption when he defines teaching as occurring within five broad skill dimensions: "content expertise, instructional design skills, instructional delivery skills, instructional assessment skills, [and] course management skills" (p. 19). Piña and Bohn (2013), conversely, identify nine representative predictors of faculty teaching quality, all of which center on interaction between faculty members and learners.

Even when researchers are purposely looking to create lists of online-only teaching behaviors, such as the frequency of instructor log-ins to the course environment, the list (including our own) inevitably includes general best practices that could apply in various teaching modalities. This is cause for hope as well as reason to continue to examine what is unique about teaching online.

The "Traditional" Teaching-Evaluation Process

In 2004, Tom Tobin was hired by a for-profit university to teach business English and communication courses at its newly opened location in Pittsburgh, Pennsylvania. Although taught in a face-to-face classroom, all courses were to be supported by online elements. Lecture notes, preparatory discussions, feedback on student work, and assignment grades were all expected to be handled within the university's learning management system (LMS).

As part of the university's procedures, Tom was slated to have his teaching observed by the chair of the communication department. The process was familiar to him, based on the many years' worth of observations he had already been part of, both as a graduate teaching fellow and then as an early-career professor.

The setup was fairly routine: the department chair selected a class meeting date and time and notified Tom that his class would be observed. With the notification e-mail message, the department chair attached a copy of the evaluation instrument that would be used and asked Tom to reply with a copy of his syllabus. The message ended with a request for Tom not to make any special changes to the content or style of teaching: "Please forget that I am even there, and just teach a normal class."

On the evening of the observation, the department chair entered the classroom a few minutes early, sat in the back of the room, and readied the observation form. A few students asked Tom who the visitor was, and he let them know that part of the university's commitment to quality education for students entailed an observation of the teaching methods of all instructors. Tom taught the class, the department chair wrote on the form, and the department chair left the classroom at the mid-point break in the ninety-minute class period.

A week after the observation, the department chair invited Tom to meet to review the results of the observation. During that conversation, the chair provided Tom with a copy of the class observation form (see Figure 1.1). The observation form seems to indicate that Tom was

FIGURE 1.1. CLASS OBSERVATION FORM, 2004

██████ University   **Class Observation Form – iOptimize Courses**

Instructor _Tom Tobin_   Course _6u410_   Center _Pittsburgh_   Room _290_

No. of Students _███_   Observer _████████_   Date _3/8/04_   Time _7:15_ to _7:45_

Topic(s) Covered _TCO B_ _____

_____

I.   Classroom Environment: Temperature _good_   Lighting _good_   HVAC _good_
      White Board _~~closed~~_ Overhead ___✓___ Tables/Chairs _in place_ Noise _none_
      Other _____

II.   **Instructions: Please circle one number. Rating Scale: 4=excellent, 3=good, 2=fair, 1=poor**

Onsite Component of Course	
Characteristic	**Comments**
Interaction: *(questioning strategy, probing for understanding, use of student names, involves all students, thought-provoking)* **④** 3 2 1	- Tom does an excellent job of probing the student - Makes the student think out the answer
Presentation: *(organization, clarity, summarizes development of theories and concepts, reference to prior and future weeks' topics, concrete examples)* **④** 3 2 1	- Extremely organized - Arrives an hour before class - Gives great examples of writing memos
Homework Review: *(proactive or reactive, teaching vs. answer-giving, calls on students)* 4 3 2 1	Done entirely in the class
Classroom Management: *(in control, use of board and other audio-visual, comfortable pace, handles student questions well)* **④** 3 2 1	Complete control - uses the board, like a Smart Board
Vitality: *(energy, enthusiasm, movement, volume, eye contact, humor, connectedness, etc.)* **④** 3 2 1	- Loves what he does Thrilled to be in the class, Connects well
Student Participation: *(interactive, active vs. passive, interested vs. bored, volunteer, prepared, enthusiastic)* **④** 3 2 1	- only one student in class. Student well prepared for class
Professionalism: *(appearance, demeanor, respect for students, fair, role-model; responsive, degree of preparedness)* **④** 3 2 1	- Shirt & tie, and always Tom ___ to ___ treats student w/ great respect
Practical Linkages: *(relevant examples, practical insights, "insider tricks of the trade," appropriate applications, integration with other functional areas)* **④** 3 2 1	- very relevant Brings the professional writing to dealing w/ a memo the student is writing for his current job.

doing very well, with high marks in all categories. The department chair offered praise for Tom's teaching, using words that echoed the suggested criteria on the form itself.

Tom was pleased that he had been able to start his teaching at this new university in such a strong manner. When he got home, he looked again at the form, and noted that it continued onto the other side of the paper. The back of the sheet held categories for the online components of the course:

- User activity
- Online component
- Discussion topics
- Feedback
- Visual appeal
- Communication style
- Posted items
- Course balance

There were also write-in spaces for strengths, opportunities for improvement, progress from previous observations, follow-up items, and an overall class rating.

The back of the form was completely untouched (see Figure 1.2). The department chair eventually confessed that because he had not himself taught using the institution's LMS, he didn't feel qualified to rate Tom's use of its tools. The chair also mentioned that he would welcome training or a "walk through" so he could get familiar with the expectations for the use of the LMS.

Deans, department chairs, faculty members, and students rate and evaluate teaching at their institutions mostly through home-grown processes and forms. Although these are often constructed to help observers and raters to provide meaningful information, it is often the case that even now, many years after the example provided in Figure 1.2, little training is provided for those using the evaluation instruments. With online teaching, observers have many more streams of information they can observe for evidence of teaching effectiveness, and there aren't clear boundaries about what counts as teaching behaviors—or even how much time an observer should spend performing an evaluation.

Further, it is common practice for state and provincial governments to require K–12 educators to receive training in not only the discipline(s) in which they are going to teach but also in pedagogy, educational psychology, and classroom management. In higher education, however, institutions typically require one to master only a specific discipline's content in order

FIGURE 1.2. CLASS OBSERVATION FORM, REVERSE, 2004

Rigor: *(appropriate level of rigor; focus on how and why [not just what]; focus on understanding, decision-making, implications, problems, and analysis)* 4 3 2 1	
Online Component of Course (use one set of numbers for each evaluation)	
User Activity: *(2.5 hours/week for faculty, 2 hours/week for students)* 4 3 2 1 4 3 2 1	
Online Component: *(other than the threaded discussion; e.g., web research, report posting in document sharing, webliography postings)* 4 3 2 1 4 3 2 1	
Discussion Topics: *(TCO-related, uses broad-based questions that generate good discussion, including follow-up questions, rather than discrete answers)* 4 3 2 1 4 3 2 1	
Feedback: *(timely, encouraging and supportive, responds to questions asked)* 4 3 2 1 4 3 2 1	
Visual Appeal *("curb appeal," aesthetically pleasing)* 4 3 2 1 4 3 2 1	
Communication Style: *(professional, grammatically correct, positive, proper "netiquette")* 4 3 2 1 4 3 2 1	
Posted Items: *(syllabus, assignments, other postings consistent with quality standards)* 4 3 2 1 4 3 2 1	
Course Balance: *(appropriate balance between onsite and online activities)* 4 3 2 1 4 3 2 1	

Strengths:_____

Opportunities for Improvement:_____

Progress Noted from Previous Observations:_____

Follow-Up:_____

Overall Class Observation Rating: _____ (i.e., 3.15 . . . 4 excellent; 1 poor) to teach in that field. Although the trend is starting to reverse, it remains true, even today, that higher-education faculty members rarely begin their teaching careers with any hands-on training in how to teach, and few avail themselves of such opportunities when they are offered on campus. This becomes a twofold concern for evaluation of online teaching: instructors who may or may not have been trained in pedagogical techniques are evaluated by peers and administrators who may or may not have a scholarly vocabulary (or the technical background) to be able to evaluate their online teaching practices.

Effective college and university teaching practices are typically learned on the job, often by trial and error, and are supported by a variety of evaluation methods that range from student feedback on end-of-course surveys to formal administrative observations in the classroom. Numerous tools and evaluation instruments have been developed and put into use to support these efforts, but the use of these tools varies widely (as evinced by Tom's former department chair). Institutions apply the results of various evaluations methods to such disparate ends as the promotion-and-tenure process, future-course staffing decisions, instructor remediation, and awards and recognition.

Add to this situation the variable of modality (teaching online via asynchronous or technology-enhanced means) and the conversation about defining best practices becomes especially diffuse. April Bellafiore of Bristol Community College recently put the problem in sharp focus:

> I think we've tried for many years to say online and face-to-face are
> the same—no significant difference. It's the same as face-to-face; don't
> treat it any differently. We're going to go set up a classroom face-to-face,
> and we'll also set up a "classroom" online. Where we're struggling
> is that we know it is different. It's been framed for our faculty that it's
> a different modality, but we can't pretend that they really are the same.
> Now, workload and effort are really coming into play on the front end,
> and evaluation effort and measurements on the back end. We have a very
> strong union as well, and we're definitely heading down that road to have
> conversations about workload and expectations. (Baird & Piña, 2014).

As online education continues to grow in popularity and becomes a mainstream practice at many institutions, faculty members and administrators face the challenge of effectively measuring the quality of online teaching. Strategies and tools designed for face-to-face classrooms are too often applied in a one-size-fits-all manner to the online teaching environment, leaving both reviewer and instructor with an ill-fitted and incomplete analysis. Designing and implementing strategies to evaluate online teaching necessarily differs from designing and implementing those used in the face-to-face environment; they vary as a function of the nature, purpose, and focus of the evaluation. Comprehensive evaluation models must balance the summative data available via formalized assessments with the formative feedback available via informal processes.

Challenges for the Evaluation of Online Teaching

Institutions share a few overarching concerns when it comes to establishing and implementing various evaluation methods for online teaching:

- What is the online equivalent to visiting a colleague's classroom for ninety minutes?
- Which elements in an online class count as "design" and which as "teaching"?
- How much time should peer and administrative evaluators spend observing online teaching?
- Should observation of online teaching take place during or after the course?
- To what purposes will student ratings, self-evaluation, peer evaluation, and administrative observation be used?

There are also some common red herrings, concerns voiced by faculty members who have not yet experienced evaluation of their online teaching:

- If the LMS suffers technical glitches, does that mean lower student-rating scores for the instructor?
- Who is qualified to perform various aspects of evaluation?
- Shouldn't my peer reviewer be from my own department?

Although these concerns can be addressed easily, they offer insight into the mind-set challenges for adoption of online-teaching evaluation in a given unit or across campus. In *Evaluating Online Teaching*, we will examine these and several additional areas in which evaluating online teaching must differ from evaluating face-to-face teaching.

Scope

In the typical evaluation of the face-to-face classroom, feedback from students, peers, and administrators is based on in-class performance only. Often, this occurs in response to a one-time observation designed to represent typical teaching behavior. Pre- and postwork (by the students and the instructor) is not observed or evaluated. For example, communications that take place outside the face-to-face classroom (e.g., office hours, e-mail messages) are not observed.

For online teaching, however, the lines between in class and out of class are blurred. Interactions among students, instructors, and materials take place in a variety of locations. Observers need to look at core course content (e.g., lecture notes, videos, readings, assignments) in order to provide context for the class, but they also need access to course communication systems (e.g., discussion forums or even e-mail) in order fully to observe student-student and student-instructor interactions.

Time Equivalence

Because the limiting factors for face-to-face classes are time and place, evaluation instruments often use time and place as the outside boundary of all observation activities. For instance, a peer evaluator might observe one ninety-minute class session in a specific room. Online teaching is not restricted to a specific geography or time frame, and it is thus more challenging to find an equivalent for evaluation.

There is a broader issue inherent in this concern as well. Because face-to-face class observations are time based (the reviewer sits in on a single class period), the assumption may be to find the equivalent of that time-based observation for online teaching as well. *Class period* is not a meaningful term within an online course, and observers must determine how much content to observe (e.g., one week or unit worth of materials and interactions). This is actually an opportunity to broaden the scope of online-teaching evaluation and to detach it from time-based criteria: the observation becomes more encompassing and includes a greater number of dimensions.

Separating Teaching from Design

In a face-to-face classroom, the teaching practices that are observed are easily separated from the tools used in the process of teaching. For example, speech patterns, body language, voice tone, eye contact, and conversational engagement are all factors that are identified as part of the observable teaching practices of the instructor, whereas textbooks, whiteboards, and PowerPoint presentations are seen as tools used in the process of teaching. These two components—instructor behaviors and course materials—can be evaluated in a face-to-face scenario, but it is clear what is under the control of the instructor and what is not when we are looking at face-to-face teaching.

Conversely, in an online environment, it is more challenging to separate elements that represent teaching behaviors from those that represent foundational or design-related parts of the course. For instance, in an asynchronous discussion tool, are the instructor's initial prompts to be considered as design elements or evidence of teaching taking place? How much instructor interaction is deemed to be "conversational engagement"? Cheryl Hayek (2012) advocates some "dinner party" suggestions for gauging optimal faculty discussion participation, whereas the rule of thumb at many for-profit institutions is to look for between 10 and 15 percent of the total posts coming from the instructor (DeVry University, 2009). Further, lecture notes, multimedia (e.g., audio and video podcasts), and narrated PowerPoint slide presentations could be seen either as tools placed within the design of the course or as evidence of teaching behaviors.

Another aspect that muddies the waters is the question of who created the content that is being reviewed. In many institutions, the faculty author who creates the content for an online course (including, say, the initial prompts for weekly discussion) may not be the same faculty member who teaches the course each term. There is already a well-established literature on creating and evaluating quality online-course materials and designing quality online-course environments, making it necessary to distinguish between "design" elements and "teaching" behaviors.

For instance, as recently as 2004, researchers have assumed that the designer of the content of a course is also the instructor. Walvoord (2004) lists three foundational questions in her "guidelines for the evaluation of teaching": "1. Are the learning objectives of the course being met? 2. Are the course material, concepts, and activities rigorous, current, relevant for students' needs? 3. Do students perceive themselves to be well taught?" (p. 94).

Measurement Equivalence

Chickering and Gamson's "Seven Principles for Good Practice in Undergraduate Education" can be observed in any course, no matter the delivery method. In many evaluation instruments, such common elements as the seven principles make for valid comparisons between face-to-face and online sections of the same course. Teaching to the course objectives, level of engagement with students, and responsiveness to learner concerns are all teaching behaviors that evaluators can observe regardless of the course modality. For example, Buller (2012) establishes six general principles for evaluating faculty teaching, regardless of delivery mode:

Practice 1: Follow your institution's established procedures to the letter.

Practice 2: Documented evidence should focus on observable behaviors and verifiable results, not on general impressions of the person's attitudes, opinions, or personality.

Practice 3: Use statistical measurements appropriately.

Practice 4: Make actual judgments when conducting summative evaluations; don't merely summarize data.

Practice 5: Remember that you already know more than you think you do.

Practice 6: Don't overlook the value of 360-degree review processes.
      (pp. 23–38)

However, evaluation instruments often contain elements that are specific to a given delivery method, such as evaluating instructor presence via tone of voice, speed of verbal delivery, and body language. Many institutions are currently using evaluation instruments that ask observers to rate instructors' use of classroom space, availability outside of class meetings, and use of class time—all of which are difficult or impossible to apply to online courses.

In this book, we will suggest some ways to redesign existing evaluation instruments to work around these measurement-equivalence challenges, such as focusing on the spontaneous interactions in online course environments, evaluating the quality of materials created by instructors in response to student questions (i.e., noncanned materials), observing the frequency and quality of instructors' interactions with students, measuring the degree of conceptual scaffolding within course discussions, and comparing the level of course inquiry at the higher levels of the cognitive domain of Bloom's taxonomy (Bloom, Engelhart, Furst, Hill, & Krathwohl, 1956).

As mentioned previously, instructors also have doubts about evaluation of their online teaching, which we will explore. Will technical glitches experienced in the online-course environment translate to lower end-of-semester student ratings? How well can a department chairperson who has never taught online courses evaluate the teaching practices that

are happening in online courses? We will examine ways that various measurement techniques can help to answer these kinds of questions as well.

Instrument Applicability

Despite significant progress in the field in the past several years, there is
still a challenge in creating, adapting, or adopting evaluation instruments
that are broadly applicable to instruction in online courses. This book will
examine a number of existing evaluation instruments in order to establish
best practices for formal and informal self-, peer, and administrative review
of online teaching. Many higher-education institutions continue to choose
to create their own instruments because of the perceived unique features
of their circumstances. Further, many existing evaluation instruments were
originally designed for face-to-face course applications. Adapting existing
instruments for use in evaluating online courses presents several forms of
potential measurement error and unintentional bias, and we will offer ways
to keep these factors in check.

Scalability

Online learning programs are more scalable than their face-to-face counterparts. There are no limits on needing to create more campus space
for teaching and residential student populations. Indeed, online courses
offer higher-education opportunities to students regardless of schedules
and geography. Likewise, online programs attract instructors from beyond
the traditional pool of campus-based faculty members. Many large online
programs depend heavily on contingent faculty members. The implementation and administration of rating and evaluation methods becomes
more challenging for larger and more-distributed online programs.
Traditional face-to-face measures, such as real-time peer-evaluation review
meetings, are not often designed to be scalable or to target contingent
faculty populations. Throughout this book, we will offer case studies and
best practices for scaling evaluation programs and for targeting specific
instructor populations.

Quality Improvement versus Record Keeping

Why do we undertake evaluation programs at all? This question is not
unique to online-teaching evaluation. However, online teaching offers a
way to move beyond the formal evaluations that are typically conducted

for reasons of hiring, continuance, promotion, and tenure. Too often, the real reason we perform evaluations is that our accrediting bodies require us to provide data based on course outcomes, and we keep the records accordingly.

We will examine ways to create and nurture a culture of evaluation that includes the use of evaluations for instructor use only, such as those provided at midterm and those used as ad hoc "how am I doing?" checks. Informal and self-assessments enable campuses to build systems that get us back to the foundational reason to perform evaluation: to make sure we are providing the best quality educational experiences to our learners.

Looking Ahead

Evaluating Online Teaching offers readers a four-stage process for establishing a culture of evaluation on their campuses, with online learning as a key component of that culture. This book provides actionable steps for campus faculty members, administrative leaders, and support staff to take in order to plan for, adopt, adapt, and institutionalize the evaluation of online teaching.

In part 1, we explore the planning process for adopting evaluation of online teaching at an institution. Chapter 1 (this chapter) introduces several challenges specific to online-teaching evaluation that campus leaders need to understand, acknowledge, and plan to address. Chapter 2 introduces the general context in which to evaluate online teaching practices. We provide readers with ways to define campus needs, important questions to ask about the institution itself and the implementation and potential impact of an evaluation program, and case studies to help demonstrate how other institutions have carried out the planning process. Chapter 3 offers tips and strategies for developing an evaluation structure amenable to your institutional context. We examine several faculty and administrator skill-building initiatives that helped to lay solid foundations for successful online-teaching evaluation programs.

Part 2 focuses on formative evaluation mechanisms that help to broaden the impact of evaluation beyond collecting data for accrediting agencies and the promotion-and-tenure process. Formative evaluations help faculty members to improve their teaching practices. Chapter 4 explores how instructors' personal use of frequent small-scope student ratings of online teaching demonstrates an institution's culture of assessment and improvement. Faculty members who engage in an informal student-review process typically see their student-retention and student-satisfaction rates increase by the time the institution's formal end-of-semester surveys roll around.

We also examine the other side of the informal-evaluation coin, offering practical advice for setting up a program of peer and self-review for online teaching practices that faculty members will want to adopt because it makes their online-classroom experiences smoother and more rewarding; because it doesn't count toward formal decisions about hiring, faculty retention, promotion, or tenure; and because it offers faculty members greater academic freedom by providing insight into how their teaching techniques are actually having an impact on their students' learning.

In part 3, we focus on data gathering for summative evaluation processes. Summative evaluation helps institutions to make personnel decisions such as promotion, tenure, continuation of contingent faculty members, awards, and remediation. Chapter 5 reviews several tools for performing the most commonly used summative-decision data-collection method: end-of-course student ratings. Chapter 6 outlines challenges and solutions specific to formal administrative evaluation of online teaching, especially when department chairs and faculty committees are tasked with deciding whom to rehire, promote, or give tenure to. Chapter 7 provides concrete tools and techniques to address the administrative-evaluation challenges from chapter 6 by examining several case studies and suggesting a set of action steps and policy statements that can help readers' campuses to implement administrative review processes smoothly. Chapter 8 examines the promise—and the hype—surrounding the use of data analytics for evaluative purposes.

Part 4 of this text offers concrete steps that readers can take in order to customize the evaluation strategies to fit their own campuses. Chapter 9 offers strategies for incorporating student, self, peer, and administrative review methods into the institution's overall assessment program of online-teaching practices. We examine several existing evaluation instruments and explore the debate between using one instrument to collect data for all course-offering modalities and using separate instruments, each specific to a different way of offering courses. We present a concise program for setting up and running a program for collecting student-rating data about online teaching, often part of the largest effort to collect evaluation data on campus.

Once institutions have created a culture of evaluation, the final stages of the process center on sustaining and strengthening that culture. Perhaps the most challenging part of this book is chapter 10, where we will offer strategies for implementing an online-teaching evaluation process on campus. Institutions that are creating brand-new evaluation programs may even have an advantage over places where there is already an evaluation process in place for face-to-face teaching practices because it enables such campuses to align their evaluation outcomes across delivery modalities. We will help readers to plan and initiate an online-teaching-evaluation program on their campuses, examine and offer advice on avoiding common missteps, and suggest how to recruit the skeptics (converts make the most convincing advocates).

Evaluation is a cyclical process, and the ease of data collection with online teaching makes a compelling case for building the entire life cycle of online-teaching evaluation into the institutional business as usual—from feedback to data gathering to reporting to interpretation to experimentation, change, and adaptation. Chapter 11 defines the various stages of the online-teaching-evaluation life cycle, and provides concrete steps that readers can take in order to move beyond bare-bones data collection for accreditation purposes into establishing a true culture of evaluation on campus.

Readers should use this book as a way to build a solid foundation for evaluation on their campuses. Once an institution has a robust evaluation culture in place, what resources and paths does that free up for accomplishing other goals related to their evaluation and quality improvement efforts? Chapter 12 and the companion website (www.wiley.com/go/tobin) for the book offer some possibilities for next steps, including a ten-minute take-away version of the book's lessons, worksheets for readers to complete in order to craft their efforts toward their specific institutions, and links to resources for sharing knowledge with the growing community of online-teaching professionals, support staff, and administrators.

Conclusion

The differences between face-to-face teaching and online teaching reflect modality and scope—but not quality. It has been well established that faculty members can be just as effective teaching online as in the classroom (Russell, 2001), and best practices for teaching online have been evolving since the mid 1990s. Online teaching has existed for long enough that we can now differentiate between traditional online teaching (with its defined course duration, number of students, and asynchronous focus)

FIGURE 1.3. CHECKLIST: CAMPUS READINESS FOR ONLINE-TEACHING EVALUATION

Please indicate your level of agreement with the following statements. "My campus today has …"

	Strongly Agree	Agree	Disagree	Strongly Disagree
a process for evaluating face-to-face teaching.	☐	☐	☐	☐
a method for communicating evaluation results to faculty members.	☐	☐	☐	☐
a method for communicating general student-rating results to students.	☐	☐	☐	☐
specific tools for collecting information about teaching.	☐	☐	☐	☐
faculty or staff members who are skilled in data analysis.	☐	☐	☐	☐
a culture that prizes teaching effectiveness.	☐	☐	☐	☐
a system for self-evaluation of teaching practices.	☐	☐	☐	☐
a system for informal peer evaluation of teaching practices (i.e., results are not used to make employment decisions).	☐	☐	☐	☐
a culture in which faculty members make teaching changes based on student-rating and evaluating feedback.	☐	☐	☐	☐
a process for evaluating online teaching.	☐	☐	☐	☐
formal policies that define the teaching-evaluation process.	☐	☐	☐	☐
faculty members who have taught online courses previously.	☐	☐	☐	☐
administrators who have taught online courses previously.	☐	☐	☐	☐

and newer forms such as massive open online courses (MOOCs), in which instructor-student interaction is more distributed and students group together to help each other work through the course materials and challenges in a self-directed fashion. Whether your campus offers traditional online courses, MOOCs, or other online-course models, the interactions that define *online teaching* remain the same, and this book aims to help you to evaluate those behaviors consistently, fairly, and productively.

Just as it has taken time for higher-education administrators, staff, and faculty members to accept that online teaching can be as effective as face-to-face instruction, the adoption of formal and informal evaluation of online teaching has lagged behind evaluation of face-to-face teaching on many campuses. This book offers concrete steps for readers who want to move their campuses beyond data collection into establishing programs that help us all to accomplish the highest goal of higher education: providing our faculty members with meaningful feedback about their teaching practices and providing learners with the best education we can provide them.

A Thought Exercise

Take a few minutes to assess the status of your own campus regarding the evaluation of online teaching. Figure 1.3 provides a process model for identifying opportunities and pathways toward online-teaching evaluation competence on campus.

You will find a series of thought exercises similar to this one throughout the book to help you apply its research and ideas to your own campus. Refer back to your responses to previous thought exercises as you complete each chapter. Doing so can help you to identify areas of current strength, new questions to pose, and strategies for customizing your efforts for the best reception and results for your institution.

CHAPTER TWO

CONTEXT FOR EVALUATING ONLINE TEACHING

B. Jean Mandernach's Story

During an informal conversation I once had with a colleague from another institution, she mentioned the challenges her university was facing as they prepared for an upcoming accreditation visit. Though well established, the university was relatively new to the world of online education and, despite her confidence that they were providing online students with a quality educational experience, they lacked a system to document teaching effectiveness and student learning. Although the university had an effective process for evaluating teaching in the face-to-face classroom, the structure for evaluating teaching in the online classroom was less clear . . . and, in truth, virtually nonexistent.

She explained that some departments that were early adopters of online education had developed their own tools and processes for gauging the quality of online instruction; other departments had ventured into the online teaching arena but were yet to conduct any formal assessments of instructional quality. Complicating matters further, evaluation structures—when they existed—had inconsistent application policies that varied depending on faculty status, with different processes being used for full-time or contingent faculty. Even worse, there was no clear indication of how—if at all—the information from teaching evaluations was being used in any meaningful fashion.

Challenged by the lack of consistency and an inability to assess effectiveness data across the university, my colleague was tasked with creating a uniform process for evaluating online teaching that mirrored the system used for its face-to-face counterpart. Recognizing that I worked at a large, well-established online program, she asked if I would be willing to share our evaluation system. Happy to assist, I provided my university's complete evaluation package including rating forms, time line, work flow, and organizational structure; in addition, I secured the necessary permissions to allow my colleague's university to adopt our evaluation tool for use at their institution.

Prepared to implement the prepackaged evaluation structure in a timely and efficient fashion, my colleague dove into the documentation to update and align with the specific nature of her own university. But her optimism and excitement soon faded as she was faced with hurdle after hurdle . . . what worked perfectly for me at my institution didn't seem altogether relevant for her institution's needs.

The evaluation system I had shared addressed many factors that were not relevant for my colleague's university. Implementation of the process was reliant on an operational structure that didn't exist at their institution. Furthermore, as she scanned the very detailed and elaborate processes underlying our evaluation system, she became increasingly concerned about the likelihood of gaining faculty and administration support for this type of evaluation.

Despite a shared goal to evaluate the quality of online instruction, the contextual differences between our institutions made it impossible to simply adopt the tools and processes of one institution for use at the other. What she was missing was an awareness of the importance of aligning evaluation structures with the processes and infrastructure of each institution. Defeated, my colleague began—from scratch—the process of adapting and customizing an online teaching evaluation system that would be applicable and relevant to the unique nature of her particular institution.

Developing an Evaluation System

Universities today are faced with the task of assessing and documenting effective teaching. Although the universal goal of all teaching evaluation systems is to ensure that instructional practices foster student learning, there are myriad unique, context-specific factors that simultaneously shape the evaluation process at each university. These institution-specific considerations exist regardless of whether the evaluation is targeting online or face-to-face teaching; yet the novelty of online education often intensifies challenges associated with developing a teaching evaluation model because of lack of acceptance, understanding, and awareness of the online modality.

As such, despite the appeal of implementing a prepackaged, comprehensive evaluation plan, universities that attempt to adopt a one-size-fits-all model to evaluate online teaching undoubtedly will be frustrated. For an evaluation of online teaching system to be effective (and provide the intended data), it must be designed with an explicit awareness of the institutional factors and practical considerations that will shape the design, structure, and implementation of the evaluation plan. Similarly, although most institutions have an established structure for evaluating face-to-face teaching, attempts to apply existing classroom-based evaluation tools to the online classroom are likely to fail. The unique nature of online teaching mandates that evaluation structures are explicitly aligned with this learning environment.

Fortunately, despite the need for a customized evaluation system, universities do not need to start from scratch. Rather, the key is an *a priori* awareness of essential dimensions and considerations necessary to effectively adapt (or build) an evaluation structure that aligns with the specific context of each institution. Equally important is reliance on empirically driven best practices in online pedagogy that anchor the evaluation with a clear focus on student learning. From this foundation, universities can construct a comprehensive evaluation of online teaching that meets their unique institutional needs, ensuring effective, efficient, and meaningful use of evaluation data.

Getting Started

When faced with the need to evaluate online teaching, universities often jump directly to locating (or creating) an evaluation rating form. Unfortunately, this is one of the last steps—not the first—in designing an effective evaluation of online teaching. Before you can determine exactly what activities and behaviors you want to measure in the online classroom, you must take a more holistic perspective and address context-specific perspectives, factors, and considerations that will shape the evaluation process. The reality is that the best evaluation tool in the world will not be effective if it can't be implemented in a consistent, efficient manner that meets the needs of the individual faculty members and the administration. Furthermore, one tool is likely not going to be enough to provide the desired information. To get started, you need to clearly identify the existing institutional, implementation, and impact considerations that will shape the evaluation system. The following steps outline key considerations and associated questions that must be addressed in order to create a functional evaluation of online teaching that is responsive to the context-specific nature of each institution.

Institutional Considerations

How do institutional considerations and factors affect the evaluation process?

- What are the current attitudes and opinions surrounding online education at your institution?
- How will your organizational structure affect the evaluation process?
- What is the role of faculty governance in approving evaluation systems?
- To what extent will funding influence evaluation decisions?
- What institutional, organizational, or programmatic barriers do you face in designing or implementing an evaluation structure?

Implementation Considerations

What are the key considerations in implementing an evaluation process for online teaching?

- Who will be responsible for conducting evaluations?
- Will evaluation stakeholders have relevant expertise in online learning?
- What dimensions (teaching, course design, other) will be included in the evaluation process?
- Who will be the target of evaluation (contingent, full-time)?
- How frequently will evaluations be conducted?
- What data are included or collected via the existing evaluation process? What additional data will be needed?

Impact Considerations

How will data from the evaluation of online teaching be used?

- How will you balance the use of student, peer, and supervisor evaluation data?
- How will the timing of evaluations affect the value of the information provided?
- Will evaluation data be a component of hiring, promotion, or continuance decisions?
- Will evaluations of online teaching be separated from generalized evaluations of teaching?
- To what extent will evaluation of online teaching be separated from evaluation of course design?

Stakeholders for the Evaluation of Online Teaching

When preparing to develop an evaluation of online teaching, it is important to consider all the stakeholders who will have an investment in this process. Exploring the institutional, implementation, and impact considerations requires a comprehensive university group. Stakeholders include the following groups:

- **Faculty members with online teaching experience** to ensure that the focus of your evaluation aligns with best practices and instructional strategies relevant to the online classroom
- **Campus faculty members** as a means of establishing equitable evaluation across modes of teaching
- **Contingent faculty members teaching online** to ensure that processes and procedures are relevant to a part-time, contingent, or geographically diverse faculty
- **Department or college administrators** to gain the perspective of those responsible for the decision making that results from evaluation data
- **Members of faculty unions or representative governing organizations** to provide insight on the relationship of evaluation systems with existing policies for promotion, tenure, and so on
- **Administrative support specialists** to ensure necessary staffing and resources to implement evaluation systems

- **Distance learning administrators** to ensure alignment across all aspects of the development, delivery, and evaluation of online courses
- **Technology specialists** to provide insight on software, programs, or systems that may be affected by evaluation data, require integration with evaluation processes, or support evaluation structures
- **LMS administrators** as a means of exploring the role of data analytics in the evaluation process
- **Faculty development and training specialists** to discuss the alignment of faculty training, remediation, and development with the evaluation system
- **Institutional assessment and effectiveness specialists** to provide insight into university needs for evaluation and assessment data to inform institutional growth, development, and reporting
- **Students** to ensure evaluation processes are relevant and appropriate to student learning, satisfaction, and experience

Step 1: Identify the Institutional Considerations That Affect the Evaluation Process

Every college and university is unique; do not underestimate the importance of identifying and embracing the unique institutional factors that will influence the evaluation process. Within any institution, there is a zeitgeist—a spirit of the times—that embodies the university's current attitudes surrounding online education, evaluation, and assessment. Recognizing the current atmosphere surrounding evaluation decisions, administrative processes, and similar topics provides important context for creating an evaluation structure that is likely to gain the necessary faculty and administrative support to be successful. You should address the following questions that are key to this discussion.

What Are the Current Attitudes and Opinions Surrounding Online Education at Your Institution? Although some institutions have seamlessly integrated online class offerings into the course mix, others have been more resistant. Similarly, although the growth of online education has been spearheaded by enthusiastic faculty at some universities, faculty members at other institutions are being pushed unwillingly to expand teaching into the online modality. The climate surrounding online education at any given institution is rarely documented in any formal manner, yet awareness of informal indicators provides valuable insight into potential challenges with implementing an evaluation of online teaching.

How Will Your Organizational Structure Affect the Evaluation Process? Identifying the organizational hierarchy in which online courses are located is essential for developing a functional evaluation system. There are two primary structural systems that typically govern online programs: (1) online courses and offerings are administered by their respective campus-based academic departments or (2) online programs are offered through a separate academic college or administrative unit focusing exclusively on distance education. Within this broad generalized structural classification, there are countless configurations that specify the working relationship among campus faculty members, administration, and operational teams. Central to this issue is the need to clearly identify stakeholders who have primary responsibility for oversight and evaluation decisions.

What Is the Role of Faculty Governance in Approving Evaluation Systems? Once an evaluation system has been developed, it must be approved and adopted for use. Unfortunately, this step is easier in theory than in practice. Depending on the institutional structure, this process may involve a number of relevant stakeholders including faculty unions, operational administrators, faculty committees, and college administration. In addition, the evaluation structure must be aligned with existing faculty contracts, collective bargaining agreements, guidelines for promotion and tenure, or other existing processes that govern the use of evaluation data (for more information, see the case study on the University of Nebraska at Kearney's experience with gaining union support for a new metric to evaluate online teaching). Development of the evaluation of online teaching must be done with *a priori* awareness of the relevant stakeholders and associated processes to ensure utility and feasibility of the final evaluation structure. This issue is particularly important when examining the evaluation of online teaching because institutions may use a different governance structure for campus-based versus online courses; although some online courses are under the academic purview of their respective departments, others are governed by a centralized distance learning administrative unit that is exempt from traditional academic oversight. It is important to recognize the time investment required to gain the necessary approvals, but it is equally valuable to identify components of the evaluation process that may be implemented during the approval process. For example, although evaluations of online teaching that will be used for faculty tenure, promotion, or retention may require a number of official approvals, you may be able to implement some of the formative, low-stakes aspects of the evaluation structure without larger institutional approval.

Gaining Buy-In for the Evaluation of Online Teaching: Unionized Campus Considerations

The authors recently spoke with Steve McGahan, Christina Jackson, and Karen Premer at the University of Nebraska at Kearney about their experiences with developing and implementing a new evaluation of online teaching. They composed the following summary of their experiences with this process.

Creating an evaluation of online teaching is a difficult task; the complexity of the task is compounded even further when the institution has a union. Not only are the key criteria that benchmark quality teaching in the online classroom difficult to quantify but also the need to gain approval from the union-governing bodies can create delays, hurdles, and unexpected barriers in the process. As discovered during the implementation of a new evaluation of online teaching at the University of Nebraska at Kearney (UNK), there can be a number of unexpected challenges associated with gaining union support.

In 2006, UNK eCampus developed a new evaluation for online instruction to monitor and promote quality teaching in the online classroom. As a unionized campus, all standards that affect faculty academic freedom and evaluation must be approved by the faculty senate; in addition, prior to implementation, evaluation standards must be formally incorporated into the collective bargaining agreement.

To begin the process, an evaluation of online teaching metric was developed in-house by the eCampus instructional designers to align with the needs of the online programs at UNK. The initial evaluation rubric was presented to the eCampus faculty senate advisory committee for approval; this committee (composed of both faculty members and administrative staff) is tasked with approval of all online education items prior to being put forward for review to the full faculty senate. Although designed as a committee to foster communication between online and campus initiatives, it was quickly discovered that the makeup of committee members presented a range of challenges for advancing online learning initiatives.

At the time the new evaluation process was being put forth for approval, several of the committee members were senior faculty members who had minimal or no online teaching experience. This general disconnect with online education led to a number of tangential debates concerning the legitimacy of online education and the value (or lack thereof) of having a unique instrument and process for evaluating online teaching. Specifically, some felt that good teaching was driven by universal pedagogical standards; thus, it was not necessary to use a unique evaluation instrument to assess online teaching. Others questioned whether evaluations of online teaching infringed on academic freedom, whether online education could compare to face-to-face instruction, and whether effective online learning was contingent on the behaviors of the faculty members versus the online course content. Although the purpose of the committee was to examine the merit of the evaluation process, a significant portion of time was spent debating the general viability of online education.

Several members of the committee, primarily those with limited online teaching experience, were adamantly against using an evaluation rubric. One faculty member vehemently stated, "I don't use rubrics to measure how well I teach in my regular classes. Why should I have to use one to evaluate my online courses?" The most strenuous arguments in opposition to the evaluation process targeted academic freedom and the union contract. Committee members expressed concern over using a standardized rubric to evaluate faculty members. As explained by one faculty member, "While I think the rubric is comprehensive, I'm concerned that using a rubric violates our academic freedom." The general committee consensus was that the union contract did not allow for the instructional practices of individual faculty to be assessed in this manner.

To address this concern, the evaluation of online teaching was modified from a rubric to a self-assessment checklist. Although most agreed that the self-assessment checklist did not fully address all concerns about instructional quality in the online classroom, these concerns were overshadowed by the need for union support and faculty buy in. Once the generalized concerns about academic freedom and contract alignment were addressed, the evaluation tool went through several additional rounds of committee review to clarify language and instructional expectations. At this point, the evaluation tool was forward to the full faculty senate for a vote on implementation. Fortunately, at the full faculty senate review, the evaluation process was approved with only minor discussion from the floor.

As is the case with committee review, the process from introduction to feedback to revision to approval can take considerable time. With most committees meeting monthly, each question, decision, and request for revisions is met with a waiting period prior to the next round of discussion. In this case, the review and approval process took three full months; this is in addition to the five months spent researching, developing, and testing the initial evaluation process. In essence, the development and approval of a new evaluation of online teaching required an academic year. Further, it took almost two more years until the approved evaluation of online teaching checklist became part of the collective bargaining agreement for the UNK faculty. When initial approvals were complete, negotiations had already been completed for the upcoming two-year contract with the union; this required waiting for the next round of negotiations a year later to have the checklist officially designated as the assessment tool for online courses.

Working with a union can have its challenges, but union-specific criteria must be met. A proposal may have to go through union-sanctioned committees, adding to the time needed for revision and approval. This can add substantial development time, stress, and resource investment for those creating the evaluation process. Conversely, working with a union can create a much higher level of faculty buy in for the new evaluation system. Giving faculty members a voice in the development, review, and approval of their evaluation processes decreases pushback and increases the utility of evaluation metrics.

Source: McGahan, Jackson, and Premer (2014a).

To What Extent Will Funding Influence Evaluation Decisions? When creating an evaluation of online teaching, it is important to examine potential budget implications that may affect the feasibility of the evaluation system. Although it is possible to create a comprehensive, targeted evaluation that integrates relevant indicators to provide valuable, meaningful outcome data, the evaluation system will not work if it requires staffing and there is no budget (or structure) from which to administer the evaluation. Budget considerations may include costs of evaluators, staffing necessary to manage the evaluation process, technology or software used to conduct evaluations, and so on. In addition, there must be a discussion of who is responsible for both initial and ongoing expenses associated with the development and implementation of an evaluation structure; because online courses may be housed in either departments, colleges, or administrative units, institutions must have explicit awareness of who is responsible for funding the various aspects of the evaluation process.

What Institutional, Organizational, or Programmatic Barriers Will You Face in Designing or Implementing an Evaluation Structure for Online Teaching? The issues highlighted here (e.g., attitudes, climate, organizational structure, faculty governance, funding) are relevant to all universities. But, it is equally important to examine unique factors that may affect the evaluation of online teaching based on specific institutional, organizational, or programmatic barriers at your institution. For example, if, similar to my colleague, your university is facing an impending external accreditation visit, there may be additional considerations that affect how you design and implement an evaluation of online teaching to fit a specified time line. Or, perhaps your university is locked into a specific software package that will be used to manage evaluation data, which may guide decisions concerning how you create and implement your evaluation plan.

Step 2: Examine Implementation Considerations That Guide the Evaluation Structure

For an evaluation of online teaching to be effective, it must be implemented in a manner that the resultant data are meaningful. Unfortunately, the nature of online education challenges traditional approaches to the evaluation of teaching. Teaching online is different than teaching face-to-face; online instruction is not limited by time, format, or physical presence. Complicating this issue, there is less awareness—or agreement—among faculty members and administrators concerning instructional practices underlying effective teaching in the online classroom. For an evaluation of online teaching to be effective, it is essential that the evaluation tools and processes are designed with an explicit awareness of the implementation considerations that are unique to each institution. The following questions serve as a guideline for examining context-specific factors that may affect the implementation of your evaluation system.

Who Will Be Responsible for Conducting Evaluations? There are a number of relevant stakeholders (i.e., administrators, peers, or students) who may be asked to complete teaching evaluations as either stand-alone evaluations or as a component of a larger evaluation package. Administrative evaluations (see chapter 6) may be completed by department chairs, supervisors, or designated evaluators. The organizational structure of the university is likely to dictate who is responsible for conducting administrative reviews.

If oversight of online course offerings is housed in individual academic departments, administrative evaluations are likely the responsibility of department chairs. If online courses are managed via academic services or a separate college, then administrative evaluations may be the responsibility of specified online teaching evaluators. Peer reviews (see chapter 4) may also be conducted by faculty colleagues, including departmental colleagues teaching similar courses or peers from outside the discipline with experience in online learning. In addition, peer mentors (see the case study of Park University located at the end of this chapter) may simultaneously provide support and guidance for online teaching while completing teaching evaluations. Student ratings (see chapter 5) are also likely to be a component of the evaluation mix; student ratings may be completed as either formative or summative indicators of teaching effectiveness.

Will Evaluation Stakeholders Have Relevant Expertise in Online Learning? The relative novelty of online education means that many individuals who may be asked to complete an evaluation of online teaching might have limited—if any—experience with the online modality. Although the potential evaluator's experience with online education is not something that can be controlled, it is important to be aware of the general experience level of potential evaluators when creating an evaluation system. If evaluations are conducted by campus-based faculty with little awareness or understanding of online education, then evaluation tools may need to be more structured or include more explanatory detail surrounding evaluation dimensions. If evaluations are going to be conducted by administrative staff with considerable experience with online pedagogy but limited disciplinary knowledge, then the evaluation system may need to include separate evaluation dimensions for online pedagogy versus content expertise. It is worth noting that participating in the evaluation of online teaching, regardless of one's experience in the online classroom, provides a rich opportunity to further campus dialogue about online teaching and learning.

What Dimensions Will Be Included in the Evaluation Process? Within a campus-based course, teaching evaluations are conducted with the assumption that the individual faculty member is responsible for curricular, pedagogical, and course management decisions. As such, evaluations of face-to-face teaching typically do not separate these dimensions but rather evaluate teaching as a holistic experience that integrates all components. In the online classroom, these traditional assumptions may—or may not—be the case. Teaching online involves two key dimensions: course design and course facilitation (i.e., teaching). In some institutions, individual faculty members are responsible for both course design and teaching. In other universities, course design is completed independent from teaching; individual faculty members are responsible for teaching an existing online course that contains instructional content, assignments, and activities.

Depending on the system used, evaluation systems need to clearly address the component(s) of the online experience that are being evaluated. Even if individual faculty members are responsible for course design and teaching, it is important to separate these dimensions within the evaluation process to ensure evaluation data are meaningful for monitoring and developing instructional practices that maximize student learning. Although a number of guidelines and rubrics exist to guide the evaluation of online course design (see MarylandOnline, 2013, for an example of an online course design rubric), the focus of this text is the evaluation of online teaching independent of course design.

Who Will Be the Target of Evaluation? Evaluations of teaching are commonplace—if not standard—for campus-based, full-time faculty members because of the need for effectiveness data to inform tenure and promotion decisions. But although the need to document effectiveness for full-time faculty is relatively universal, evaluation of contingent faculty is less consistent because of variability in schedules, differential retention criteria, and the irrelevance of promotion and tenure guidelines for faculty members in this role (Langen, 2011; Marble & Case, 2013). Although institutions typically implement student ratings as an indicator of contingent faculty effectiveness, they are less likely to be subject to the same administrative or peer evaluations as their full-time counterparts (Langen, 2011; Marble & Case, 2013).

This issue is intensified in the online environment in which universities may be more reliant on contingent faculty to teach online course offerings (Allen & Seaman, 2008; Lyons, 2007). Universities must examine how evaluation processes may vary as a function of faculty status (e.g., contingent, full-time, tenure-track, tenured, etc.) with particular focus on emphasis on barriers to implementation. For example, if a university has a large online contingent teaching population, it is not feasible to rely on a single administrative evaluator to conduct evaluations of online contingent faculty because of the heavy workload of such a task. Despite challenges associated with the evaluation of contingent instructors teaching online, it is important that they are included in the evaluation process when this population is responsible for a significant portion of online course offerings.

How Frequently Will Evaluations Be Conducted? Although it is standard practice to have students complete teaching evaluations at the conclusion of every course, the frequency of conducting administrative and peer evaluations is more variable. Similar to the campus-based environment, it takes considerable time and effort to complete thorough course evaluations. As such, it is important to determine a schedule of evaluation that balances the need for timely data with the desire to invest time and resources most efficiently. In an ideal world, administrative and peer evaluations of teaching would be conducted every semester to ensure students are receiving high-quality instruction, but repeatedly investing precious time to evaluate a consistently high-rated instructor wastes evaluation time or resources. However, failure to evaluate an instructor who is not an effective teacher may lead to a host of issues related to student learning, satisfaction, and retention.

Although the challenge of determining an effective and efficient evaluation schedule is universal for all modes of teaching, this issue is even more complex in the online environment. First, the relative novelty of online instruction means that many instructors are not as proficient with online teaching and, thus, may require additional assistance to ensure their effectiveness. Second, because online courses are often offered in an accelerated format (Wlodkowski, 2003), the pace at which courses are offered dictates that scheduling for upcoming terms must be completed before evaluation data are available from previous terms (Dobbins, 2011; Mueller, Mandernach, & Sanderson, 2013). As such, the rapid pace of course scheduling may prevent the timely use of evaluation data to ensure courses are being taught by the most effective instructors. Third, if online courses are being taught primarily by contingent faculty (Allen & Seaman, 2008; Lyons, 2007), the inconsistent scheduling of these faculty (i.e., contingent faculty members may teach a term, then take a term off, then teach again; scheduling is a by-product of faculty interest and scheduling demands) may create challenges in ensuring that all faculty are receiving consistent, timely evaluations of teaching.

What Data Are Included or Collected Via the Existing Evaluation Process? What Additional Data Will Be Needed? In a face-to-face classroom, there is a relatively standard, limited set of information that can be evaluated. In the case of student ratings, there is a generally a small number of questions that students reply to with a quantitative rating as well as a few opportunities for students to provide open-ended qualitative feedback. When implementing an administrative or peer evaluation, there is also typically a set of questions that evaluators reply to with quantitative ratings (often based on rubric scoring if an evaluation tool is used) or evaluators are asked to provide holistic qualitative feedback based on their observations. Although this type of information can be collected through similar evaluations of online teaching, the nature of the online classroom provides a host of other available data via artifacts in the LMS and course analytics. Such data may include the following:

- Frequency of log-ins
- Time spent in the LMS
- Number of threaded discussion posts
- Nature and quality of threaded discussion interaction
- Timeliness of interaction
- Timeliness of grading and feedback
- Nature and quality of feedback
- Proportion of instructor-to-student posts
- Days on task
- Time on task

The possibilities of data that can be generated are limited only by the analytic functions of the LMS. But, with an awareness of the plethora of data that are potentially available, it is important to determine what data are relevant to the evaluation—and equally important to determine what data are *not*. Universities must examine what data are available via LMS analytics and then determine the relevance of those data in relation to best practices in online teaching.

Step 3: Determine How Data from the Evaluation of Online Teaching Will Be Used

All evaluations of teaching produce data; the challenge lies in ensuring that the data produced via the evaluation process align with the specific needs and goals of the university, departments, faculty, and students. If the only goal of a teaching evaluation is to gauge effectiveness so that an individual faculty member can modify instruction to better meet the needs of the students, the evaluation will elicit very different data than if the impetus for evaluation lies in documenting instructional equivalence between various modes of teaching for an external accreditation visit; these data, in turn, will be very different than evaluation data used to prioritize which faculty members are given scheduling preferences for online course offerings. Although all these motivations share an underlying emphasis on effective teaching, each mandates differences in how data will be collected, what information is deemed most valuable, and who has access to evaluation findings.

In reality, there are a number of competing—and overlapping—motivations for conducting evaluations of online teaching; as such, it is essential to identify all stakeholders who will use the evaluation information to ensure the data are collected in a format amenable to each stakeholder. Equally important is awareness that the original impetus for creating an evaluation system may be very different from the ongoing systems and processes that rely on the data produced. Consider the following questions when determining how data will be used at your institution.

How Will You Balance the Use of Student, Peer, Administrative, Self, and Analytic Evaluation Data? As previously discussed, there are a number of sources for teaching evaluation data (i.e., student, peer, administrative, self, and analytic). Although the most comprehensive evaluation systems will include information from multiple—if not all—of these sources, it is important to note that not all data are considered equal. Within the context and guidelines of each university, it is important to examine the relative weight of the information provided via each data source for making associated decisions.

For example, if the primary impetus for conducting teaching evaluations is to monitor teaching activities to improve student retention in the online classroom, increased importance may be placed on student ratings of teaching. By contrast, if the key motivation for conducting teaching evaluations is to document equivalent teaching time on task between online and campus courses for accreditation reports, then priority might be given to analytic or administrative data. Recognition of the value of each data source for providing specific evaluation information ensures that data are collected in a meaningful way to make informed decisions.

How Will the Timing of Evaluations Affect the Value of the Information Provided? Teaching evaluation data can be divided into two primary types: formative and summative. Formative evaluations of teaching are designed to provide faculty members with feedback to enhance their teaching and foster development. By contrast, summative evaluations of teaching are designed as outcome measures to evaluate an instructor's effectiveness. In reality, rarely are evaluations of teaching exclusively formative or summative because of the cyclical nature of the teaching process.

Even evaluations geared narrowly to measure a faculty member's performance for use in summative decision making (such as tenure or promotion) provide faculty with valuable formative information to guide future teaching. Likewise, evaluations conducted midsemester with a primary focus on providing feedback to enhance teaching may be used as an indicator of faculty performance (see the Park University case study on page 44). The nature of online learning complicates challenges inherent in determining the most appropriate timing of evaluations.

Because many faculty members are not as experienced, knowledgeable, or comfortable with the online format, it is helpful to provide formative evaluations and feedback to guide their development (as opposed to waiting until the end of a course to discover that the faculty member failed to use appropriate pedagogy for the online modality); yet, early investment of time and resources to provide formative feedback may limit the feasibility of reevaluating at a later point to judge overall effectiveness. And, as mentioned previously, if evaluation data are a component of scheduling, waiting until the end of one term to conduct summative evaluations may mean that important evaluation data are not available in time to inform changes to teaching strategies or scheduling decisions for the subsequent term (particularly with respect to contingent faculty working in an accelerated format). When developing an evaluation time line, institutions should consider the number of faculty members involved, frequency of evaluation data, and the timing of associated decisions informed by evaluation outcomes.

Will Evaluation Data Be a Component of Hiring, Promotion, or Continuance Decisions? Evaluations of teaching are an integral component of personnel, scheduling, award, and promotion decisions at a university. As such, evaluation tools, processes, and outcomes should be designed with clear awareness of how evaluation information is going to be reported, who has access to evaluation information, and the alignment of evaluation standards with existing faculty guidelines. Although these expectations are not unique to evaluations of teaching in the online modality, the relative novelty of online programs and course offerings often translates into less explicit understanding of how this information fits into the larger university context. In addition, because many faculty members are not as experienced with online education, they may be more hesitant to teach online if they fear negative repercussions of a lower evaluation ranking. The high-stakes nature of hiring, promotion, and continuance decisions mandates that faculty members and administrators consider the impact of the resultant data when designing evaluations of online teaching.

Will Evaluations of Online Teaching Be Separated from Generalized Evaluations of Teaching? Traditionally, evaluations of teaching have been examined as a comprehensive indicator of one's teaching; evaluations were not a function of individual course, course level, or delivery style of the course (e.g., lecture, discussion, lab). Although this has been the standard for the majority of campus-based courses, institutions must determine if data from evaluations of online teaching are going to be used as a component of the overall evaluation of instructional effectiveness or if teaching effectiveness should be examined as a specific function of the mode of delivery. For example, if an instructor has outstanding teaching evaluations for face-to-face courses but poor teaching evaluations for online courses, it is useful to make a priori decisions that dictate whether that information is presented in aggregate (resulting in the instructor having an average mean rating) or whether evaluation data should be reported via the mode to indicate relative strengths and weaknesses. Although this distinction may seem detail oriented when discussing at the onset of creating an evaluation system, the high-stakes nature of using evaluation data for tenure, promotion, or continuance decisions forces a more thorough examination of how teaching evaluation data are reported, organized, and disseminated.

To What Extent Will Evaluation of Online Teaching Be Separated from Evaluation of Course Design? As discussed previously in this chapter, depending on the organizational structure of the university, there are two broad approaches to online course design: (1) online courses are designed by the individual faculty member who teaches that course or (2) courses are created independently of the faculty member who designed the course (i.e., the course may be taught by someone other than the original author or designer). The evaluation of online teaching must be structured in a manner that focuses on dimensions of the teaching experience that are within the control of the instructor. Even if individual instructors are responsible for both course design and teaching, it is essential to differentiate evaluations of the course design from evaluations of the instructor activity (e.g., facilitation of online discussions, quality of feedback on student work, coaching students as they work on course assignments) so that evaluation data provides meaningful, relevant information that can be used in both formative and summative capacities. For example, an instructor can design an outstanding online course but may fail to facilitate the course in a manner that is engaging, responsive, or timely (or vice versa: a poorly designed course with outstanding teaching).

Conclusion

As in the case of Jean Mandernach's colleague, the need to document teaching effectiveness for external accreditation requirements often serves as the impetus for creating a system to evaluate online teaching. But beyond external constituents, data from evaluations of teaching are important components of the professional development of individual faculty members, departmental decision making, and university benchmarking. Recognizing the widespread value, utility, and importance of teaching evaluations, it is imperative to create an evaluation of online teaching that is aligned with the context-specific needs of each institution. Equally important is recognition that an effective evaluation of online teaching is more than simply finding (or creating) an evaluation tool; if evaluation data are going to be meaningful, they must be couched within a comprehensive evaluation system.

Fortunately for Jean's colleague, this doesn't mean that universities start from scratch to create a context-specific system for evaluating online teaching. There are a host of available evaluation tools and processes from which a customized evaluation system can be created. Throughout this text, we will examine a range of existing tools and processes for conducting peer and self-reviews (chapter 4), student ratings (chapter 5), and administrative evaluations (chapter 6) that are specific to the unique nature of the online classroom. In addition, we will explore the decision-making process underlying how to adapt and expand existing tools to fit your institutional context. As you examine the available tools and approaches, we encourage you to refer back to the questions presented here to help guide the development of your own online teaching evaluation strategy.

Case Study: Park University

The evaluation model for online faculty at Park University was created to meet the unique demands of an evolving online program. Although Park University was founded as a small, private, liberal arts college in 1875, the original campus in Missouri has grown to include graduate programs, forty-two nationwide campus centers, and an extensive online program supporting forty-five thousand annual student enrollments in seven online degree-completion programs and four fully online graduate programs. Culturally, Park University is a teaching-oriented institution, with emerging expectations for faculty scholarship, research, and service. The institutional complexity at Park University samples challenges found across a host of institutions targeting two- or four-year degrees, public or private settings, and traditional or adult student populations. As such, the university's online faculty evaluation model is potentially translatable to an equally wide range of higher-learning institutions. With the increasing popularity and growth of online learning, it is essential to establish clear, direct, relevant guidelines for evaluating online faculty that maintain instructional quality and promote best practices in online education.

Rationale for Online Faculty Evaluation System

The legacy online faculty evaluation system at Park University was inadequate for evaluating the unique expectations and demands faced by online instructors within the institution. Prior to the development of a new online evaluation system, online instructors were evaluated by a formal evaluator using a generic instrument designed for face-to-face distance instructors at the university's campus centers across the country. Because the evaluation was based on traditional classroom concerns, the instrument's evaluative criteria did not emphasize key competencies for effective online instruction, such as instructor response rate and availability, frequency and quality of presence in online classroom, facilitation of discussions in writing, usability of instructor-created supplemental content, and overall management of the administrative aspects of the course (e.g., approving final examination proctors, connecting students to university support resources, completing required administrative tasks).

Also in keeping with traditional face-to-face evaluation models, the evaluator completed his or her review at the end of the term in a singular exchange with the instructor. Although this type of singular formal interaction may be effective in the more intimate environment of the on-ground campus, where evaluators have ongoing opportunities to interact informally with instructors because of proximity, this practice does not translate meaningfully to the virtual classroom. In the online environment, the evaluation process often proved the first and only time the instructor and evaluator interacted. The limitations of this model were compounded by the fact that many online instructors were relatively new to the virtual classroom. Not only were the evaluation and recommendations for these instructors' online teaching practice being provided *after* the point at which suggestions could be effectively implemented into the classroom but also the legacy evaluation instrument did not account for the limited online teaching experience of many of the university's online instructors. Thus, the assumptions undergirding face-to-face faculty evaluation models limited the effectiveness of an online evaluation system based on traditional models.

In addition to the flaws in the timing and content of the legacy evaluation system, there were growing concerns about the lack of peer support and professional guidance for instructors working within a geographically diverse and highly individualized environment. Larger university concerns included the need to educate the key departmental leaders who were expected to work with online learning staff to evaluate online instructors. The legacy evaluation system did not provide these individuals, only some of whom had experience with online instruction, with the context and education needed to understand the differences between online and face-to-face methods. As such, the Online Instructor Evaluation System (OIES, which is described in greater detail in chapter 7) was developed to reinforce key competencies and expectations unique to online faculty members, provide significant professional development exchanges and resources for online faculty members, and ensure a high-quality learning experience in all virtual classrooms. Looking outward, a tertiary goal of the OIES was to educate the broader university community about benchmarks and best practices of online learning to promote reciprocal exchange between online and face-to-face practitioners and practices.

Theoretical and Institutional Foundations

When evaluating the effectiveness of an online course, two distinct components are under review: the content (curriculum) provided within the online course and the instructor's facilitation of the learning experience. At Park

University, the core content of each course is created by a faculty content expert. Once the core content is reviewed and approved by the relevant department chair, all instructors teaching that course use the same core content. In addition to ensuring compliance with university-wide learning outcomes and promoting academic equivalence and curricular coherence between delivery methods, this type of standardized curriculum enables the evaluation of online faculty to emphasize the facilitation and instructional skills of faculty members rather than their ability as instructional design-ers. This curriculum development model also acknowledges the realities of developing and facilitating content within an accelerated format by providing instructors with a full course of instructional materials they can then supplement as desired to reflect their expertise and to suit learner needs. Because Park University uses a standardized curriculum, there is less emphasis during evaluation on the content of a course. As such, the OIES was designed to focus exclusively on online teaching while relying on departmental oversight to ensure content quality.

The OIES was developed out of a comprehensive review of the literature on benchmarks and best practices of online teaching to achieve the goals of educating online instructors concerning accepted standards in online education and holding them accountable to these best practices through evaluation and professional development. Based on Chickering and Ehrmann's (1996) guidelines for integrating principles of good practice in undergraduate education into technology-enabled learning environments, the OIES emphasized reciprocal student-faculty contact, inclusion of active learning strategies, prompt feedback, promotion of student time on task, clear communication of high expectations, and respect for diversity in student talents and ways of learning.

It is important to note that the OIES was *not* founded solely on the literature and research findings. Rather, these generalized best practices in online education were considered and adapted in ways that reflected Park University's institutional history, current context, and future goals, as synthesized in the university's "Online Course Standards and Principles." The development of the OIES occurred simultaneously with the conversion of the online program to a different online course delivery platform. The new platform provided increased instructional resources and thus enabled evaluators to expect more rigorous and varied interaction in the online classroom from instructors. At the same time, the initial training of online instructors was streamlined and condensed into a self-paced, individualized online format, opening up an opportunity to extend the instructor training and orientation processes with an individualized first-term evaluation. All of these programmatic changes were implemented during a paradigm shift in which there was increased emphasis on faculty collaboration, communication, and integration across all modes of course delivery. As such, the OIES at Park University was developed in light of institutionally specific dynamics combined with an empirical basis of online pedagogy. The effectiveness of the OIES is a direct result of this type of tailoring: in order for an evaluation system to be effective, it must have a foundation in generally accepted practices, but these best practices must be tailored to meet the needs of the particular institution.

Overview of the OIES

The OIES serves the dual purpose of mentoring and faculty evaluation. As such, the model contains two distinct phases of interaction: formative reviews and summative evaluation.

The purpose of the formative reviews is to provide feedback and guidance to instructors on critical online learning components essential to successful facilitation of an online course. The formative reviews are no-stakes evaluations in which the evaluator provides detailed feedback relevant to the instructor's online course as well as suggestions for overall enhancement of the online learning experience. Although the formative reviews are shared with the instructor (and instructors are encouraged to use reviews as a starting point for further dialogue), they are not included in the overall course review sent to the instructor's academic department.

During an eight-week course term, the instructor is evaluated with five formative reviews, each focusing on a critical aspect of online instruction. The topics for each review were selected based on the guiding principles outlined in the best practices for online education and were sequenced according to logical use within the course or term:

- **Preterm review.** The preterm review is completed prior to the start of the term and focuses on the setup of the online course. While completing the preterm review, the evaluator ensures introductory items (i.e., course home page, home page content items, and syllabus) are updated, personalized, and reflect university requirements. These set-up activities are especially important in orienting learners in an accelerated format when students often access their online classrooms prior to the start of the term to obtain textbook ordering information and other preparatory materials. In addition, the evaluator provides targeted suggestions for enhancements related to course organization and the use of course tools and features.

- **Review 1.** Review 1, which is completed at the end of the second week, examines community building and promotion of an interactive climate. The purpose of this review is to examine the use and implementation of discussion threads, including an overview of participation expectations, tips for grading discussion items, instructor availability, instructor presence, and student-to-student interaction.
- **Review 2.** Review 2 is completed during the fourth week and focuses on discussion facilitation, feedback, and grading. During this review, the evaluator provides guidance on instructor interactions, specifically addressing feedback and participation in the discussion threads as well as comments and use of the grade book. Reviews 1 and 2 emphasize discussion facilitation and feedback because meaningful, consistent instructor interaction is an ongoing essential of effective online learning.
- **Review 3.** Done at the end of week six, review 3 examines assessments and final exam preparation. The evaluator reviews the implementation of formative and summative assessments as well as preparation for the final exam and the proctored exam process. In addition, interactions include an opportunity to share ideas about supplemental formative assessments that may be added to the course. Although instructors are expected to use the core curriculum provided, they are also encouraged to add supplemental content to their courses.
- **Review 4.** Implemented during the final weeks of the term, review 4 focuses on instructional materials and overall course climate and organization. As such, evaluators will review all supplemental information to ensure adherence to general instructional design principles and specific university curriculum standards and expectations.

These formative assessments provide an avenue for peer mentoring and professional growth by promoting ongoing reflection and dialogue about practice. Although the formative reviews are not explicitly presented as an informative or prescriptive resource, they serve as consistent and concrete mechanisms to educate instructors about best practices and serve as a valuable professional development resource.

In contrast to the low-stakes nature of the formative reviews, the final summative evaluation is an overall reflection of the course and is used to inform the instructor and the academic department (who will use the summative evaluation along with the instructor's self-review and student ratings to make final decisions concerning instructor retention). Although the summative evaluation is focused on an overall evaluation of the course, it emphasizes the instructor's ability to incorporate suggested changes and required modifications (including an evaluation of instructor responsiveness and adherence to administrative requirements) from the formative reviews; although the formative reviews, in keeping with their function, are not included in the summative package, the particulars of those reviews are generalized to reflect either the instructor's strengths as a reflective, improved practitioner or to note unresponsiveness and lack of participation in the process.

The summative evaluation package is particularly effective as a means of online faculty member evaluation because it incorporates multiple perspectives to present to the department a comprehensive portrait of the instructor. This integrative evaluation emphasizes an instructor's growth throughout a term rather than simply highlighting the mistakes made throughout the instructional process.

Implementation

The OIES is implemented by designated instructor evaluators. The instructor evaluator position is a full-time, faculty-classified role, with 50 percent administrative release time granted to evaluate and mentor approximately fifteen instructors per eight-week term. The faculty classification of the evaluators enables them to be fully integrated into the life of the campus, participating on curriculum and other university-wide committees and meeting institutional expectations for research, scholarship, and service. A dual benefit of this classification is that the online learning program gains faculty representatives in the disciplines, faculty members who can serve as ready sources of accurate information about the online learning program, its academic oversight, and the processes related to developing and teaching courses online. The representative-liaison function of the evaluator role enables stronger relationships between the online learning program and the disciplines, paving the way for increased collaboration. Pragmatic implications of structuring the position in these ways include working with university academic administration and candidate departments in the hiring process to ensure that the candidates possess appropriate credentials and the hires respond to departmental needs in addition to needs within the online learning program.

At the conclusion of the first year of the OIES pilot, extensive reflection on the evaluation system resulted in the creation of a university review board composed of full-time faculty, administrators, and contingent instructors to provide annual feedback and guidance on the faculty evaluation system. As part of the first review board process, additional instructor evaluators were hired to meet the demands of the university's pool of approximately three hundred active online instructors and to ensure sound evaluation loads. Based on pilot analysis, it was determined that five instructor evaluators were needed to mentor and evaluate fifteen faculty members per eight-week term, four terms each academic year. This load would enable each instructor evaluator to complete sixty OIES evaluations in one academic year, resulting in a total of three hundred evaluations completed across the university each year. Although there exist ongoing budgetary considerations associated with the additional faculty members hired as instructor evaluators, these costs are offset by the economic value of retaining qualified instructors compared to the high cost of faculty turnover.

Source: Adapted from Mandernach, Donnelli, Dailey, and Schulte (2005).

A Thought Exercise

Chapter 2 raises many questions, most of which help to determine the environment in which evaluation of online teaching takes place. Before you can set up the foundation of an online-teaching evaluation program, it's imperative to know what purposes the evaluation itself will serve. Here is a recap of the major questions from this chapter: the "three I's" of institution, implementation, and impact (see Figure 2.1).

See how many of these questions you are able to answer for your own campus as it is right now. Don't worry if you are not able to answer every one, but mark those as opportunities to learn more about the climate in which your program must operate. Your answers will help you as you begin thinking about the elements you will need to provide the foundation for a program at your institution.

FIGURE 2.1. THE THREE I'S: INSTITUTION, IMPLEMENTATION, AND IMPACT

	I can answer.	I can't answer yet.
What are the current attitudes and opinions surrounding online education at your institution?	☐	☐
How will your organizational structure affect the evaluation process?	☐	☐
What is the role of faculty governance in approving evaluation systems?	☐	☐
To what extent will funding influence evaluation decisions?	☐	☐
What barriers do you face in designing or implementing an evaluation structure?	☐	☐
Who will be responsible for conducting evaluations?	☐	☐
Will evaluation stakeholders have relevant expertise in online learning?	☐	☐
What dimensions (teaching, course design, other) will be included in the evaluation process?	☐	☐
Who will be the target of evaluation (contingent, full-time faculty members)?	☐	☐
How frequently will evaluations be conducted?	☐	☐
What data are included or collected via the existing process? What additional data will be needed?	☐	☐
How will you balance the use of student, peer, and supervisor evaluation data?	☐	☐
How will the timing of evaluations affect the value of the information provided?	☐	☐
Will evaluation data be a component of hiring, promotion, or continuance decisions?	☐	☐
Will evaluations of online teaching be separated from generalized evaluations of teaching?	☐	☐
To what extent will evaluation of online teaching be separated from evaluation of course design?	☐	☐

CHAPTER THREE

ESTABLISHING A FOUNDATION FOR EVALUATING ONLINE TEACHING

B. Jean Mandernach's Story

While attending the annual Sloan-C (now the Online Learning Consortium) International Conference on Online Learning, I had the opportunity to chat with a number of different faculty members about the challenges and successes their universities had experienced throughout the growth of their online programs. Regardless of the institution type (community college, private, public, or for-profit) a common theme emerged from the discussions: everyone was confident that online instruction could be as dynamic, interactive, and educational as face-to-face instruction, yet no one believed that their own university had an effective system for monitoring whether this type of effective instruction was actually occurring in their online classrooms. As highlighted by one faculty member,

Knowing the importance of documenting effective teaching, three years ago our institution created a task force to develop a system for evaluating online teaching. Yet, despite a plethora of meetings, e-mails, and heated debates, we still have no evaluation plan. In fact, if anything, we are even further from having an evaluation structure today than we were when we started. The more we discuss, the more questions we generate. Our committee is in a perpetual questioning spiral, with no tangible outcomes to show for all our efforts.

Through our discussions of this faculty member's situation, it became clear that—although dedicated and well-intentioned—the task force lacked the necessary information to create an effective evaluation system. The task force had little agreement on the focus, nature, and intended purpose of the evaluation plan and struggled to determine where to start. Although some faculty members emphasized the need for summative evaluations of online teaching performance, others highlighted the importance of formative feedback for those new to online teaching. Similarly, there were ongoing debates surrounding the extent to which online teaching could be evaluated independently of course structure. Furthering the challenge, faculty members struggled to establish boundaries for what instructional activities should and should not be included in evaluations of online teaching.

The failure of this task force highlights the challenge that faculty members face in developing an effective evaluation program for online teaching: the relative novelty of online education often leaves faculty members with more questions than answers. Although institutions typically have an established structure for evaluating teaching in the face-to-face classroom, variability in the structure, timing, and format of online courses makes it virtually impossible to simply adopt campus-based strategies to the online format.

Ron Berk knows this well. He spent his career at Johns Hopkins University examining how best to create, implement, and use student ratings of teaching. In his latest book, one of the flashpoints he identifies is the quality and applicability of home-grown rating scales when they are either administered online or are used to rate teaching modalities other than the face-to-face classroom (Berk, 2013b, pp. 35–38). When we spoke to him recently, he also mentioned that when he taught a blended course, his research on evaluation suggested that:

> the issue seems to fall into two camps. There are people who have been using face-to-face, and professionals such as the IDEA Center, who will argue that in all their studies that they have done comparing face-to-face and online classes, that there's no significant difference between the two. What they're measuring is basically face-to-face ratings and the factors that contribute to face-to-face [teaching quality], so they are looking, in

terms of their form, at the common-denominator elements between the two modalities.

The other perspective is that after I read all of the material in the online-teaching literature, the bottom line is that there is a strong common core of teaching methods and course characteristics that is similar for both face-to-face and online, but there are unique elements to each, especially online, that can be measured and would provide a more comprehensive assessment of the online evaluation of teaching than just saying "these are equal."

Being a measurement person, it's the latter position that I have adopted, and I just tested it out in the last year with the development of a couple of versions of a scale that I was involved in consulting on for the Johns Hopkins School of Engineering. The issues came up there in terms of what was going to be measured, and the committee got into a whole discussion of what are the common elements, and then what is unique to online teaching. They really got into a thicket, so to speak, and it was a challenge to help them get to an instrument that they could actually use and make planning decisions with. (Berk, personal interview, March 31, 2014).

Berk's expertise helped the engineers at Johns Hopkins to put together the student-ratings portion of their overall evaluation program; our focus in this chapter will be similar but takes a broader perspective to account for the myriad considerations present when developing an evaluation of online teaching.

A Decision-Making Process

In this chapter, we provide a sequential decision-making process for considering the focus, nature, and purpose that drive the development and implementation of an effective overall evaluation of online teaching. By addressing the questions posed in each step of the process, you can create a foundation from which to build an evaluation of online teaching that meets the unique needs of your institution. Through this decision-making process, you will accomplish the following:

- Identify the focus of the online teaching evaluation
- Operationalize evaluation components in order to measure effective teaching in the online environment
- Create an implementation plan that aligns the evaluation system within the institutional structure

Step 1: Identify the Focus

The first step in developing an evaluation of online teaching is to determine exactly what you want to evaluate. This step is much easier in theory than in practice: the reality of online education is that a number of related factors affect the quality of the teaching and learning experience. These factors include the following, as seen in Figure 3.1:

- University resources (e.g., access to online library resources)
- Curriculum design (e.g., sequencing of courses within a program of study)
- Course materials (e.g., learning objects or instructional resources)
- Prior student learning (e.g., impact of experience on knowledge)
- Student satisfaction (e.g., enjoyment, interest, or engagement in the course)
- Teaching behaviors (e.g., activities and behaviors of the course instructor)

Following are some questions that target these aspects of the online learning experience. Also note that some of the sample questions ask for ratings of nonteaching aspects of the course, such as library resources and instructional materials—in fact, "teaching" is just one category in the sample questions.

FIGURE 3.1. TARGETS OF EVALUATION

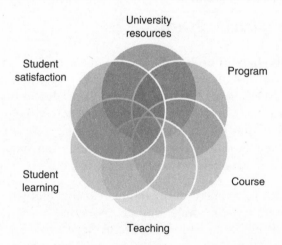

Sample Student Rating Questions and Directives Targeting Aspects of the Online Learning Experience

University Resources

- Rate the effectiveness of the online library for locating course material.
- Based on your experiences in this course, how helpful is tech support in assisting with technology-related challenges?
- Rate the value of the writing center in enhancing the quality of your written communication?

Curriculum

- To what extent did the prerequisites prepare you to succeed in this course?
- Rate your preparation to take more advanced courses in this discipline.
- Indicate the relevance of this course in relation to your degree program.

Course

- To what extent did the online resources enhance your understanding of the learning objectives?
- Rate the usefulness and value of the instructional materials in this course.
- Did the assignments in this course adequately measure your knowledge of the course content?

Student Learning

- Did this course prepare you to take more advanced courses in this area?
- Rate your mastery of the course learning objectives.
- What is your anticipated grade in this course?

Student Satisfaction

- Based on your experience in this course, how likely are you to take future online courses?
- Rate your level of interest in the topics, concepts, and theories discussed in this course.
- Indicate your desire to take additional online courses if taught in a format similar to this course.

Teaching

- Rate the instructor's ability to respond to questions in a timely manner.
- Rate the helpfulness of the instructor's feedback in enhancing your understanding of course content.
- Indicate your desire to take another online course taught by this instructor.

Clearly, evaluations of online teaching should include a clear and direct emphasis on *teaching*, but it is also important to consider other factors that may be included in your evaluation process, especially those that help to situate teaching practices within your specific institutional context. Within this scope, there are three primary levels of measurement: rating of experiences (students), evaluation of teaching practices (peers, self, administrative), and evaluation of contextual support structures (peers, self, administrative). The administrative and functional structures of each institution inform the focus and scope of necessary evaluation components. To determine which of these components to include along with your evaluation of online teaching, consider the following questions.

Do You Have a Centralized Administrative Unit That Oversees Online Course Offerings? If your institution has a centralized structure that coordinates online courses, it may be more efficient to separate the evaluation of institutional resources from the evaluation of specific courses. Because university resources are broadly relevant across all online courses, they can be evaluated in a more holistic fashion that examines their impact across disciplines and degree programs. But, if your institution does not have a centralized system for coordinating among colleges or programs, then you might consider including a focus on university resources in the overall evaluation structure. Likewise, many student satisfaction factors are used to inform broader questions addressing retention and intent for future enrollment. The focus of student satisfaction issues are often more aligned with general evaluations of the university experience.

Do Academic Departments Have Oversight Over Course Development? If the content of the online course was developed under the supervision of the academic department, many of the questions concerning the alignment of the course curriculum within the overall program structure will be addressed as a function of course development. As such, you would not need to target the role of the course within the program in your evaluation of online teaching. Conversely, if online course content is developed by individual instructors or if it is coordinated through a centralized administrative office parallel to the academic department, you should include evaluation components addressing the course fit within the program.

Do Faculty Members Develop Their Own Online Courses? In some online programs, the instructor is responsible for the development of the online course as well as for the facilitation of the learning experience (i.e., teaching). In these cases, it may be desirable to focus the evaluation simultaneously on the course content and the teaching. But, in other online programs, the online course is developed independently from the facilitation of the course. In these cases, it is necessary to separate evaluations of teaching from evaluations of the course, because each component is under the control of a different individual. There are a number of existing evaluation tools that assess online course development (e.g., Quality Matters and similar rubrics). As such, our focus is exclusively on the evaluation of online teaching (independent of course development). Although the remainder of this text will emphasize the evaluation of teaching, it is important to remember that including an evaluation of the online course design is an important aspect of a comprehensive evaluation system.

Although your evaluation of online teaching should clearly highlight *teaching* considerations, within this broad focus there is a wide range of teaching behaviors that underlie an effective online learning experience. The section on "Best Practices in Online Teaching" provides an overview of principles found to be central to quality online education.

At the onset of developing your institution's evaluation of online teaching, you should review the established best practices in online education to determine the relevance and value of each within your institution. These generalized best practices can be adapted, refined, and focused to target your specific university needs. Once you have determined the principles on which to base your evaluation, you are ready to move from theory to practice by aligning each principle with associated teaching behaviors.

Best Practices in Online Teaching. Since online teaching was introduced, researchers have proposed their lists of the essential teaching behaviors that are specific to the online medium. Here is a brief chronology of the most useful definitions, culminating in the "Faculty Competencies for Online Teaching" from Pennsylvania State University, developed by Ann H. Taylor (2011).

Principles of Good Practice: Technology (Chickering & Ehrmann, 1996; Chickering & Gamson, 1987)

1. Encourage student-faculty contact.
2. Develop reciprocity and cooperation among students.
3. Use active learning techniques.
4. Give prompt feedback.
5. Emphasize time on task.
6. Communicate high expectations.
7. Respect diverse talents and ways of learning.

Be VOCAL: Characteristics of Successful Online Instructors (Savery, 2005)

- Visible
- Organized
- Compassionate
- Analytical
- Leader-by-example

Best Practices for Online Teaching (McCullom, 2010)

1. Make learning goals and paths clear to students.
2. Use deliberate practice and mastery learning strategies.
3. Provide prompt, constructive feedback.
4. Provide a balance of challenge and support.
5. Elicit active, critical reflection.
6. Link inquiries to genuine issues of high interest to the learners.
7. Develop learners' effectiveness as learners.
8. Create an institutional environment that supports and encourages inquiry.

Best Practices in Online Teaching Strategies: Instructional Behavior (Hanover Research Council, 2009)

1. Planning and development
2. Teaching in action
3. Student assessment and data evaluation

Faculty Competencies for Online Teaching: Pedagogy (Taylor, 2011)

1. Attend to unique challenges of distance learning.
2. Be familiar with unique learning needs.
3. Master course content, structure, and organization.

4. Respond to student inquiries.
5. Provide detailed feedback.
6. Communicate effectively.
7. Promote a safe learning environment.
8. Monitor student progress.
9. Communicate course goals.
10. Provide evidence of teaching presence.

Step 2: Operationalize Evaluation Components

After identifying the focus and scope of your evaluation, the next step is to determine how you will operationalize the focus into measurable components. Key to this process is an awareness of how your focus aligns with the purpose of the evaluation, the source(s) of data available to you, and the perspectives from which the evaluations may be conducted. Consider the following questions.

What Is the Purpose of the Evaluation Program? Broadly speaking, evaluations of online teaching are done for two primary purposes: to improve teaching (formative evaluation) and to assess performance (summative evaluation). Formative strategies tend to be low-stakes evaluations with a primary emphasis on providing extensive feedback to enhance the ongoing teaching and learning process. The focus of formative evaluations lies in the use of data to guide future improvements. Because of the low-stakes nature of formative feedback, data is typically restricted to the instructor for use in the improvement of teaching. By contrast, summative strategies are more formalized processes designed to assess proficiency. Summative evaluations typically occur at the end of the teaching and learning process and are used as a means of comparing performance against existing benchmarks or standards. Unlike the private nature of formative evaluations, summative evaluations typically provide data to stakeholders to assist with decision making (e.g., tenure, promotion, course scheduling, awards, or remediation).

In many cases, evaluations of online teaching include both formative and summative components, but in order to operationalize principles so that you produce meaningful data, it is important to have *a priori* awareness of the *primary* purpose of the evaluation. For example, if the primary purpose of the evaluation is to provide formative feedback to instructors to help improve their teaching, you may choose to collect rich qualitative data that provides robust detail about the impact of specific teaching behaviors on the learning experience. However, if the primary purpose of the data is to inform tenure and promotion decisions, then concise quantitative data that enable a comparative examination of teaching effectiveness over time may be more appropriate. There is no single right way to collect evaluation data; rather, you need to look at the alignment of the purpose and focus in relation to the type of data you collect.

When determining the primary purpose of the evaluation of online teaching, it is important to consider the longevity, status, and resources of your online program. Unlike the established nature of face-to-face education, many instructors have limited awareness of or familiarity with online education. Similarly, many institutions new to online education may have limited faculty development, technology, or support resources available for faculty teaching online. In these cases, you may choose to prioritize formative evaluations as a means of supporting faculty members as they develop their online teaching skills. By contrast, more established programs may offer extensive training and faculty development resources in online teaching; there may be less need for formal formative evaluation and a greater emphasis placed on summative evaluations.

The same logic may be used to justify different evaluation processes as a function of the experience of the online instructor. As highlighted in the case study of Park University's Online Instructor Evaluation System (see chapter 2), formative evaluations can be used to provide weekly feedback to new instructors with a summative evaluation conducted at the completion of the first course. Central to Park's evaluation process is emphasis on providing additional support and feedback to instructors who are new to online teaching (done through the formative evaluations) while simultaneously evaluating the instructor's ability to use the formative feedback to more effectively facilitate the online learning experience (measured by the final summative evaluation). Because the need for extensive feedback decreases after successfully teaching one's first online course, the sequence of formative evaluations are used only for new faculty members, and all faculty members (regardless of experience) are evaluated with equivalent summative measure.

What Are the Sources of the Evaluation Data? In addition to examining the purpose of the data within the teaching and learning process, it is also important to consider potential data sources. In general, there are two approaches to gathering data: *asking* and *looking*. The quickest and easiest way of gathering data to evaluate an online course is simply to ask the primary stakeholders their opinions and perspectives in relation to the focus of the evaluation. In the case of evaluations of teaching, this may include requiring faculty members to complete a self-evaluation of their teaching effectiveness or administering surveys to gauge student perspectives of a learning experience. The value of the survey data rests in the ability to efficiently assess the attitudes, perspectives, opinions, and experiences of a wide number of individuals at the same time.

Complementing the individualized perspectives and attitudes available via survey data, it is equally important to examine the teaching behaviors that occur in the online classroom. Evidence-based data on instructional activities in the online classroom may include the following:

- Number of announcements posted per module
- Number of contributions to the asynchronous discussion boards
- Quality of contributions to asynchronous discussion boards
- Timeliness of posting student grades
- Quality of feedback on student work
- Frequency of log-ins to the online course environment

Although quality-based indicators (e.g., quality of contributions to asynchronous discussion board, quality of feedback on student work) must be evaluated by peers or administrators, many LMSs offer analytic functions that can provide frequency data (e.g., number of posts to discussion board, number of days logged into a course, time spent in the online classroom). When determining the type of data to be used in the evaluation of online teaching, you should include a discussion with the administrators of the LMS to determine the scope and availability of analytic data.

It is important to note that evaluations of online teaching should integrate analytic data with an explicit awareness on the limits of this type of data. Chapter 8 provides a detailed discussion of the value (and limitations) of using prescriptive data analytics in evaluating online teaching.

Who Will Provide the Data? For an evaluation of online teaching to be relevant and valid, it must ask for the right data, for the right reason, and from the right source. In addition to the analytic and archival data available via the online classroom, there are a number of different stakeholders who can inform the evaluation process, including the instructor (self), students, peers, and administrators.

Recognize that each stakeholder provides only one perspective on the teaching and learning process. It is important to ensure that evaluation processes target the sources who can provide the most accurate information for the focus and purpose of the evaluation. For example, although students are the best raters concerning the ability of the instructor to respond to questions, they may lack the necessary background to assess the quality of an instructor's feedback to students. Conversely, although peers may be able to evaluate the quality of feedback most effectively, they may lack the ability to determine how well an instructor can relate to students in the online classroom. Figure 3.2 provides an overview of the evaluation questions and issues relevant to each stakeholder.

Ideally, your evaluation of online teaching will include feedback from all stakeholders, but all stakeholders do not have to participate in all aspects of the evaluation process. Rather, it is best to begin with a list of best practices that you or your institution have elected to focus on for the evaluation. From this list, determine which stakeholders are able to assess the target dimension. At this point, you are ready to start building the tools that support your evaluation structure. Notice, it is not a matter of building a single tool. An effective evaluation system will include a series of tools that can be used either alone or in combination to provide data to meet the purpose(s) of the evaluation. The remainder of this text is devoted to providing specific guidance on how to adopt, adapt, and build the tools for your evaluation of online teaching.

Although you do *not* need to start this process with a blank slate, you must carefully analyze each dimension and criterion carefully to determine its relevance and fit for your particular institution. Even if you elect to adopt an existing set of best practices as the foundation of your evaluation of online teaching, you will need to operationalize how to measure those best practices within the confines of your unique situation.

For example, assume that your institution has chosen to base your evaluation on "Implementing the Seven Principles: Technology as Lever" by Chickering and Ehrmann (1996), which states that effective teaching with technology accomplishes the following:

- Encourages student-faculty contact
- Develops reciprocity and cooperation among students
- Uses active learning techniques
- Gives prompt feedback

- Emphasizes time on task
- Communicates high expectations
- Respects diverse talents and ways of learning

Focusing just on the first dimension of encouraging student-faculty contact, you will find a number of ways that this may be operationalized in the online classroom. If we return to the ask-look paradigm, there are two directly involved stakeholder groups (instructors and students) who can be

FIGURE 3.2. SAMPLE EVALUATION ISSUES FOR INSTITUTIONAL STAKEHOLDERS

Stakeholder	Relevant Evaluation Questions and Issues
Self	• Were there unique barriers that affected teaching? • What is my technological competence for facilitating online learning? • What is my level of engagement and investment in the online course?
Students	• Did the instructor communicate effectively? • How timely did the instructor respond to the questions? • Did the instructor stimulate discussion interaction through questions, posts, and/or prompts? • Was the instructor professional in all communications and interactions?
Peers	• Did the instructor provide useful feedback to enhance student learning? • Did the instructor demonstrate competence in the discipline? • Was the instructor knowledgeable and current with trends, issues, and theories in the discipline? • Was the instructor responsive to various learning styles and preferences? • Did the instructor enhance the quality of the online learning experience through integration of relevant resources, experiences, and readings?
Administrators	• Did the instructor follow institutional policies for course setup, grade submission, and so on? • Did the instructor follow institutional expectations for frequency of interaction? • Were students provided with grades and feedback in a timely manner? • Did the instructor meet institutional expectations for professionalism?

TABLE 3.1. SAMPLE ONLINE-TEACHING EVALUATION QUESTIONS

	Formative	**Summative**
Instructor	• How were discussion forums used to encourage interaction in the online classroom? • What barriers have you faced in connecting with your students? What strategies can you implement to overcome these barriers?	• On a scale of 1 (never) to 10 (always), rate your ability to stimulate ongoing interaction in the asynchronous discussions. • Rate your use of course tools to interact with your online students.
Students	• What can the instructor do to more effectively engage with you in the online classroom? • What has the instructor done particularly well to facilitate your learning experience?	• On a scale of 1 (not at all) to 7 (completely), how comfortable are you asking the instructor questions? • Rate your agreement with the following statement: My instructor stimulates ongoing interaction and discussion in the online classroom.

asked to evaluate the student-faculty contact. Possible questions and evaluation items that evaluate this target dimension are illustrated in Table 3.1.

In addition, there are artifacts in the online classroom that we can examine as indicators of "encouraging student-faculty contact," such as these:

- Tone of instructor posts and interactions
- Responsiveness to student introductions
- Initiation of a welcome e-mail to students
- Facilitation of a course "lounge" or informal asynchronous discussion
- Use of multimedia to personalize the online learning experience
- Responsiveness to questions
- Active engagement in threaded discussions
- Integration of questions, reflective prompts, or critical thinking activities in the online classroom
- Personalized nature of feedback to student assignments
- Use of announcements to connect with students
- Integration of faculty biography or introduction

Beyond these specific instructor activities in the classroom (which must be evaluated via peer or administrative stakeholders), there are also analytic indicators of student-faculty contact:

- Ratio of faculty-to-student posts
- Number of instructor log-ins per week
- Time spent in the online classroom
- Number of announcements posted
- Response time for providing feedback to students

All of these indicators provide insight into the ability of the online instructor to encourage student-to-faculty interaction. So, which do you choose? The answer to this question depends on the structure and resources of your particular institution. You must select the processes and tools of your evaluation of online teaching to align with your institutional structure.

Step 3: Create an Implementation Plan

The final step in preparing the foundation of your evaluation of online teaching rests in examining the unique circumstance of your institution that will affect the evaluation process. In this step, you must ensure your evaluation of online teaching measures the desired outcomes within the bounds of what is practical, possible, and sustainable at your institution. Consider the following questions.

Who Will Have Primary Responsibility for Conducting Evaluations? There are three general levels from which evaluations of online teaching may be mandated: (1) the department, (2) the college, or (3) a centralized distance-learning administrative unit. In most institutions, there is a clear hierarchy of teaching oversight for face-to-face courses starting at the department level and progressing up to the college or university level. But oversight of online teaching often presents a challenge because of the intersection of specialized administrative structures targeted specifically at online or distance education.

If your institution does not have a centralized administrative unit that oversees online education, you will likely want to use the same evaluation oversight for evaluation of online teaching that is used for face-to-face teaching evaluations. Most likely, this will mandate that evaluations be conducted at the department or college level. However, if your institution has a centralized administrative unit targeting online education, then it is essential that you clearly specify who has primary responsibility for overseeing evaluations of online teaching. Keep in mind that the evaluation process may include self, student, peer, or administrative review.

Regardless of the source of data, there must be a designated entity that is responsible for oversight of the entire evaluation process.

In determining who will have oversight of online teaching evaluations, there are a number of interrelated considerations.

Do Evaluators Have the Necessary Qualifications? An evaluation of online teaching is going to include two primary considerations: instructors' knowledge of disciplinary content and their ability to teach that content within the online classroom. Therefore, you must make sure that evaluations include insight from individuals who have the prerequisite knowledge of each of these aspects of the teaching process. If evaluations are conducted solely at the department level, this may prove challenging because departmental peers or administrators who are able to assess disciplinary expertise may lack sufficient experience in online teaching. Conversely, if evaluations are conducted solely via a centralized administrative unit, evaluators may be able to assess online teaching proficiency but would likely lack specific disciplinary knowledge.

Within your particular institution, you need to determine if either departmental or centralized evaluators possess the necessary background to evaluate both dimensions of teaching. If so, you can structure the evaluation process within the singular line of oversight. If not, you will need to structure the evaluation process to integrate information from both sets of stakeholders (while ensuring to clearly establish who has final authority over evaluation-related decisions).

Do Evaluators Have the Required Time Available to Complete Evaluation Requirements? How Frequently Will Evaluations Be Conducted? The time required to complete an evaluation of online teaching varies dramatically as a function of how the evaluation is structured and how many individuals must be evaluated. This issue becomes intensified when examining the evaluation of online teaching as the scalability of online education increases potential course offerings through the use of contingent instructors. You should start by determining how many evaluations must be conducted per year (based on your institutional size) and what the potential time investment for evaluation oversight will be as a function of the type of evaluation process used. For example, see Table 3.2.

The "Scenarios of Time Investment" case studies provide several examples of the time required as a function of evaluation oversight and university size.

TABLE 3.2. TIME ESTIMATES FOR COMMON EVALUATOR TASKS

Type of Evaluation	Evaluator Role	Estimated Time Investment per Class
Student ratings	Review a summary report of student-rating statistics and numbers.	5–10 minutes
LMS analytics report	Review a summary report of specified LMS data.	5–10 minutes
Instructor self-evaluation	Review a self-evaluation submitted by the instructor.	5–10 minutes
Formative peer observation	Review online course according to specific dimensions and provide instructor feedback.	15–120 minutes, depending on evaluation tool and process
Summative peer or administrative review	Review online course according to evaluation tool and provide evaluative judgment of instructor quality.	30–120 minutes, depending on evaluation tool and process

Scenarios of Time Investment

Scenario 1

University X handles all evaluations directly through the academic department; it is a traditional university that has recently began offering online programs to supplement its face-to-face course offerings. Most departments currently offer six online courses per semester. These courses are taught primarily by the campus-based faculty. Because of their small size and novelty with online education, they have elected to use a combination of formative peer observation (sixty minutes each) along with summative administrative review (sixty minutes each). This requires that each department dedicate a minimum of twelve hours per semester to the evaluation of online courses.

Scenario 2

University Y is a traditional university with a rapidly growing online program. Similar to University X, evaluations have traditionally been conducted through the academic department. But, unlike University X, the rapid growth of University Y's online program has required the extensive integration of contingent faculty members to teach the increasing number of online courses. At present, departments are averaging thirty online sections per semester and numbers continue to grow. Mirroring the evaluation process used for face-to-face courses, University Y adopted a once-a-year, summative administrative review of each course. Within this system, department administrators are required to invest more than thirty hours in the evaluation of online courses.

Scenario 3

University Z has a large, well-established online program. In a typical semester, University Z will offer more than three hundred online course sections taught by more than two hundred instructors. Similar to University X and Y, University Z relies on a summative peer evaluation (in addition to student ratings and analytic data). Each semester, this requires more than 350 hours dedicated to online evaluations. The extensive time commitment mandates that evaluations be handled out of a centralized administrative unit devoted to online education.

The selection of an evaluation strategy and the responsibility of evaluation oversight must be done in tandem in order to balance the practical constraints associated implementing any evaluation system. But, even within this structure there are a number of ways to maximize the impact of the evaluations while being as efficient as possible. Because student ratings and analytic data can be collected, analyzed, and reported quite efficiently, it is wise to collect this data every time that an online course is taught. But, because of the time investment required for peer or administrative review, you may elect to evaluate on an interval schedule or to set the evaluation schedule as a function of the outcome of the previous review (low scores might force more frequent evaluations whereas high scores could extend the time frame between evaluations).

What Funding Is Available to Support the Evaluation Process? Evaluation tools, in and of themselves, are not expensive. But the administration of the evaluation tools and the staffing necessary to conduct evaluations may involve additional expenses. When selecting your evaluation processes, you will want to consider any necessary software, equipment, or implementation expenses that are required for either start-up or ongoing evaluations.

What Processes Already Exist? Although evaluations of online teaching are, in fact, different than evaluations of face-to-face teaching, there may (or may not) be existing processes at your institution that you will want to take into consideration. For example, many face-to-face courses use online systems for administering end-of-course evaluations; these systems may be amenable to implementing student ratings in online courses as well. Likewise, some institutions use e-portfolios for tracking faculty evaluations over time, so you may want to examine how these types of systems could be used to implement evaluations of online teaching.

In addition, depending on the specific needs of your institution, there may be a need to gauge equivalence between online and face-to-face education (whether in reference to learning gains, instructor quality, student satisfaction, etc.). You may wish to examine existing indicators of teaching effectiveness to intentionally mirror some of the evaluation strategies that are currently used in the face-to-face environment in your evaluation of online teaching; this type of data will enable comparisons across teaching modes within the institution.

Conclusion

As highlighted at the beginning of this chapter, one of the greatest challenges to developing an effective evaluation of online teaching is knowing where to start. The sequential decision-making process outlined in this chapter provides a foundation for considering the focus, nature, and purpose that drive the development and implementation of your evaluation of online teaching:

1. Identify the focus of the online teaching evaluation.
2. Operationalize evaluation components to measure effective teaching in the online classroom.
3. Create an implementation plan that aligns evaluation system within the institutional structure.

For your evaluation system to be effective, it must be tailored specifically to address the unique needs of your institution and the structure of your online program(s). By clearly identifying the focus of the evaluation, you can then operationalize evaluation components to create an implementation plan that aligns the evaluation of online teaching within your institutional structure.

A Thought Exercise

Perhaps the names of specific people on your campus came to mind as you read in chapter 3 about the various stakeholder roles that typically support an evaluation program. Take a few minutes and see how many specific people or areas of your institution can be matched against the questions asked throughout chapter 3. Again, don't worry if some questions are difficult to assign right now. Note those as areas for exploration.

- Do you have a centralized administrative unit that oversees online course offerings? If not, what areas or people on your campus perform this function?
- Do academic departments have oversight over course development? If not, what areas or people on your campus perform this function?
- Do faculty members develop their own online courses? If not, what areas or people on your campus perform this function?
- What is the purpose of the evaluation program? Who on your campus has the final authority to say so?
- What are the sources of the evaluation data? Who on your campus is responsible for gathering this information?
- Who will have primary responsibility for conducting evaluations?
- Do evaluators have the necessary qualifications? Who on your campus certifies this?
- Do evaluators have the required time available to complete evaluation requirements? Who on your campus has the say-so to make time for the processes needed?
- How frequently will evaluations be conducted? Who on your campus is part of making this decision?

To conclude this exercise, share this list of questions with a colleague and compare your responses, especially if they differ. This is a good way to expand your project by identifying likely team members to invite to become part of the creation and implementation processes.

PART TWO

FORMATIVE EVALUATION

CHAPTER FOUR

CONDUCTING FORMATIVE REVIEWS TO ENHANCE ONLINE TEACHING

B. Jean Mandernach's Story

Being immersed in virtual education, I have frequent discussions with colleagues about the trials and tribulations of teaching online. One theme of these discussions is clear: virtually everyone worries that their online teaching is not as effective as it could—or should—be.

During a recent chat, a fellow online educator mentioned her constant struggle to find the right balance of instructor postings in the asynchronous discussion. As she explained the challenge, "If I post too much, the students become passive and rely on me to carry the discussion; if I post too little, the conversation becomes shallow and fails to explore key issues. I'm just not sure where the tipping point is."

Although my colleague was likely hoping I would provide the magical (nonexistent) formula to accurately address her challenge, I responded with a simple question. *Have you asked your students?* This question produced an immediate burst of nervous laughter and an equally rapid "no"; she explained that she never seeks this type of informal feedback from students because she worries that it implies a lack of competence with online education.

In a sincere attempt to be helpful, I chose to ignore the fallacies of her logic and offered to peek at her online course to offer insights as to how she might improve the quality of asynchronous discussions. This suggestion prompted another round of robust laughter with an "absolutely not" response. My colleague explained that letting me see her online course was akin to teaching naked and she did not feel confident enough in her skill as an online instructor to take that risk.

Despite my objections and solemn promises not to judge, my colleague didn't budge; she refused to seek informal feedback during the course of the semester and opted to wait it out for the required summative student ratings of teaching. The conversation ended with her resolve to read the end-of-course evaluations in more depth this year to attempt to discern any insight that the open-ended questions might offer on this issue.

The Value of Evaluation

There are two primary goals that drive the evaluation of online teaching: (1) to gauge instructors' overall effectiveness or skill in an online classroom in order to inform their subsequent teaching experiences (summative evaluation) and (2) to gain feedback during a course to improve the ongoing teaching and learning process (formative evaluation). Despite the complementary and overlapping nature of each type of evaluation, significant differences exist in the purpose, use, integration, and reliance of each. Although summative evaluation is generally accepted as a necessary component of accountability and quality control in a comprehensive evaluation system (especially in terms of making employment decisions to rehire contingent faculty members or promote tenure-line faculty members), one is less apt to see a role for formative feedback in most online teaching evaluation plans. This is not to imply that instructors are opposed to receiving informal feedback, but rather that the private, behind-a-password nature of online teaching may not seem to lend itself as naturally to formative evaluation. Although face-to-face instruction may be informed by hallway observations or students' nonverbal cues, seeking formative feedback in an online course requires more deliberate planning and implementation.

As highlighted in the opening case, instructors regularly subject their online teaching to required summative evaluations, such as end-of-course student surveys, but the use of less formal feedback with the explicit goal of enhancing in-progress teaching is less common. Summative and formative evaluations *both* provide important information about the quality of online teaching and *both* provide instructor feedback to help enhance teaching strategies. How each is implemented, however, varies a great deal, particularly with regard to what information is gathered, when data are collected, who has access to the feedback, and how the feedback is used.

Comparing Summative and Formative Evaluation Approaches

Summative evaluations emphasize an overall judgment of one's effectiveness in teaching online. Conducted at the end of a course or program, the focus of summative evaluations is to measure and document quality indicators for decision-making purposes. Although information gained from summative evaluations may be used to improve *future* teaching performance, the information is not provided in a timely fashion to provide opportunities for revision or modification of instructional strategies while the teaching and learning is still in progress.

Summative evaluations are designed to measure instructor performance following a sustained period of teaching with the focus on identifying the effectiveness of instruction. Summative evaluations provide a means of accountability in gauging the extent to which an instructor meets the institution's expectations for online teaching. Because summative evaluations are a central component of gauging instructional effectiveness at most institutions, the high-stakes nature mandates that these evaluations are valid and reliable. Summative evaluations provide the following:

- Information concerning instructor adherence to teaching expectations
- A basis for comparing instructor performance to reference groups and external performance criteria
- A means of determining the effectiveness of instructional activities
- Objective information for determining course assignments
- Comparative data to determine employment decisions (continuation, tenure, promotion, etc.)
- Diagnostic information about strengths and weaknesses in instructor performance
- Data to determine achievement of departmental or curriculum performance expectations

By contrast, formative evaluations aim to gain quick feedback about the effectiveness of *current* instructional strategies with the explicit goal of enhancing teaching during the target course. The focus of formative evaluation is on soliciting feedback that enables timely revisions to enhance the learning process. Formative evaluations are designed to provide information to help instructors improve their online instruction. Formative evaluations may be conducted at any time throughout the instructional process to monitor the value and impact of instructional practices or to provide feedback on teaching strengths and challenges.

What differentiates formative evaluation from summative evaluation is the role of feedback obtained; this feedback enables instructors to modify instructional activities midstream in light of their effectiveness, impact, and value. Because formative evaluations are designed to guide the teaching process—and are not used as outcome indicators—they are generally individualized evaluations that are under the control of the instructor and target specific instructional issues or concerns. Unlike the more general summative evaluations, formative evaluations may include any targeted attempt to gain feedback for the purposes of enhancing instruction during the teaching and learning process. Formative evaluations provide the following:

- Insight on pedagogical strengths and challenges in relation to specific course concepts
- Guidance to improve teaching strategies
- A means of monitoring progress or growth in teaching effectiveness
- Diagnostic information concerning the impact of instructional practices
- A nonthreatening environment to identify and correct challenges in instruction (Chatterji, 2003)

For formative evaluation to be effective, it must be goal-directed with a clear purpose, provide feedback that enables actionable revisions, and be implemented in a timely manner to enable revisions within the active teaching-learning cycle. Formative evaluations are most effective when they are focused on a specific instructional strategy or concern. Focused formative evaluations produce more specific, targeted feedback that is amenable to actionable change. For example, rather than ask a general question, such as "How can the instructor be more effective in the online classroom?" one might ask about a specific aspect of the online classroom, such as "What can the instructor do in the asynchronous discussion threads to foster more engaged dialogue?" This type of targeted question encourages a richer, deeper response that is more likely to provide insight into how specific instructional strategies can be improved.

See Table 4.1 for more details on the relative strengths and drawbacks of each evaluation approach.

TABLE 4.1. ADVANTAGES AND DISADVANTAGES OF SUMMATIVE AND FORMATIVE EVALUATION

	Advantages	*Disadvantages*
Summative evaluations	Necessary for determining faculty effectiveness teaching online	Tendency for overreliance on summative measures
	Promotes instructor, department, and college accountability	Does not provide information for correcting errors during the teaching and learning process
	Provides a means of evaluating the impact or value of instructional activities	Fails to capture improvements or gains in instructional ability
	Monitors instructor's adherence to institutional expectations for online teaching	May be inappropriate to apply equally to all instructors because of differences in experience, discipline, or instructional goals
Formative evaluations	Enables the identification and correction of ineffective instructional practices	May be difficult to motivate voluntary inclusion or use (if not required)
	Promotes active reflection on the effectiveness of instruction	Requires acknowledgment, inclusion, or revision based on feedback
	Encourages feedback that enhances quality of online teaching	Often dependent on individual faculty for effective inclusion
	Low-stakes nature encourages feedback-revision-improvement cycle	

The Unique Nature of Formative Evaluation in the Online Classroom

Formative evaluation is particularly important in the online classroom because of the unique circumstances surrounding this learning environment. Consider the following factors:

- **Novelty.** Although virtually all instructors have experienced effective face-to-face teaching at some point in their lives, the same assumption cannot be made for online teaching. For many instructors (and students), online teaching and learning is a novel experience. Lacking an established background to serve as a guide, teachers may feel that the novelty of online teaching creates an increased need for informal feedback to guide effective instructional development.

- **Teaching expectations.** Depending on how established the online program is at each institution, there may be variability in the expectations for teaching online. In more formalized programs, there may be very clear standards and expectations for online teaching so less informal feedback may be necessary. By contrast, the less that established standards and expectations exist, the more formative feedback may be necessary to guide teaching practices.

- **Training variability.** There is considerable variability in how faculty development and training is conducted in relation to online teaching. At some institutions, instructors who teach online are provided extensive training in how to use the LMS and related instructional technology but are provided little in the form of pedagogical instruction; in these cases, instructors may need more informal feedback to assist in the development of effective teaching strategies. Conversely, some institutions provide increased training information on online pedagogy so less formative feedback may be necessary.

- **Privacy and isolation.** The majority of online classes are supported via an LMS with password-protected access. As such, online teaching occurs in an isolated environment with limited opportunity for casual, unplanned feedback from peers. Likewise, many instructors are teaching their online courses remotely and may not have access to informal peer networks to casually discuss teaching challenges. This lack of spontaneous informal feedback increases the need to intentionally plan and implement formative evaluations to foster effective online teaching.

- **Rapidly changing technology.** The field of educational technology is rapidly evolving; the number of tools, techniques, and applications to support online education is growing at an astounding rate. In response to changing technology, it is important that instructors seek informal feedback on the value, relevance, and application of the various technologies integrated into the online classroom.

- **Lack of unsolicited feedback.** Instructors who teach online also recognize that they will not be able to rely on the expressions on their students' faces or the questions students ask in the hallway after class as evidence of their teaching effectiveness, as they may do for their face-to-face teaching. To learn how things are going in the online classroom, they will need to devise a more structured way to get feedback from their students. Such feedback can be particularly helpful in online courses in which it is more difficult to read student's reactions ... and in another course or even another institution, it is just a click away. Instructors who take the time to ask for feedback while their course is in progress and who act on that feedback help to ensure that the learning experience is successful for both their students and themselves.

Making Room for Improvement along the Way

Unlike the regimented options of published summative evaluation tools, formative evaluations of online teaching are often more organic. Although some instructors may use preplanned formative evaluation instruments such as a standardized midsemester student survey, the need, approach, and strategy for seeking more informal feedback often arise as an unstructured—even unanticipated—opportunity in response to attempting a new pedagogical approach or tackling an instructional challenge. Despite their organic nature, in order for these more informal formative evaluations to be effective, they must still be intentionally structured and implemented to produce the intended feedback.

To ensure your all of your formative evaluations meet your needs, you must consider the five Ws: who, what, when, where, and why:

- **Who.** Unlike summative reviews of teaching that are conducted for administrative purposes, such as promotion or staffing decisions, formative reviews are typically conducted by and for the instructor (perhaps with the support of a learning design team). As such, each online instructor must determine the relevance, focus, and timing of their formative evaluations. Instructors need to be knowledgeable about formative evaluation strategies so that they can be implemented on an as-needed basis in the online classroom. There are many options for formative evaluations, including self-evaluations, peer evaluations, and student ratings of online teaching.
- **What.** Formative evaluations typically differ from summative reviews of teaching with regard to the type and amount of feedback that is sought. Instructors seeking formative feedback on their teaching typically focus their efforts on specific aspects of their teaching that they are seeking to improve. For example, instead of an end-of-course student survey that asks about a wide variety of aspects of the course—from questions about the structure of the course to those that address instructor-student interactions—a formative student-rating instrument might ask only about a new technique that the instructor had recently tried out in

order to gain the perspectives on how well the technique had been implemented.

- **When.** Because formative evaluations are short, direct measures conducted in response to specific pedagogical questions, formative reviews of teaching are typically conducted more frequently than formal reviews. Although instructors must balance the need for feedback with a respect for students' and peers' time, formative reviews may be conducted at multiple points throughout an online course.

- **Where.** Although summative end-of-course student surveys or peer reviews are the most common ways to elicit feedback, those take place only at the end of the course and may not be conducted each time the course is taught. Many instructors have discovered the value of asking for formative feedback much earlier in their courses. Midsemester surveys and even instruments that are given more frequently, such as end-of-lesson or end-of-week questionnaires, enable instructors to find out how things are going in their course in time to make adjustments that will benefit current students.

- **Why.** Instructors should conduct formative evaluations when they are personally interested in improving their teaching and desire feedback in order to do so. Formative evaluations should not be conducted simply for the sake of doing so. Of course, part of their motivation may still be related to ultimate goals of promotion or ensuring that they will continue to be hired to teach a given class in the future, but the primary motivator should be a focus on teaching improvement. By conducting formative reviews of their teaching, instructors are not waiting for periodic summative reviews to get a sense of how they are doing in the online classroom but are actively soliciting feedback to improve their teaching skills for the benefit of the students currently in their course.

Making the Most of Formative Feedback: The SCARF Loop

To get the most value from formative reviews, Thomas J. Tobin has created the concept of the SCARF loop (see Figure 4.1). This simple mnemonic reminds instructors to do the following:

Solicit the desired information.

Compile and analyze findings.

Adjust teaching based on the feedback.

Report Feedback to stakeholders.

FIGURE 4.1. THE SCARF LOOP

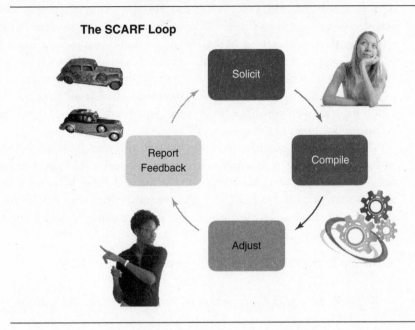

The SCARF Loop

S: Solicit the Desired Information

The first step in the SCARF loop is to figure out what it is you want to learn. Although it is tempting to ask a lot of questions, keeping your questions to a minimum helps to ensure that stakeholders provide you with the targeted, meaningful feedback you desire. Ask yourself what you most want to find out about the following issues:

- Concerned about whether your students are grasping the main concepts for the current lesson?
- Wondering if anyone is actually getting anything out of the video clips you worked so hard on and embedded into your course?
- Worrying that there may be problems with the team project you assigned last week?
- Scared that lack of activity in your discussion forums means that no one is completing your reading assignments?

The questions you have about your course should dictate what you want to ask. Try to limit yourself to the key aspects of your course that concern you the most. We will return to the topic of writing good questions in a moment.

The next step is to determine how you will to find out that information. In an ideal world, you could have a lengthy, rich discussion with each stakeholder to explore their thoughts, ideas, and suggestions. Practically speaking, that is probably not feasible ... particularly if you are interested in students' perspectives. So what technique can you use to solicit the information you need? A multiple-choice survey? An open-ended questionnaire? A peer review? Some combination? Something else? It all depends on how much information you hope to receive. Sometimes a simple "yes" or "no" response is all you need.

For example, one instructor we worked with wanted to know if anyone in his class was using a supplemental web page he had created to share related resources with his students. He worked hard to keep it updated with the latest from his field, but it occurred to him that maybe he wasn't spending his time wisely if his students weren't using it. So he created the following online poll:

Do You Ever Look at the "Supplemental Resources" Page?

☑ Yes, I use on the supplemental resources page and will continue to do so.
☐ Yes, I visited it, but I don't plan to return.
☐ No, I didn't realize it was there ... but now I will!
☐ No, I haven't and I don't plan to.

Within twenty-four hours, he had the information he needed. Despite his assumption that no one was using the page (and that he shouldn't bother with it anymore), he found that either his students were already using the web page and planned to return to it or they didn't know it existed, but plan to use it now that he'd called their attention to it. The poll was a quick and simple way to get the information that he needed. With this new information in hand, he was motivated to continue updating the resource for his students, knowing it was making a difference to their learning.

However, sometimes we have questions about our teaching that cannot be answered by simply checking a box or answering a quick poll. For example, perhaps you want to know what your students thought were the most important concepts from the current reading assignment so you can make sure you have helped them to focus on the right information. You might ask them to share their thoughts with you in the form of a brief narrative.

In the soliciting feedback step of the SCARF loop, you will also need to consider the frequency with which you do so. Is this feedback you will seek only at one point during your course (perhaps because it focuses on a time-specific aspect of the course) or might you solicit feedback more regularly? Will you ask the same question(s) each time? In addition to the question of what it is you are trying to learn, the frequency also depends on formal feedback mechanisms that might be in place in your course because of institutional requirements (e.g., the institution might have a midsemester survey that all courses must include or a required annual peer-review process), the length of your course, and the amount of effort that you, your students, and your peers are willing to contribute to the process. Let's look at each of these in turn.

First, how do other, more formal feedback instruments required by a department or institution factor in? A well-documented phenomenon in research is "survey fatigue," in which the respondent tires of answering survey questions as they progress through an instrument and the quality of their responses diminishes as a result (Lavrakas, 2008). A similar phenomenon occurs when individuals are surveyed too frequently or with multiple instruments simultaneously. For this reason, it is important to consider other solicitations for feedback when planning opportunities for formative feedback. For example, your department may require a formal midsemester survey to be completed in all of its courses. Because your students will already be asked to complete that instrument, you will want to avoid adding your own midsemester survey. Instead, you might consider asking for feedback at the end of the first quarter of the course, the end of the third quarter of the course, or even at both of those points. Likewise, if your department requires peer reviews, you will want to avoid asking the same peer to informally review your online teaching if that individual will have to conduct a formal review in the near future so you don't overburden that individual.

Next, how does course length factor in? For a course that lasts twelve to sixteen weeks in length, asking for student input on a weekly basis can be a reasonable approach. For a shorter course that may only be a few weeks in duration, however, you may want to limit how often you solicit formative feedback to mirror how quickly you will actually be able to make changes as the course is being conducted. Remember, formative feedback is intended to affect current students. If you will not have time to address the feedback in your current offering, then it doesn't make sense to ask for that feedback midcourse. If students, in particular, are asked for their feedback and then do not see any response to that feedback, the entire process loses credibility.

In addition, how does the amount of effort the instructor, students, and peers contribute to the process factor in? Whether you have questions that can be answered with the click of a box or a narrative or both, you should keep in mind the amount of time it will take you to review the feedback you receive. After all, being able to review the feedback you receive is the goal! As suggested, there is no sense asking for input if you are not going to be able to respond to it. Make sure that you will have time to review the feedback that you receive and to make sense of it. This can be particularly challenging in large classes. When faced with collecting student feedback in a class that contains large numbers of students, you may want to consider strategies that will keep your workload reasonable, such as limiting the number of open-ended questions you ask or inviting only a random sample of your students to complete your instrument instead of the entire class.

You also need to consider the time your students and peers are being asked to spend on your query. Think of the last time *you* were asked to fill out a survey or questionnaire. Most of us decide whether or not to complete such requests based on how long it will take us to do so. Our students and peers are no different. When faced with a lengthy instrument, most will likely breeze through it quickly in order to get it over with. Likewise the types of responses they are being asked to provide can influence how much effort they give to the instrument. For example, answering a series of multiple choice or Likert-scale questions will seem less daunting than being faced with a series of questions that require open-ended responses.

Although soliciting formative feedback can be as easy asking stakeholders to e-mail their feedback to you or to have students use your institution's LMS (e.g., Blackboard, Canvas, Desire2Learn, Moodle) to submit a one-minute or muddiest point paper, there are also many web-based tools available—often for free—that make doing it yourself easy. Some popular online survey tools include the following:

- Qualtrics (http://qualtrics.com/)
- SurveyMonkey (www.surveymonkey.com/)
- Survey Gold (www.surveygoldsolutions.com/)
- Google Template (search for existing templates at https://drive.google.com/templates)

These tools typically require instructors to enter their desired questions into a web-based form, then provide them with a URL to give to their students so they can complete the instrument. Results are reported in clear, easy-to-read formats. The hardest part, as we have discussed, is figuring out what to ask.

Having determined what it is you want to learn from your formative review and the best way to solicit that information, it is time to return to the task of writing specific questions to ask of your stakeholders. Writing your questions is actually trickier than one might think. Subtle nuances in wording make a world of difference in how the question is perceived by respondents. In order to get the information you seek, great care must be taken in crafting your questions. Most online survey tools provide helpful guidelines to assist one with creating a good instrument. (See "Creating Good Survey Questions.") Remember, you don't have to start from scratch. A simple online search using words such as *course survey questions* will lead to many existing examples. Of course, not everything you find online will be well written. You may need to adapt the questions you find in order to make them work for your needs (particularly if the examples you find were created for use in a face-to-face course environment) and to follow the advice given in the next section.

Once you have written your questions, it is a good idea to pilot test your instrument to make sure the questions are clear, unbiased, and provide you with the information you seek. Colleagues and trusted students are a good source for feedback.

Creating Good Survey Questions

Creating good survey questions is more challenging than it might seem! There are a number of things to avoid:

- **Jargon and acronyms.** Be careful not to use language that your students might not understand or find confusing. This can be especially true for populations that include international students. For example:
  - **Original question.** Was the feedback provided to you via ScoreCard helpful in facilitating your learning?
  - **Revised question.** Was the feedback provided to you via ScoreCard, our online gradebook tool, helpful in facilitating your learning?
  - **Original request.** Please rate the effectiveness of the training provided for the OBS.
  - **Revised request.** Please rate the effectiveness of the training provided for the One Button Studio.
- **Complex questions.** Keep your survey questions simple. If you ask about multiple things in a single question or make your questions too wordy, it

will be hard for your students to answer your question and also difficult for you to make sense of what the responses you get actually mean. For example:

- **Original question.** Do you agree that the textbook used in this course is outdated and that an alternative textbook should be used instead?
- **Revised question (now two separate questions).** How do you rate the adequacy of the textbook used in this course in terms of explaining the course concepts? Do you think an alternative textbook should be used instead of the one currently used in this course?
- **Original question.** Do you believe that this course is difficult because of the number of assignments required and the amount of reading that is assigned or do you believe that this course has the appropriate amount of rigor for a standard three-credit course in geography?
- **Revised question.** What is your opinion of the level of difficulty of this course as compared to other three-credit, hundred-level courses offered by our department?

- **"Loaded" language.** Make sure your survey questions aren't biased or leading in their tone so you don't lead your students into responding the way that you would like them to (or to give the perception that you are doing so). For example:

  - **Original question.** Don't you agree that the video interviews embedded in the course materials aid in your understanding of the course concepts?
  - **Revised question.** Do the video interviews embedded in the course materials aid in your understanding of the course concepts?
  - **Original question.** There are many people who believe that the amount of work required for this course is appropriate for a three-credit course. Are you one of them?
  - **Revised question.** How does the amount of work required for this course compare to the other three-credit, hundred-level courses you have taken at our institution?

- **Vague language.** Using vague terms within your questions or asking about vague concepts will confuse your students and runs the risk of being misinterpreted. Be clear and concise in your wording. Try your question out on a few colleagues or students and ask them what they think the question is about.

  - **Original question.** What do you think about this course? (This is confusing because the question isn't clear about what it is specifically asking

about ... the quality of the course? The content covered in the course? The attentiveness of the instructor to the students? Something else?)
- **Revised question.** What assignments in this course helped you the most to understand the subject matter?
- **Double negatives.** Sentences that contain double negatives can confuse the reader and might not be interpreted correctly.
  - **Original question.** Do you agree or disagree that students should not be marked down for not including a complete citation at the beginning of their reports?
  - **Revised question.** Should students who do not include a complete citation at the beginning of their report be marked down?

There are many resources available online that provide additional help in writing effective surveys. One particularly useful document available for download is "Questionnaire Design: Asking Questions with a Purpose" by Ellen Taylor-Powell (1996).

C: Compile and Analyze Findings

As the saying goes, "Be careful what you wish for." When asking for feedback, we need to be prepared to listen. Take time to review your feedback carefully and thoughtfully. Do you agree with the feedback? Where do you see room for improvement? Is there anything that surprises you? Do you see any trends? What comments seem to be outliers?

Interestingly, we all tend to focus on the negative when reviewing our feedback. Even if just one stakeholder makes a comment that hits us hard, that comment will jump out at us as if it is the only salient point in a sea of otherwise glowing reviews. That is human nature. The trick is to neither obsess with the negative nor to dismiss it entirely by rationalizing it away. Instead, reflect on the troubling comment. Is there an element of truth to what the feedback says? It may be worth asking a close peer to review the comment and help assess its worth. If there is an element of truth, determine how to address it. If the comment doesn't ring true to either individual, however, it is probably best to let it go.

A: Adjust Teaching Based on the Feedback

Once the feedback has been analyzed, the next step is to make a plan of action for addressing that feedback. What steps will you take to improve your teaching with the information that has been gained? Are these steps you can accomplish on your own or will you need assistance from someone else, such as an instructional designer or an assessment expert?

Baby steps work best. You may find yourself faced with feedback on many different aspects of your course, and not all of them will necessarily be widespread. You may even find you have conflicting feedback. For example, one student might complain that the course has too many required discussions, and another requests even more. Another student might feel you are not "accessible" or "present" enough in the course, and another student might think you send too many communications to the class. Tackling the entire course at once can be overwhelming. Prioritize the improvements that you want to make and address what seem to be the key ones in time for the next course offering. See what works well and what needs further adjustment. Some of the changes made may have unforeseen positive or negative impacts on other aspects of the course. By taking small steps, adjustments can be made more easily along the way.

If additional resources will be needed, do you have those readily available to you or do you need to make a special request of your supervisor? Institutions vary widely in the amount of teaching support that is available to their instructors. Fortunately, there are many websites and online forums where instructors can find free assistance. The following list provides some good, general starting points.

Help Wanted! A Sampling of Faculty Development Resources

- MERLOT Faculty Development Portal
  (http://facultydevelopment.merlot.org/)
- Michigan State University's Online Instructional Resources
  (http://fod.msu.edu/oir/online-instructional-resources)
- The Dutton Institute's Faculty Development Site, Penn State
  (http://facdev.e-education.psu.edu/)
- The Professional and Organization Development (POD) Listserv
  (http://podnetwork.org/pod-listserv/)
- The Online Learning Consortium (formerly Sloan-C) Listserv
  (http://onlinelearningconsortium.org/mailing_list)

You may find that there are aspects to what you are hearing from the feedback that you do *not* plan to act on. For example, maybe some of your students requested that you post the previous semester's exams online so they can be used for practice. You, however, may only have a couple of versions of your exam, so you worry that posting them will make it too easy for future students to cheat. In our next section, we will look at how to convey decisions like this to your students.

R and F: Report Feedback to Stakeholders

Although the purpose of soliciting formative feedback is personal in nature, instructors will find it useful to report their findings and plans to their students and even to their supervisors, because both are also stakeholders in this process. Sharing feedback and your action plan with students and peers is a valuable way to let them know that their feedback indeed matters, which is particularly important if you want to solicit their feedback again at a later date! Let them know what you will be doing differently in the future and why, as well as what requested changes you will *not* be making. Without sharing the last, your reviewers may think you did not consider all of their feedback and that the entire process was a waste of their time. Letting them know the rationale behind your decisions also serves as a valuable teachable moment—a point when you can provide them with helpful insights about your teaching practice.

Think back to our previous example of not wanting to share previous exams with your students. By sharing your rationale (i.e., there aren't enough versions of the exam available and creating new versions may be too complicated or lengthy of a process given their content), you will be helping them to understand why their request isn't as simple as it may seem. It might also prove to be a way to open a discussion with your students about other strategies that might meet their needs. For example, if they wish to have more practice tests, perhaps they would each be willing to make up potential test items of their own that could be shared among the class for practice purposes. Students often ask tougher questions in these cases than the instructor.

Sharing formative feedback as well as your action plan with your supervisor can also be a great way to show that individual that you are listening. It demonstrates that you value input and are concerned with continually improving your teaching practice. It is also a great way to share the positive feedback you receive. It is hard for many of us to toot our own horns. By sharing both the positive and constructive feedback you receive from your students, along with your action plan for continuing to improve your practice, a supervisor cannot help but be impressed with your dedication.

. . . And Repeat!

Remember, the SCARF process is a loop. To continually improve the quality of your teaching, it is meant to be repeated. As the familiar saying goes, "Insanity is doing the same thing over and over again but expecting different results." As you progress through the SCARF loop you will be trying new things, not the same thing over and over again. You will actually be *hoping* for different results—results that will reflect an improvement in your teaching! So you will, again, want to **S**olicit feedback on your new teaching plan, **C**ompile and analyze that feedback, **A**djust your teaching by creating an action plan for improvement, and **R**eport your **F**indings to your stakeholders ... and repeat!

The Sources of Formative Feedback: Self, Peers, and Students

Recognizing that formative evaluations arise in response to specific teaching questions or challenges, it is no surprise that there is a wide range of approaches for generating formative feedback. Likewise, depending on the purpose and scope, there are a number of different stakeholders that can provide informal feedback to enhance the quality of online teaching. In this section, we review strategies for conducting self, peer, and student formative evaluations.

Self

Although your immediate instinct may be to look to others for feedback and guidance, self-evaluation is the first step in a comprehensive plan for evaluating online teaching. As explained by Pettifor (2012), self-evaluation can assist you to do the following:

- Improve the educational experiences you provide for your students
- Identify the professional education you need to further develop your capacity to teach well
- Prepare for your performance review with your supervisor
- Assess your readiness to apply for promotion and tenure

Although self-evaluation may be as simple as dedicated reflection on your teaching strategies, the use of structured tools or checklists can help to focus your attention on key aspects of the teaching experience. For example, Castley (2005) outlined stages of reflective analysis and evaluation in which faculty self-reflect on the following questions in relation to their teaching strategies, learning activities, and curriculum design:

- What did you do?
- How did you do it?
- Why did you do it that way?

- How else might you have done it?
- How did you feel about it?
- How do you know it worked or didn't work?
- What will you do next time?

Alternatively, you may elect to use a more directive checklist to guide self-reflections on teaching; for an example, see Table 4.2, "Quick Online Teaching Self-Evaluation." In addition, you may want to take the

TABLE 4.2. QUICK ONLINE TEACHING EVALUATION

How well did I ...	Very Well	Satisfactory	Not Very Well	Poorly	Does Not Apply
link the threaded discussion to previous information?					
introduce this module?					
make the goals of the threaded discussion clear to students?					
emphasize key points throughout the threaded discussion?					
summarize the module?					
capture students' interest through personalized interaction?					
maintain students' interest via the introduction of relevant information, resources, or questions?					
ask thought-provoking questions that stimulated further discussion?					
handle student questions and responses in the online forum?					
provide feedback to student assignments in a timely manner?					
integrate multimedia to foster learning for a range of student learning styles?					
update course content to be relevant and timely?					
provide individualized feedback in response to student assignments?					
integrate formative assessments to gauge ongoing learning progress?					
use announcements in a meaningful fashion?					
convey my enthusiasm in the online classroom?					
provide a model of good interaction?					

Source: Adapted from Gibbs, Habeshaw, and Habeshaw (1997).

Teaching Perspectives Inventory (www.teachingperspectives.com/drupal/take-survey) to gain insight into the beliefs and intentions that underlie your personal teaching philosophy.

Record with a tick in the appropriate column the comments that come closest to your opinion of your performance in each of the following areas.

Beyond these quick checklists, there are a number of more detailed self-evaluations that can be used to guide reflections on your online teaching:

- Online Teaching Survey (http://sln.suny.edu/teachingsurvey/)
- Self-Assessment of Online Teaching Skills (www.pioneerresa.org/Documents/PL/OTEselfassessment.pdf)
- Faculty Self-Assessment: Preparing to Teach Online (https://weblearning.psu.edu/FacultySelfAssessment/)
- Instructor Growth Self-Evaluation Form (www.abmp.com/instructors/SelfEvaluationForm1.pdf)

Self-evaluations of online teaching provide meaningful information to explore targeted instructional issues, but it is important to keep in mind that it is difficult to be objective with any form of self-judgment. As such, instructors should supplement formative self-reviews with complementary feedback from peers and students.

Peers

Often, there is no better source of feedback than to ask someone who is struggling (or has struggled) with the same issues you are contemplating. Formative peer review is "a process for gathering feedback on teaching, reflecting on the alignment of teaching strategies with objectives, activities and assessments, and improving the fit between teaching approaches and student learning" (Center for Enhancement of Learning and Teaching, 2014, para. 1). As is the case with all formative evaluations, the purpose of an informal peer review of online teaching is to seek expert feedback to foster the quality of the online teaching and learning dynamic.

There is no standardized format or structure for informal peer reviews of online teaching; formative peer evaluations can range from an unstructured review of an online course to more formalized investigations to reflect on targeted issues. For informal reviews to provide helpful feedback, it is essential for instructors to clearly identify the goal and target of the review. The following sample questions can help you to understand the context of a peer review (adapted from Erickson & Sorcinelli, 2012):

Course Context

- How does this course fit in the curriculum?
- What are the learning goals of the course?
- How do you know if students are meeting the learning outcomes?
- What learning materials do you use to support your online course?
- To what extent are you in control of the content, assignments, and other features of your online course?
- What do you perceive as the strengths of the course?
- What do you feel are the greatest challenges of the course?

Student Context

- Describe the background, experience, and goals of a typical student in this course.
- In general, what are the students' perceptions about the quality, focus, and assessments of this course?
- Is there anything about the course that students find especially challenging?
- What kind of relationship do you try to establish with the students? How satisfied are you with your relationships with students? What online teaching techniques do you use to connect with your students? Do they feel you are accessible when they need your assistance?
- Have you modified your online teaching strategies in response to student feedback?

Instructor Context

- How long have you been teaching online? How comfortable are you with online teaching techniques?
- How long have you taught this course online? How have you changed the course or your approach to online teaching since the first time you taught it?
- What do you think are your online teaching strengths?
- What would you like to improve or change in your online teaching?
- What would you like us to focus on for this review?

Unlike a face-to-face course in which there are clear bounds on a class period, it is important to establish the scope of the review within an online course. The scope and target of the review will be dictated by the instructor seeking the review; components of an online course that may be reviewed include, but are not limited to, the following:

- Syllabus
- Online lectures
- Online course structure
- Asynchronous discussion facilitation strategies
- Techniques to engage students in an asynchronous learning environment
- Strategies for personalizing the online learning experience
- Role of announcements
- Value of feedback

Because of the vast range of instructional artifacts available in the online classroom, it is essential that instructors specify which components to include in the review and highlight the role of each component within the structure of that particular online course. It is also important for peer reviewers to have experience with online teaching so that feedback can be provided with respect to the unique pedagogies of the online environment. Finally, peer reviews of online courses should clearly distinguish components of the online course within the purview of the instructor (i.e., facilitation of asynchronous discussions or strategies to engage students) and aspects of the online course that may—or may not—be under the control of the instructor (i.e., course structure, assignments, materials, and so forth at institutions that use a standardized curriculum for online courses).

Recognizing the explicit focus on development of teaching strategies, formative peer reviews should not attempt to evaluate, train, or direct how one should teach online. Rather, effective formative peer reviews create a collaborative environment in which instructors seek the experience, advice, and expertise of their colleagues to address specific instructional challenges (Chism, 2007). Effective formative peer reviews share the following characteristics (Wilkerson & Karron, 2002):

- Focus on improving teaching and learning
- Be context specific, relevant, and focused
- Faculty ownership over the focus, goal, and format of the review process

- Collaborative agreement on purpose, focus, and criteria
- Private exchange of information between colleagues
- Based on a consultative (not evaluative) relationship between equals
- Provides constructive feedback to foster effective instruction (see the following list of best practices for providing constructive feedback for more information)
- Voluntarily initiated by individual faculty

To be most effective for facilitating growth and development, feedback should be the following (adapted from Berquist & Phillips, 1975):

- Descriptive rather than evaluative
- Specific
- Focused on behavior, not personality traits
- Bidirectional in sharing information and seeking input from the faculty member
- Well-timed to prevent information overload
- Clearly communicated
- Focused on faculty member's goals, not reviewer's opinions or standards
- Directed toward behaviors within the instructor's control
- Solicited rather than imposed

Students

Asking students for feedback on our teaching is an obvious mechanism to find out how we are doing in the online classroom. There are many ways to solicit informal feedback from students, from simple survey questions and polls to techniques that gather more substantive feedback. A few of our favorites follow:

- **Minute papers**. In a face-to-face class, instructors typically use the final few minutes of class to ask students to spend one minute answering two questions: (1) "What was the most important thing you learned during this class?" and (2) "What important question remains unanswered?" You can do the same thing in an online course by posting these questions at the end of an online lesson or module. Reviewing your students responses can reveal areas where students might be going astray (i.e., maybe what they felt was most important was not what you most wanted to convey!) or where your materials can be improved.

- **Muddiest point**. This simple technique asks students to identify the "muddiest point" they encountered in a lecture, video, discussion, homework assignment, and so on. In short, ask, "What was least clear to you? What questions do you still have about what we have covered this week?" Asking students to provide this information by posing these questions at pertinent points in your online course can help you to identify aspects of the course that might need to be strengthened or clarified.

- **Electronic survey feedback**. You can use the "Email All Users" feature of a course's LMS (e.g., Blackboard, Moodle) or even a formal survey tool to pose an on-the-fly question to students, asking them for their feedback on a specific aspect of the course or your teaching strategies. For example, perhaps you have been providing students with short video explanations each week that address concepts they seem to be struggling with on their assignments. You might send a note to all students several weeks into the course, asking them to let you know if they are finding these videos to be helpful to their learning and inviting them to suggest ways they can be made even more effective. Or perhaps you are concerned about how little your students seem to be engaging with you via your office hours, e-mail, and discussion forums. You might take a quick survey to find out which methods of communication work best for them and whether there are other ways they would like to interact with you.

- **The suggestion box**. Have you ever put a comment in a suggestion box at a local store or service provider? Why not provide your students with an online suggestion box where they can provide feedback at any point in your course? You might be surprised at the kind of useful feedback you receive through this very open-ended format!

Conducting strategies such as these in the online environment is easy. You can use tools such as e-mail, discussion forums, and surveys to collect the data. Be sure, however, to consider whether anonymity is needed when selecting the right tool. Most students will feel more comfortable providing their answers anonymously.

There is much more we should consider when conducting student reviews of teaching. Chapter 5 will address student ratings in greater depth, looking at issues and tools applicable to formative and summative student ratings of online teaching.

Conclusion

As highlighted by the faculty experience shared at the beginning of this chapter, the first steps to integrate formative evaluations can be daunting. Much of this apprehension and nervousness lies in the organic nature and flexibility of the formative review process ... there is no set time, place, format, or focus that drives the informal collection of feedback. To help embrace the important role of formative evaluation, instructors must create their own structure by reviewing the five Ws: who, what, when, where, and why:

- **Who.** Formative evaluations are conducted under the guidance and discretion of the instructor.
- **What.** Formative evaluations should focus on gaining feedback to improve specific aspects of online teaching.
- **When.** Formative evaluations are conducted as short, frequent opportunities to gain feedback throughout a course.
- **Where.** Formative evaluations are implemented during active courses in time to enable instructors to make adjustments that will benefit current students.
- **Why.** Formative evaluations are driven by the desire to improve online teaching.

Essential to the success of informal evaluation is a clear and constant focus on the purpose of formative feedback: the desire to improve online teaching. By embracing the formative nature of the process, evaluation apprehension (i.e., fears concerning perceptions of incompetence) can be overcome and replaced with a willingness to approach online teaching as an evolving skill: a skill developed through targeted exploration, feedback, and revision.

A Thought Exercise

Formative feedback, because it is focused on improving teaching practices and is not typically used for making institutional decisions about individual faculty members, is both (1) ideally suited to experimentation and customization for specific online courses and (2) difficult to implement (or at least track) as part of a campus culture because it depends on the interest of each faculty member to adopt it as a regular practice.

Think for a few minutes about your role on your own campus and respond to the following questions:

- Who on your campus is currently using formative evaluation methods?
- How do you know that (that is, what communication methods exist on campus to share good practices)?
- Does your institution (or an area within it) have a process for sharing best practices among faculty members, especially across disciplines?
- Is there formal language at your institution to guarantee that formative evaluation feedback received at the request of individual faculty members will not be used for summative purposes (e.g., hiring and promotion decisions)?
- What resources on your campus can help faculty members who want to set up formative evaluation processes for the first time?
- How receptive would faculty members on your campus be to sharing their experiences with formative evaluation, either anecdotally or as part of a repository of shared practices?
- What incentives would help to increase voluntary adoption of formative evaluation methods across campus?

Some of these implementation questions will come up again when we examine student ratings and administrative evaluations in chapters 5 and 6, so revisit your responses to this thought exercise after reading those chapters.

PART THREE

SUMMATIVE EVALUATION

CHAPTER FIVE

STUDENT RATINGS OF ONLINE TEACHING

Ann H. Taylor's Story

In 2013, the lead faculty member of one of Penn State University's online programs faced a problem common to many program administrators. She had helped launch her academic department's first fully online, undergraduate degree program three years before. Situated within a large research university that had embraced distance education almost since its inception, her college already had a great deal of experience in the online education realm. She and her fellow program faculty members, however, had never ventured into the online arena themselves. They had a lot to learn about how to design, develop, and deliver high-quality online instruction. Fortunately, the college had a robust instructional design unit in place that was charged with supporting online education. Her team worked closely with the instructional design unit to create fourteen new online courses. The new courses were then combined with the university's existing online curriculum to create a new degree program that could be completed entirely at a distance.

Three years later, the program's faculty felt like seasoned online veterans. Nine terms had passed since the program had been launched and each course was now regularly offered at least once a year. One hundred and twenty-eight students were currently enrolled in the program, making it one of the largest majors offered by her academic department. The program had graduated its first four students this past spring.

As the lead faculty member reflected over the past three years and the growth of her program, she felt things were really going well. Or were they? She realized she really had very little information about the quality of the courses being offered in her program. She was confident that they were well designed, but what did she actually know about the delivery other than what her colleagues self-reported?

She knew, all too well, that just because a course was well designed did not mean it was being well taught. It seemed easier on campus to find out how well a class was being taught. She could walk right up to someone in the student union and that student could readily tell you who were "good" and "bad" teachers. She needed to get that same kind of insight about the teaching that was taking place in her online program, but how? The many ratings websites like RateMyProfessor.com could provide some help, but she worried about the validity of those ratings and doubted they would give her an accurate picture of what was transpiring in her classes.

Her first thought was to put in place the standard end-of-course student survey instrument that the university provided for their face-to-face courses. A reexamination of that instrument, however, revealed that many of the questions it included were outright inappropriate for an online class. Items such as "Rate the effectiveness of the instructor as a speaker" were not going to work for their online, text-based courses. Using the existing survey instrument was clearly not an option, but she wasn't sure what options did exist. Clearly she was going to need to explore this further.

What Good Are Student Reviews?

As the consumers of our courses, students are a logical source for feedback on course quality. After all, they are the ones who sit through our classes, week after week (we hope). They are eyewitnesses to our teaching efforts. Anyone who has asked students knows that they can quickly tell you what was good or bad about each course they have taken. Although there are many ways to gather information about an instructor's teaching practice, student reviews are a time-honored mechanism for doing so. In reality, however, no single source of data about teaching practices can provide a complete picture of what is happening in our classrooms. We need a variety of data points from a variety of sources. Student ratings are but one source for this information. As we will discuss in the next few chapters, administrative reviews, peer reviews, and self-reviews of teaching are additional, valuable means for collecting valuable data.

Persistent misconceptions about student ratings of teaching have led many to dismiss their value in revealing any true insights into teaching practices. Faculty members have expressed ongoing doubt about the reliability of student ratings and the qualification of students to conduct such reviews, going as far as to claim that ratings of instructors by their students are nothing more than popularity contests. Decades of research have demonstrated, however, that well-designed mechanisms for conducting student reviews of teaching can, indeed, elicit reliable information that can help instructors improve their teaching practice.

Did You Know?

A review of fifty years of credible, scholarly research on "student evaluation of teacher performance" in higher education revealed the following findings (Benton & Cashin, 2011):

- Student ratings from multiple classes provide more reliable results than those from a single class, especially when ratings are based on fewer than ten students.
- Ratings of the same instructor across semesters (i.e., same class, different students) tend to be similar.
- The instructor, not the course, is the primary determinant of students' ratings.
- Students' ratings of their instructor's communication, motivational, and rapport-building skills most closely relate to their overall global rating of that instructor.
- Student ratings consistently and significantly relate to their level of achievement of course learning outcomes, their instructor's self-ratings, administrator and peer ratings, and even ratings by trained observers.
- A number of factors are *not* related to student ratings, including the student's age, gender, year of study, GPA, and personality. In addition, time of day and time during the term when ratings are collected are *not* related to student ratings.
- Student ratings of face-to-face and online courses are more similar than they are different.

In addition to their value as a professional development tool, many institutions routinely rely on student reviews of teaching as evidence for promotion and tenure decisions, contract renewal, quality assurance, or even when selecting winners of teaching awards. Students have been known to use their peers' reviews of teaching when selecting courses, too (think of websites such as RateMyProfessors.com). As online course offerings have been increasingly introduced in college curricula, concern for the quality of online teaching has likewise risen. As a result, many faculty members and administrators have used student reviews of online teaching as important evidence to validate online education.

What Are Students Qualified to Review?

Students who take our courses are still learning our disciplines. Although asking them to provide feedback on our content expertise may seem premature, there are many aspects of college teaching that students are well qualified to address. Whether sitting in classrooms on our college campuses or logging in to our courses online, students spend more time with our faculty members in a teaching environment than anyone else. Who better than our students to ask how things are going?

In reviews of teaching, whether online or face-to-face, students are typically asked questions about their instructors that fall into the following categories:

- **Course organization and structure** (e.g., "Rate the clarity of the syllabus in stating course objectives, course outline, and criteria for grades.")
- **Communication skills** (e.g., "Rate the effectiveness of the instructor's explanations of why certain processes, techniques, or formulas were used.")
- **Teacher-student interactions** (e.g., "Rate the students' freedom to ask questions and express opinions.")
- **Course difficulty and student workload** (e.g., "Rate the instructor's skill in making class materials intellectually stimulating.")
- **Assessments and grading** (e.g., "Rate the effectiveness of exams in testing understanding and not memorization.")
- **Student learning** (e.g., "Rate the instructor's skill in emphasizing learning rather than tests and grades.")

Of course, the possibilities of which questions to ask are limitless. As we have discussed in previous chapters, the first step to take is to determine what, exactly, you want to learn about what is taking place in the course. From there, reinventing the wheel is not necessary. There are many highly regarded instruments and tools already available (we will explore several later in this chapter). Once you have considered the specific aspects of teaching you want to focus on, the next step is to identify and review existing instruments to assess which items will help you in your quest and which ones might serve as a good starting point but will require adaptation first. Gaps where the existing instrument(s) doesn't address all of your needs will become apparent, too, suggesting new questions that you will need to add.

Most of the instruments you will come across, however, have been developed with the face-to-face classroom environment in mind. That doesn't mean they cannot be used for online course evaluation. The trick is to make sure that each and every question is appropriate for the delivery environment.

The sample questions provided previously, for example, would make sense regardless of the nature of the course environment. Some questions one might find on an instrument designed for a face-to-face classroom, however, might not lend themselves so easily to the online world. For example, the face-to-face course instrument might include an item, such as "Rate the instructor's skill in establishing and maintaining eye contact with students." If the same instrument were used for an online version of the same course, students would surely find that question odd. Likewise, there may be questions that would be desirable to include on a student rating of an online course that would not make sense for a purely face-to-face offering, such as "Rate the organization of course website."

How Much Is Enough?

As you think about the many things you would like to learn from the students in a given course, it will be easy to get carried away. You could quickly find yourself with something that would take students an hour to complete. Although the information you would glean from the results would undoubtedly be helpful to faculty members and administrators, getting students to actually complete something that lengthy would prove difficult.

To get the rich, meaningful feedback you desire, you need to limit the questions that you ask. Focus your questions on the key elements of the course you want to learn more about. Consider using a Likert scale for items such as "Rate the instructor's skill in … " and open-ended response items for areas where you seek more detailed responses, such as "What helped you learn in this course?" Remember, questions are not worth asking if you won't be able to take the time to carefully review the responses. If the class size is quite large, you will likely want to limit the number of open-ended questions you ask in order to make reviewing the feedback a manageable process.

The Classic Approach: Formal Student Surveys

End-of-course student surveys have become a standard tool that college administrators and faculty members use to determine how well things are going in our classrooms. Often referred to as "smile indexes," these surveys commonly ask students to rate everything from the overall quality of the course to the adequacy of the eye contact the instructor makes with the students. Although end-of-course surveys can provide instructors with helpful information that can lead to improved teaching in future offerings, they fail to directly benefit the students who complete them. Students, therefore, have a hard time taking them seriously because they do not see themselves as the beneficiaries of their efforts. Faculty can increase their response rates by demonstrating that they genuinely care about and listen to the feedback they receive from their students. This is especially important when these surveys are conducted in online courses, where research has shown completion rates tend to be lower than those for surveys given in a face-to-face classroom (Nulty, 2008). One way to effectively demonstrate that level of commitment is to create a culture of feedback in the course by soliciting student feedback long *before* the end of the course.

Increasing Student Rating Response Rates

Here are some ideas to help faculty members encourage students to take the evaluation process seriously. Some may work better for you than others or work better with a faculty member's personal style. Try them and see which work best for your particular situation (adapted from the University of Oregon's Office of the Registrar, 2014):

- **Early reminder, two to three weeks prior.** Although we already automatically send reminder messages to students during the evaluation period, one study (Norris & Conn, 2005) noted a great increase in student response rates when students were given an early notification that evaluations were approaching. A reminder at around two to three weeks before the term ended was found to be ideal, raising response rates an average of 17 percent.

- **Reminders into term to check how students are doing.** If classes aren't submitting evaluations at the rates you'd like to see, remind faculty members to mention the evaluations to them in class, letting them know how important their feedback is to them and administrators. Johnson (2002) followed up with nonresponding students in his study, and found that 50 percent of the nonresponders reported having no idea that the survey was available to be taken, and another 16 percent forgot.

- **Make it an assignment.** Many faculty members are against offering credit for students to do evaluations. The good news is, you don't have to. Making an evaluation an assignment, even with no point value attached, raised response rates 7 percent in one study (Johnson, 2002).

- **Give instructions.** If they can't find the online evaluation instrument, they can't evaluate. One study found that courses in which faculty members demonstrated how to find and use the evaluations system had a 24 percent higher response rate than in courses with no demonstration given (Dommeyer, Baum, Hanna, & Chapman, 2004).

- **Stress the importance of evaluation.** Students are more likely to complete course evaluations if they understand how they are being used and believe their opinions matter (Gaillard, Mitchell, & Kavota, 2006).

- **Detail how the institution uses evaluation feedback.** Many students don't realize that their evaluations may be looked at by department chairs and by promotion and tenure committees campus-wide. Let them know that these data are valued and used by administrators.

- **Detail how the course instructor will use evaluation feedback.** One of the best ways to let students know that their opinion matters and that it will be used to improve teaching is to give them an example of how that has been done in the past. Share with the students some past feedback and let them know the changes that were made as a result. Although it is likely valuable to let students know how the institution uses their feedback, that's not what their biggest concern is. Chen and Hoshower (2003) found that students consider an improvement in teaching to be the most important outcome of an evaluation system, followed closely by an improvement in course content and format. If the university listens, great. But what students really want is to know that their instructor listens.

Making Room for Improvement along the Way

Although end-of-course surveys are the most common way to elicit student feedback, many faculty members have discovered the value of asking for formal feedback much earlier in their courses. Midsemester surveys and even instruments that are given more frequently, such as end-of-lesson or end-of-week instruments, enable faculty members to find out how things are going in their course in time to make adjustments that will benefit current students. Such feedback can be particularly helpful in online courses when it is more difficult to read student's reactions. Faculty who take the time to ask for feedback while their course is in progress, and who act on that feedback, help to ensure that the learning experience is successful for their students and themselves. We explored these types of formative feedback instruments in chapter 4, and we will examine student feedback from a formative perspective later in this chapter, as well.

A Look at Three Existing Tools

As we've discussed, there are many well-designed student ratings instruments already in existence that can be used as is or adapted. Here we will explore three such tools: the Students' Evaluation of Educational Quality (SEEQ), the Student Assessment of their Learning Gains (SALG), and Penn State University's Student Rating of Teaching Effectiveness (SRTE). We will also discuss taking a do-it-yourself approach using the many free web-based resources that are available today.

Students' Evaluation of Educational Quality (SEEQ)

The SEEQ is a widely used survey instrument that was developed by educational psychologist Herbert Marsh in 1982. The full questionnaire asks students how well each of thirty-five statements describes their teacher or their course, using a five-point scale from "very poor" to "very good." The statements reflect nine dimensions of effective teaching:

- Learning value
- Instructor enthusiasm
- Organization and clarity
- Group interaction

- Individual rapport
- Breadth of coverage
- Examinations and grading
- Assignments and readings
- Workload and difficulty

The instrument concludes with two open-ended questions:

- Which characteristics of this instructor or course have been most valuable to your learning?
- Which characteristics of this instructor, course, or classroom or teaching environment are most important to improve on (particularly aspects not covered by the rating items)?

The SEEQ instrument has been heavily researched and normed across more than one million respondents in more than fifty thousand courses. As a result, the instrument is highly trusted to provide useful results. It can be used in its entirety or by selecting only the items of interest. Although certainly valuable as an end-of-course evaluation instrument, many faculty members have found the SEEQ to be a useful midsemester feedback instrument to inform the remaining part of the course.

The SEEQ survey is copyrighted by Dr. Marsh and can be used with permission. Many institutions have already secured permission to use the instrument in their courses, so check with your own institution to see if it may already be available for you to use. Detailed information about the SEEQ can be found in Marsh (1982).

Student Assessment of their Learning Gains (SALG)

The Student Assessment of their Learning Gains (SALG) instrument is a popular tool that was developed in 1997 by Elaine Seymour, director emerita of ethnography and evaluation research at the University of Colorado at Boulder. The instrument grew out of a desire by project faculty for a course evaluation instrument that would focus on how well specific course features and activities were enabling student learning. They wanted an instrument that would do more than reveal what students *liked* about a course—they wanted to know what "learning gains" had been made as a result of specific aspects of the course. In 2007, Carroll, Seymour, and Weston revised the SALG to address evaluation needs beyond their originally targeted chemistry courses.

The SALG now includes five overarching questions, each of which can be customized by the instructor through subitems:

- How much did the following aspects of the course help you in your learning? (Examples might include class and lab activities, assessments, particular learning methods, and resources.)
- As a result of your work in this class, what gains did you make in your understanding of each of the following? (Instructors insert those concepts that they consider most important.)
- As a result of your work in this class, what gains did you make in the following skills? (A sample of skills includes the ability to make quantitative estimates, finding trends in data, or writing technical texts.)
- As a result of your work in this class, what gains did you make in the following? (The subitems address attitudinal issues such as enthusiasm for the course or subject area.)
- As a result of your work in this class, what gains did you make in integrating the following? (The subitems address how the students integrated information.)

The instrument also includes an area where the instructor can ask open-ended questions.

Because it was developed through funding from the National Science Foundation, the SALG is free to use. Faculty can create customized SALG instruments through the SALG website, located at www.salgsite.org. A handy feature of the website is the advanced search tool, which faculty members can use to find SALG instruments that have been developed by other SALG users. An existing instrument can then be used as a base template for the faculty member's own SALG. Once customized, the faculty member's SALG is made available to students online through the SALG website, with results provided in the form of a statistical report.

Other features of the SALG instrument include the ability to password-protect access to an instrument, statistical results that can be cross-tabulated and disaggregated (comparing the results of one question against another question, even if that second question is from a separate instrument), and the ability for departments to create SALG templates and provide access to those templates to its faculty members so they can incorporate those templates into their own instruments.

Guests are welcome to try out the SALG website via the "Take a Tour of SALG" link on the home page before creating a personal version. The guest account is a lightly restricted version of a regular account.

Student Rating of Teaching Effectiveness (SRTE)

At Penn State University, policy dictates that the evaluation of teaching effectiveness for purposes of promotion and tenure must be based on both peer and student input. In 1985, the Office of the Executive Vice President and Provost, in consultation with faculty members and administrators from each unit and the Committee on Faculty Affairs of the University Faculty Senate, created a standard method to enable students to evaluate face-to-face instruction that would make it possible for them not only to monitor quality but also to make comparisons across courses. The result of their efforts was the creation of an end-of-course student survey instrument, the Student Rating of Teaching Effectiveness (SRTE).

The SRTE consists of four mandatory multiple-choice items and two mandatory open-ended items. From there, departments can select up to fifteen questions from a predefined list of 177 question options. The full set of questions can be found in the companion website (www.wiley.com/go/tobin) for this book.

The question bank includes general and specific items in the following areas:

- Organization
- Structure or clarity of the course or course material
- Teacher-student interaction
- Teaching skills
- Instructional environment
- Specific instructional settings

Questions from the bank are rated on a seven-point scale, with identifiers provided at the end points and the midpoint. Instructors can also add up to five more questions from the bank. Although decisions about when SRTEs are conducted are left to individual academic units, the intention is for evaluations to be conducted over a period of years and in a variety of courses.

In 2005, The Schreyer Institute for Teaching Excellence at Penn State began a pilot of an online version of the SRTE. At the time of this writing, the online SRTE has been fully implemented across the university and continues to be managed by the Schreyer Institute. Gone are the days of the paper-and-pencil form. The new format and growing number of online course offerings led the university to make changes to the requirements for selecting questions. Although up to fifteen questions are still to be selected from the list of 177 questions in the question bank, up to ten additional questions can be added that do not have to be from that bank. This has enabled the SRTE to include questions that better address some of the unique aspects of online teaching and learning than those questions originally created in 1985.

Findings from Penn State's pilot test of the online SRTE found that, contrary to faculty concerns, response rates were not significantly lower for the online instrument than they had been for the paper version. Focus groups conducted with students also revealed that they would be more likely to complete the survey if they are convinced that the information will be used to improve the course. Faculty members are, therefore, advised to explain to students how they have used past feedback in their course improvements.

The following is an example of a SRTE survey that has been customized by the College of Earth and Mineral Sciences at Penn State for use with its online courses. The questions selected from the SRTE question bank and created for the departmental section reflect the primary areas of concern for which the college wanted to gather data. The full SRTE question bank can be accessed through this book's companion website (www.wiley.com/go/tobin). In addition to these items, individual instructors are encouraged to add course-specific questions of their own either by selecting relevant questions from the SRTE bank or by creating their own survey instrument for separate administration (more on the do-it-yourself approach later in this chapter).

MANDATORY UNIVERSITY-WIDE ITEMS

A1 Are you taking this course as an elective? (If uncertain, omit.)
A2 What grade do you expect to earn in this course?
A3 Rate the overall quality of this course.
A4 Rate the overall quality of the instructor.

SRTE Question Bank Items (up to 15 allowed from the pool of 177—see www.srte.psu.edu/SRTE_items/)

- Rate the instructor's availability for individual help and consultation. (Question 42)
- Rate the effectiveness of the instructor's responses to student questions. (Question 48)

- Rate the instructor's skill in keeping the course on schedule. (Question 70)
- Rate the promptness with which graded exams, reports, and other materials were returned. (Question 101)

Additional Departmental Questions (up to 10 are allowed)

- Rate your agreement with the following statement: "The instructor initiated communication with students on a regular basis."
- Rate your agreement with the following statement: "The instructor responded to my inquiries in a timely manner."
- Rate your agreement with the following statement: "The instructor provided meaningful feedback on my class assignments."
- Rate your agreement with the following statement: "I would recommend this course to others."

Mandatory University Open-ended Questions

- What helped you learn in this course?
- What changes would improve your learning?

Source: John A. Dutton e-Education Institute, College of Earth and Mineral Sciences, the Pennsylvania State University (2013).

Open-Ended Feedback

A word is needed about student responses to open-ended questions, especially where the results from the student-ratings instrument are used as an element in employment decisions. As we saw in chapter 4, many faculty members use their own open-ended formative feedback mechanisms throughout the course in order to collect student perceptions about the progress of the course:

> I usually do a "feedback form" 4–6 weeks into a 16 week semester. I let students know that their responses will be anonymous, and that I am the only one who will see them. I let them know that the end-of-semester evaluations are also important, but that their responses on those are really for my benefit and for the benefit of the students who will take the class the next time I teach it. I let them know that the feedback forms are so that I can try to make improvements to the course while they are still taking it.

The questions I include vary from semester to semester and course to course; I really want it to be formative, so that they can let me know their opinions on how things are going, and what (if anything) needs to be done to make things better. I then take a look at their responses and decide if any changes should be made. It helps me make adjustments, and hopefully helps students feel like they have a voice, as well. (Mueller, 2014)

Such feedback is seldom shared with the institution and almost never goes into the summative decision-making process. In online courses, formative, open-ended feedback like this is easier to employ than in a face-to-face environment: for example, most LMSs have survey tools so there is no chance of handwriting being recognized.

The ease of collecting open-ended feedback for online courses may lead some end-of-semester student-rating instrument designers to include more open-ended questions in order to learn more about an institution's overall online program. We strongly suggest using multiple-choice or other closed-ended questions for such purposes. Rosenbloom (2014) studied the psychological impact of open-ended feedback in end-of-semester ratings, and found, not surprisingly, that an unconscious bias exists to weigh open-ended responses greater than other types of feedback.

This is also true of campus administrators, who are also likely to base their employment decisions more heavily on the open-ended feedback from student-rating instruments—even though doing so risks introducing biases into what should be as objective a process as possible. This creates a potential liability of the fact that students using online rating instruments tend to respond in greater numbers to open-ended feedback and write more per response than their paper-and-pencil counterparts. The lesson for online ratings instruments is to separate open-ended feedback for formative purposes and either do not show open-ended feedback to summative decision makers at all or provide it to them at a separate time than other data.

So What Is the Right Mix for You?

In this chapter, we have explored the SEEQ, the SALG, and Penn State University's SRTE. In fact, we have barely scratched the surface. A quick web search on terms such as "student ratings online teaching" will reveal many other tools and resources. The possibilities can be overwhelming. Our advice: take baby steps. Doing something is better than doing nothing.

Some questions to consider as you move forward:

- What kind of feedback are you looking for? What do you want to learn about your online course? What do you want to learn about your online program?
- What strategies are already in place for your institution's face-to-face courses?
- What adaptations could be made to make those work for your online offerings?
- Will those adapted instruments give you all of the information you are looking for? If not, what is still missing?
- Are there other tools available (perhaps some you've seen here?) that could better meet your needs or that could complement the institutional resources you adapt?
- How will you use the feedback you receive?

Conclusion

Let's return to the lead faculty member's challenge that we introduced at the beginning of this chapter. Similar to most of us, this program administrator wanted to learn more about how she and her program faculty were doing as teachers by asking their students for feedback. She recognized, though, that her university's standard end-of-course evaluation instrument wasn't going to give her the information that they needed. Furthermore, the questions on that instrument were clearly written for use with a face-to-face class, whereas all of the courses in her program were taught online. So what happened next?

In this particular case, the lead faculty member turned once more to her college's instructional design unit for help. Together they explored the very strategies we have discussed in this chapter. She quickly learned that her program's needs were not unique at her institution. The college had already created a version of the university's end-of-course evaluation instrument that was appropriate for use in online courses, a tool that she and her team could immediately incorporate into their own courses. Colleagues in the college had also been using a midsemester feedback tool that she thought would also meet her program's specific needs. Finally, the learning design unit shared with her several weekly feedback strategies that the lead faculty member and her program team could incorporate into their courses to elicit regular feedback from their students. With these resources in hand, the program team designed a program-wide strategy for gathering and using student feedback that has helped them to continuously improve their courses. The information they now have in hand has helped the program to ensure that things are, indeed, going well.

A Thought Exercise

Student ratings of teaching practices are already their own large segment of the research about teaching effectiveness generally. Focus your thinking for your own institution on what elements of student ratings can tell you important information related specifically to online teaching.

- Does your campus currently use a single form for end-of-course student ratings generally (or perhaps a common set of mandated questions to be added to departmental or individual ratings feedback)?
- What questions in your current ratings instrument(s) are biased toward the face-to-face classroom (e.g., questions related to voice tone or eye contact)?
- What questions might you ask online students to help differentiate teaching behaviors from concerns about the medium itself (e.g., asking about what portion of online activities students completed or asking about the frequency of access and connectivity concerns)?
- Students are qualified to rate instructors' facilitation of learning, communication of ideas, and respect and concern for students, regardless of delivery mode. How can survey instruments on your campus address these ratings areas while being either modality neutral or specific to online delivery?
- What people or areas on your campus would need to be involved in order to test and then approve proposed instruments or changes?

Student ratings can be used for both formative and summative purposes. Your responses to this thought exercise will help you to set up the more summative uses of student ratings. In chapters 6 and 7, we will examine how supervisors and administrators can best evaluate online teaching for the purposes of making employment decisions.

CHAPTER SIX

ADMINISTRATIVE EVALUATION OF ONLINE TEACHING

Tom Tobin's Story

At many institutions, part of the promotion-and-tenure process is a visit by the department chair to observe the teaching practices of a candidate faculty member. For example, at Northeastern Illinois University, the adoption of online courses posed a challenge for "observing" online teaching. In early 2013, a faculty member was getting his portfolio ready for the retention, tenure, and promotion process toward becoming full professor, and he had asked his department chair to observe his online course.

The department chair stopped by the Center for Teaching and Learning with a quick question for the technology coordinator: "We just need to know one thing. Our observation form has an item on it: 'Instructor demonstrates enthusiasm.' How can instructors demonstrate enthusiasm in an online course? After all, the students can't see the professor or hear his voice." It wasn't a quick question to answer. After some more conversation, four pertinent facts emerged:

- This was the first time that anyone would be doing a formal administrative observation of an online course in the entire college. Even though the department in question had offered online courses for several years, they were not part of the regular peer and administrative observation cycle that was already set up for face-to-face courses. Similar to many colleges and universities (Shelton, 2011), Northeastern Illinois University has a formal process in place for conducting retention, tenure, and promotion reviews. The steps in the process, format for submitted documents, and time line for observation and review are all delineated in university policy and the collective-bargaining agreement (University Professionals of Illinois Local 4100 and Northeastern Illinois University Board of Trustees, 2009). However, each college and department has the flexibility to perform the tasks within the review process how they see fit.

- Many years ago, the department had created an observation rubric for use by the department chair and peer reviewers when visiting classrooms so that observers would ask the same questions from visit to visit.

- The department chair had never developed or taught online courses himself, and the enthusiasm concern was the tip of the iceberg. He was unsure how many of the items on the department's observation form might apply to online teaching. He was also skeptical whether some of the items from the form could even be observed at all, given the nature of an online course.

- The faculty member had taught the course to be observed as a face-to-face course for many years, and the department chair had sat in on a ninety-minute Thursday afternoon session some years back. The chair was concerned that he would not be able to estimate how much of the faculty member's online course he should observe: "How much online is the same as ninety minutes?" The chair was also concerned that he would be able to see things in the online course that he could not observe in the face-to-face classroom. "So [the faculty member] has already e-mailed me his syllabus, his grading rubrics, his study guides, his lecture notes, and a whole bunch of other stuff. Do I have to read all of this in order to see his online course? Heck, *should* I read all of it? I don't get to see that kind of stuff in the classroom."

The department chair paused and said, "You know, to get down to the brass tacks, this whole thing used to take an hour and a half for me to sit in the classroom, and then another hour to type up my report. Now, I'm going to have to spend who knows how long reading and reading and reading before I even see the teaching happening, aren't I?"

The technology coordinator suggested that they schedule a meeting at the end of the week to work together to get the department chair ready to perform the observation.

Administrators Today

The traditional model for face-to-face course observation is one in which an administrator, typically a department chair, is responsible for visiting the classroom of an instructor in order to perform the evaluation. Although some department chairs and deans have taught online courses themselves (and thus have a feel for the challenges and flow of online teaching), many more administrators conducted their teaching careers exclusively in the face-to-face classroom. Especially for those administrators who moved away from teaching in the early 2000s, they are likely not to have developed or taught courses in a mode other than face-to-face (McCarthy & Samors, 2009).

The skeptic may speak up, here, to say that online teaching has been in existence long enough that most administrators will have had some first-hand experience with online teaching practices. The more likely situation is that administrators have not addressed the challenge of "what is good online teaching" until forced to do so, as shown in the scenario with the department chair and review committee. Even when department chairs have taught online themselves, there is often a gap between their own teaching practices and the institutional processes in place for evaluating those practices. Further, institutions will find varying levels of administrative familiarity with online teaching methods from department to department.

The Elephant in the Room

There are purposes for evaluating online teaching that are largely apolitical: we evaluate our online teaching practices so that we can improve our teaching methods, retain students, and best support students in accomplishing their educational goals. Student, self, and peer evaluations—especially informal ones—fall into this category.

In the specific situation of administrators and their proxies observing and evaluating online teaching, evaluations typically are performed in order to determine whether the instructor is rehired for the following semester (in the case of contingent faculty) or whether the instructor progresses through the promotion-and-tenure process (for tenure-line faculty).

Because the purpose of administrative review is so narrowly conceived, many institutions have already created or adopted an administrator-observation instrument that is separate from peer- and student-evaluation instruments. For example, Columbus State Community College (2009) includes a "Faculty Online Observation Report" form as a separate instrument in its *Faculty Promotion and Tenure Handbook*. The form instructs administrators to indicate yes, no, or not applicable on observed elements of an online course. Interestingly, the directions include some of the challenges of administrative observation of online courses:

- Perform the online observation jointly with faculty and collaborative reviewer(s).
- Provide information to help differentiate course design from faculty instruction.
- This observation is to review one lesson or learning activity.

These directions are intimately linked to the online format of the course. Administrative evaluators for face-to-face courses seldom need guidance about determining the people with whom it is appropriate to conduct the review session, differentiating between teaching behaviors and course materials, and the length of the observation period. These and other challenges are addressed more fully in the following sections. The existence of separate administrator-observation instruments—however open-ended—is an opportunity for opening the conversation about what behaviors constitute good teaching practices, what evidence of those behaviors can be observed, and how those behaviors can be quantified and evaluated (rather than merely noted as existing or not).

Observational Bias

Before we can create an instrument to evaluate teaching behaviors toward retention and promotion, we must confront several myths about the observable qualities of good teaching. The administrative-observation instruments developed for face-to-face teaching typically share some common observational biases, which are invisible until we start thinking about shifting the modality of teaching from face-to-face to online.

Bias 1: Good Teaching Is Embodied

In the scenario that opened this chapter, the department chair was skeptical as to whether it would be possible to observe instructor enthusiasm in the faculty member's online course, worrying that "the students can't see the professor or hear his voice." The bias inherent in the question is that body language and voice inflection are integral to effective teaching. Although it is true that varied voice inflection and open body language help to keep face-to-face learners engaged (Betts, 2013), such indicators are not the only means of demonstrating instructor involvement with class participants.

For online courses that incorporate video of the instructor, another bias is revealed. Evaluators may wish to observe online video content in the same way they would observe a face-to-face lecture. Evaluators with an embodied-teaching bias may be swayed by professional-style production values in longer lecture-capture-style videos and disappointed by brief, bare bones videos of instructors discussing course concepts. Flashy presentation skills can mask a lack of instructor subject knowledge even in a face-to-face environment, and chunking of video content is an established best practice for course-related multimedia regardless of the course-offering modality.

By expanding beyond the bias, we can see that the communication between the instructor and the learners is the key measurement here, especially with regard to its frequency, nature, and quality. Administrators can think of all of the signals that face-to-face instructors send to their students, and they can look for similar kinds of signals in online courses, such as the frequency of instructor posts to discussion boards and the regularity of follow-up communication with learners about posted video content.

Bias 2: Good Teaching Is Intuitive

The department chair in this chapter's narrative is lucky. At least his department has an instrument from which to begin the conversation about observing online teaching. In many cases, the evaluation of face-to-face teaching is based on the subjective feelings of the administrative observer. Even when there are score sheets, rubrics, or other observation instruments, the questions asked sometimes do not lend themselves to quantifiable responses.

Using "I know it when I see it" as an observation criterion exposes a bias for the observer's own learning preferences. Administrators who themselves learned best in lecture courses will rate lecturers as more competent teachers than instructors who favor other teaching practices. This bias exists in face-to-face observations, and it persists even when departments use specific instruments as guides to the observation.

The impact of the bias is magnified when observing online courses. The department chair's concern that "the students can't see the professor or hear his voice," is also a coded way of saying that he can't see the professor or hear his voice, either. Especially when administrative evaluators' experiences have been primarily as classroom-based instructors, they lose some of their ability to use an "I know it when I see it" gestalt to judge instructor quality when the course modality moves from the classroom to an online environment.

To expand beyond this bias, administrators can shift their thinking away from charismatic traits (e.g., ability to hold students' attention, strong classroom "presence," and student eagerness to be involved in the class) and toward the support-behavior analogues to those charismatic behaviors (e.g., providing multiple ways for students to consume course content, reaching out to every student with a personal communication at least once per unit, and supporting student achievement by recognizing effort, milestones, and accomplishments).

Bias 3: Good Teaching Happens in Real Time

Questions often raised by administrators unfamiliar with online teaching include "how does one hold class online," "does everybody log in to a live video feed or something," and "where do the students go to actually have a conversation with the instructor?" There is a strong bias toward synchronicity as a hallmark of effective teaching. Although online teaching can happen synchronously (e.g., via Skype or Adobe Connect real-time class meetings), one advantage of online learning is its any time, any place nature.

Although it is true that a real-time conversation provides instructors and students with the opportunity to explore issues together and have immediate feedback within the conversation, it's not the case that every course member can be involved in a synchronous class meeting at the same level. In many face-to-face classrooms, it is only the instructor and a small core of students—between five and ten students, regardless of class size—who are engaged in the class discussion at any given time (Weaver & Qi, 2005). Many students remain silent throughout the entire class period.

Administrative evaluators can move beyond the real-time communication bias by focusing on opportunities for students' participation in and their direction of the learning experience, as well as the instructor's ability to engage students both through the course content and through ad hoc interactions with students throughout the course. In fact, this ability to engage directly, one-on-one with learners asynchronously, is a teaching behavior unique to online teaching. For example, online discussion forums offer all students the chance to reflect on the ideas and statements of others and offer instructors the opportunity to facilitate student learning in a dynamic environment. Administrators should look for evidence of teaching practices that invite learners and instructors to share and shape the conversation through such discussions, collaborative group work, and the like.

Bias 4: Good Teaching Appears Effortless

Readers of this book who have taught for many years may remember the very first time they taught. It was likely a nervous time, preceded by a lot of preparation. Often, we entered the classroom with a legal pad filled with information and notes or with a PowerPoint™ presentation bristling with notations and resource links—reminders for ourselves of the things about which we did not want to forget to talk with the class. Over time, as we taught the same kinds of courses again and again, that legal pad got put aside in favor of an index card with a few key phrases or bullet points to remember. Some of us now have retired the memory aids all together and rely on our experience and memory in order to facilitate each class session.

Theatricality, or the appearance of effortlessness, is the most common mental shortcut that administrators use to stand in for "effectiveness" in face-to-face teaching. Administrator-observers are often biased toward the faculty member whose ability just to wing it from memory indicates mastery of the subject and comfort with the processes of sharing it with learners. In online teaching, however, instructors are brought back to the legal-pad stage of their teaching: much of what instructors typically speak and perform in face-to-face classes ends up as documentation in the online environment—and is thus not observed as an online teaching practice.

Further complicating this bias is the situation where in online courses, the person who designed the course outline, lecture content, assessments, videos, and initial discussion prompts may not be the person who is teaching the course. To the biased eye, this suggests that all that is needed to teach online is a warm body, one who can occasionally answer student questions, grade the tests and quizzes, and report on student achievement at the end of the course.

In order to work against the sage-on-the-stage bias, administrative evaluators should avoid confusing information delivery with teaching behaviors. Observers should define ahead of time what behaviors are to be evaluated as online teaching practices. One of the most common forms of face-to-face information sharing, even today, is lecturing. In an online environment, the lecture content (whether text, audio, or video) is more a source of information delivery, akin to the textbook readings in a face-to-face course: it's a piece of media to be consumed by the learners in their own time rather than an interaction to be shared with the class together. Although it is important that media elements in online courses be expertly created, it is the delivery of the online course—the teaching—that is key to administrative reviews conducted for staffing and promotion decisions. We will discuss this distinction between content media and interactive experiences again later in this chapter.

Equivalence

Especially when administrative observation of teaching occurs for the purpose of determining whether to rehire or promote an instructor, the overarching goal is to make the observation process as standardized as possible: to observe each instructor under conditions as similar as possible to those used to observe his or her peers and to evaluate instructors using a common set of criteria. Hence, it is tempting to want to create a comparative table of equivalences between face-to-face and online course delivery. If one observes ninety minutes in a face-to-face course, where (and to what extent) should one look in an online course environment to see the same amount of teaching happening?

This would be a much shorter book if such a goal were possible to achieve. Part of the confusion about observing face-to-face and online versions of the same course has to do with the visibility of the content and behaviors that fall within (and outside of) the scope of what can be seen by the observer. For example, in a face-to-face class, the administrative observer typically does not come to the instructor's office hours to observe one-on-one interactions with students, nor does the observer review a sample of the instructor's e-mail communication with students. The observer does not typically ask to see the instructor's notes for the class period. The observer may get copies of assignments or in-class worksheets only if the instructor shares them with the observer—and only then so the observer can follow along with the activities taking place in the classroom. Furthermore, the observer does not usually request a copy of the syllabus before the observation takes place or see samples of student work that is handed in during the class being observed.

In an online course, however, the observer has access to all of these elements and often more. He or she can see the course syllabus, the lecture content and multimedia for every unit of the course, students' interactions with the instructor in the threaded discussion forums, and even student submissions for assignments and sample instructor feedback on these (when provided to the reviewer), as well as the grade book that the instructor is keeping for the course. In fact, pretty much the only element of the educational transactions for the entire online course that remains invisible to an administrative observer is the flow of e-mail between students and instructors (and that can even be made available in many cases).

What is Unique about Administrator Evaluation?

Because of these differences in visibility and access between face-to-face and online courses, it is helpful to reexamine some general online-course-review strategies through the lens of what actions administrators can take that other reviewers cannot. For example, a department chair can do the following:

- Phone or e-mail current students to follow up on the observation
- Look up past performance data on current students' previous courses
- Compare observation data from the instructor's previous classroom and online-course visits
- Recommend (and often enforce) instructor remediation actions for noted challenges
- Provide incentives for improved teaching practices, retention, and student satisfaction

All of these actions take place outside of the observation itself, and administrative observers are in a unique position to be able to integrate the observation of online teaching practices into an overall program of feedback to the instructor. Thus, when administrators are the observers, they should employ the process that follows.

Step 1: Define Behaviors

Instead of looking for specific behaviors or affective elements of the instructor (such as "speaks clearly" or "maintains the interest of students"), administrative observers can find modality-neutral, measurable criteria for evaluation by focusing on the effects of instructor behavior. For example, "the instructor communicates in a way that students respond to throughout the range of observation." By observing the behaviors of the instructor for what those behaviors elicit from the learners, administrative evaluators can make a yes or no determination and further assign a measurable value to the behavior. In their seminal article, "Seven Principles for Good Practice in Undergraduate Education," Chickering and Gamson (1987) analyzed a wealth of research on good teaching in colleges and universities. They revealed seven core principles of effective teaching practice that are themselves modality independent:

- Encourage student-faculty contact.
- Develop reciprocity and cooperation among students.
- Use active learning techniques.
- Give prompt feedback.
- Emphasize time on task.
- Communicate high expectations.
- Respect diverse talents and ways of learning.

By seeking instructor behaviors that help to meet each of these core areas, administrative observers can tailor their observations to the tools and methods being used, regardless of the course-offering modality. For online courses, especially, focusing on Chickering and Gamson's principles enables administrators who may not have taught online themselves to look for evidence of effective teaching interactions throughout the online environment: everything that is not an interaction can be seen as a piece of media.

By categorizing elements of online courses as either media or interactions, administrative observers can make more fine-grained determinations than, say, the informal student- and peer-observation processes from chapters 4 and 5 about which parts of the online course are actually examples of teaching behaviors. Table 6.1 illustrates one way to match teaching principles against commonly observed teaching behaviors in online courses.

Chickering and Gamson's principles also serve as a foundation for other types of formal review processes. We will explore some specific observation instruments that can be used for this purpose in chapters 7 and 8.

Step 2: Agree on the Scope of the Observation

There is no hard and fast equivalent in an online course to the sixty- or ninety-minute period typical of face-to-face observations. Because face-to-face courses are fixed in time and place, those parameters are the

TABLE 6.1. OBSERVABLE ONLINE TEACHING BEHAVIORS

Teaching Principle (Chickering and Gamson)	Common Online Teaching Behaviors
Encourage student-faculty contact.	Set aside regularly scheduled times for online office hours or implement a maximum turnaround time for responses to communications. Facilitate regular course discussions. Post course announcements or news updates on a regular basis.
Develop reciprocity and cooperation among students.	Assign group or dyad projects. Require discussion responses to peers. Offer encouragement in public ways (e.g., on the course discussion forum); offer criticism privately (in grade-tool feedback seen only by individual students).
Use active learning techniques.	Ask students to summarize and propose next steps. Assign "butts out of seats" tasks to give online learners tasks away from the keyboard (e.g., interview experts near students' homes) and ask students to report back to the class. Have students create and post study guides.
Give prompt feedback.	Respond to each student at least once in each graded threaded discussion topic, or for very large courses, at least once per course unit. Keep to turnaround time expectations for instructor responses to graded work. Give students encouragement, reflection, and correction feedback.
Emphasize time on task.	Give students estimates of how long assignments will take. Communicate progress of the whole class toward week and unit goals. Provide individual progress milestones for graded work.
Communicate high expectations.	Give preview, status, and review communications. Provide samples of good practice on assignments and discussion. Spotlight students who do good work or improve their efforts (e.g., post an "everyone look at Kevin's response" message in discussions or ask improved students to lead group study sessions).
Respect diverse talents and ways of learning.	Provide multiple ways for students to respond to assignments (e.g., write an essay, record an audio response, create a video). Allow students to respond to discussions using a variety of media. Present learning material in a manner that enables a range of possible learning paths.

givens of the observation. The givens for online courses are not time or physical location (both of which are variable) but the online environment itself. In order to assist administrators who are observing online courses, agreement should be reached on five key factors:

- Definition of teaching practices
- Communication between observer and observed
- Which elements are in bounds
- Duration of the observation
- Assistance available to the observer

Definition of Teaching Practices

In an online course, there are many analogues to face-to-face teaching practices that may not be considered "teaching" for the online course. For example, in a face-to-face class, lecturing is a key teaching practice. However, video clips or lecture notes in an online course are part of the course media and are not themselves direct evidence of teaching behaviors—especially if the person who developed the lecture notes or videos is not the person facilitating the class.

As mentioned in the discussion of the "effortlessness bias," one strategy for making clear what counts as a teaching practice in an online course is to examine those elements that lead directly to interaction among the students, instructor, and course content. Items that present information but do not then directly ask the learner to respond may be considered to be parts of the course design. Course content items may be either design elements or teaching practices, depending on their structure and use.

For example, a set of lecture notes that is presented as a single web page and that presents information—in the manner of a textbook or article—is part of the course design and would not be considered in an administrative observation of the online course. Likewise, videos, audio podcasts, and the like are also as part of an online course's materials and do not count as observable teaching behaviors.

However, if an instructor responds to student questions in an online-course discussion by posting a mini-lecture or video to explain a concept, that certainly counts as an observed teaching behavior because the content is created or shared as a result of interaction between the learner and the instructor. The overall question to apply is one of information presentation versus interaction. As a final caveat, items that were created by a person other than the course instructor should never be counted toward administrative observation of online courses. This leads to the second area needing agreement: communication (see the next section).

Consistent instructor presence in an online course is one of the most important components of online teaching practice, helping students feel less isolated and more supported in their learning. In fact, instructor presence supports each of Chickering and Gamson's seven principles. In online instruction, in which another course or even institution is just a click away, instructor presence goes a long way toward student retention, academic success, and building a sense of community. Piña and Bohn (2014, p. 32) identify specific behaviors unique to the online environment that administrators perceive as effective indicators of teaching quality:

> Our desire was to identify a set of criteria that would yield objective data easily examined by supervisors and peers during an online course observation and serve as a balance to the more subjective data gathered from student surveys. This study focused upon quantitative measures of instructor actions and behaviors that could be readily observed in the online course and/or collected using the reporting tools of the learning management system:

- Has the instructor logged in at least an average of every other day?
- Has the instructor posted a biography of at least a paragraph, in addition to contact info?
- Has the instructor posted announcements at least weekly?
- Is there evidence that the instructor answers student inquiries in two days or less?
- Does the instructor participate in discussion forums where appropriate?
- Does the instructor provide feedback on assignments?

Communication between Observer and Observed

For face-to-face classes, the usual communication that takes place prior to the observation is to let the instructor know that he or she will be observed on a given day and time. Perhaps the observer asks for a copy of the course syllabus or for any handouts that will be provided to the students. There is typically little communication between the observer and the instructor during the actual observation.

For online courses, similar needs arise: the observer must still notify the instructor that observation will take place. Instead of requesting copies

of documents (which, *de facto*, may be accessible during the online observation), the observer will want to establish whether the instructor is also
the author of the course content. Likewise, the instructor may communicate ahead of time to the observer about where the observer may wish
to focus attention or about anything unique regarding the context of the
instruction, especially if there are interactive elements in the online course
environment that are in different places than, or go beyond, the usual
places where interaction occurs.

A further difference for online courses is that communication, in the
form of clarifying and directional questions, is often beneficial during the
observation period. For example, the administrative observer may want to
see supplemental content that is released to students only after they accomplish various course tasks (and which the observer is unable to complete
in order to unlock). This brings up the next area in which agreement is
needed: the extent of the observation.

Which Elements Are In Bounds

Agreement on which elements of the online course represent teaching
practices is often the most contentious discussion on a campus because
many elements may be considered part of the course design or teaching
practices, depending on their structure and function, as seen in the
example of lecture content previously discussed. However, it is possible to
create a core agreement that identifies elements of online courses:

- Those that are *always* counted as teaching practices (e.g., discussion
  forums, group-work areas, and feedback on student assignments)
- Those that *may* be counted as teaching practices, depending on
  structure and interactivity (e.g., supplemental materials, spontaneous
  mini-lectures, news or announcement items)
- Those that are *never* counted as teaching practices (e.g., preconstructed
  lecture content, graded tests and quizzes, major course assignments,
  links to websites, and content created by third parties such as textbook
  publishers)

A secondary concern about the scope of what administrative observers
may use for evaluation has to do with the boundaries of the course-delivery
environment. Many instructors, whether teaching face-to-face or online,
perform teaching actions outside of formal instruction. For instance,
instructors in both types of classes may meet with students for office-hour

consultations and engage in student consultations via e-mail and telephone calls. In the face-to-face environment, such contact, although it definitely meets the definition of "teaching," is not counted toward administrative observation because it is not readily visible and measurable to the observer.

However, in the online environment, these behaviors may or may not be visible, depending on the technical setup used at the institution. In institutions where the course-delivery environment includes text-based chat and synchronous-environment features, faculty office hours may be recorded and stored in logs accessible to the instructor and students in the course. More commonly, many instructors have a Q&A or "water cooler" topic in their online discussion forums that is intended for general questions about the course—but such discussion topics are almost never a required element of the course design.

One way to resolve the question of where observers may look is to think about the boundaries present in both face-to-face and online class observations. In a face-to-face class, the boundary is the classroom itself. Interactions that take place outside of the physical location of the classroom, including office-hour consultations, phone calls, and e-mail messages, are not counted toward the observer's evaluation. An easily defined boundary in online courses would be to consider excluding those same types of outside-of-formal-instruction communications from the observation and evaluation process.

Consider that a discussion of where to draw the boundary lines will result in different combinations of interactions being in play at different institutions and may even result in some interactions coming into consideration when a change is made to the institution's course delivery environment that adds new features. For example, if an institution adds a synchronous-online-classroom software feature to its course environment, then logged recordings of the use of that feature would come into the scope of what is possible to be observed.

One final word is necessary about the level of access granted to the observer. In most online course environments, observers can be granted student- or instructor-level access to the environment. The best practice is to allow administrative observers student-level access to online courses, unless there is a compelling reason for access to an instructor-only area of the course. Agreement on this point, and a process for making the request to see instructor-access parts of a course, are best made in advance of the observation. Such agreement helps to keep the focus of the observation on the interactions accessible to students.

Duration of the Observation

For face-to-face courses, the temporal boundary of an administrative observation is well defined, usually one class-meeting period. The observer spends fifty to ninety minutes watching the class unfold in real time. The challenge for observing online classes is that the observer's time spent examining the online environment does not correlate directly to the amount of time spent observing a face-to-face class covering the same scope of ideas and content.

The best practices for defining the time period for observation are to allow the evaluator access to the online course environment over a set period of days and to communicate time-spent expectations up front. For example Penn State University advises evaluators to conduct their reviews toward the end of the semester so that there will be a rich and complete set of interactions to evaluate. If observations take place too early in the course, there may not yet be a lot of teaching behaviors in evidence. At Penn State, administrative evaluators are also told that the observation instrument was designed to take approximately two hours to complete. Communicating time-spent expectations helps observers to know how much attention and detail is required for completing a thorough observation, enables observers to focus on the must-observe areas of the course environment, and offers an opportunity for evaluators to examine other areas of the course environment to determine whether they fall into the "leads to interaction" category.

Assistance Available to the Observer

In the face-to-face classroom, there is little concern about the observer's required technical skills. He or she arrives at the classroom and takes notes about the class. For online courses, however, administrative observers may not be skilled at navigating the online course environment or may need technical help in observing various elements in the online course. Agreement about the availability, extent, and role of technical staff is needed prior to the observation.

If administrative observers of online courses require sherpas who will guide the observation process, first determine from what area(s) of the institution the technical assistants should come. For example, at Northeastern Illinois University, retention, tenure, and promotion observations may be facilitated by staff members from the teaching and learning center. Center staff have to draw a bright line about being able to answer process-related questions when assisting administrative observers, leaving the domain of what to observe squarely in the hands of the administrative observers.

Further, the role of the technical assistant should be defined. The continuum of assistance can range from fully embedded (in which the assistant is at the keyboard all the time and takes direction from the administrative observer) to consultative (in which the administrative observer is at the computer and the assistant offers verbal help) to on call (in which the assistant is not initially involved in the observation and is brought in only if the observer requests help).

A final concern about assistance for the administrative observer is to make clear that any assistance offered is facilitative in nature and not evaluative. For instance, a technical assistant may show an evaluator the discussion forums in a given online course and may mention that the instructor appears to be responding to students at the rate of about one message per ten student messages. The assistant should not, however, provide evaluative or comparative advice during the observation, such as saying that a good benchmark for instructor postings is to post between 10 and 20 percent of the total number of messages in online discussions. This can be challenging for assistants who are, outside of the observation setting, resources for the institution on precisely these kinds of issues. In institutions where teaching-center staff members train administrators in the process of observing online courses, it is a good practice to source the pool of technical assistants from another campus unit, such as the information technology area, to avoid potential conflicts regarding who is providing the evaluative response in an observation.

How to Fool an Administrator in Three Easy Steps

A dean in charge of a well-established faculty at a large four-year college in New York is asked to perform an administrator observation for two instructors' courses. One of her instructors is Sal, a tenured faculty member who teaches food safety courses in the hotel management BA program, and another instructor is Mel, a contingent faculty member who teaches film history in the liberal arts program. Both Sal and Mel recently began to teach online courses for the college. Both took the required online-instructor training provided by the computer-support folks on campus, and both instructors have developed syllabi, lecture notes, and class discussion content for their online classes. Both Sal and Mel have been teaching online since 2000, but neither has yet been evaluated on his performance in the online classroom, despite both having been evaluated at least once per year for their classroom-based courses.

The dean, anticipating the upcoming visit from the college's regional accreditation association, wants to demonstrate that she is evaluating the performance of her faculty in online as well as face-to-face courses, so she asks both instructors to allow her to observe their online classes.

Sal invites the dean to come into his online course environment at any time without first making arrangements. He provides the dean with a copy of his syllabus and asks her to drop in for an hour whenever she likes. The dean studies the syllabus, and she notes with satisfaction that it contains all of the required elements for college syllabi: faculty contact information, course objectives, textbooks, and a course calendar with due dates and assignments. The dean, with help from one of the computer-support techies, looks in on Sal's class on a Thursday afternoon. She sees Sal's home page, which contains a short video clip introducing himself to the class, and it appears professionally designed, with a maroon background that helps to tie the whole site together visually. The dean visits Sal's threaded discussion for unit 3, where she discovers that Sal has answered every one of the students' questions; his name appears on almost every other line. Finally, the dean looks at Sal's "webliography," where she finds more than sixty links to outside resources—plenty of help for students.

The dean contacts Mel to ask for a copy of his syllabus in anticipation of a visit to his online course. Mel provides not only the syllabus but also an expectations sheet for unit 3 that lists the tasks students should do in the order in which they are expected to do them. Mel requests the dean to visit the course as if she were a student engaged in unit 3's assignments. The dean notes that Mel's syllabus deviates from the typical model, omitting due dates for assignments but including sections on how to submit work online and netiquette. When the dean visits Mel's course on the next Thursday afternoon, she goes first to the course home page (where she notes only text with a white background); then to the lecture notes (same format); then to the PowerPoint slides (mostly text with a few pictures); and finally to the class threaded discussions, where she notes that Mel seems to be somewhat "absent." His postings appear only once in eight or ten postings. The dean notes that a student asked a question on Monday, and Mel has responded with his thoughts on Thursday. Granted, many other students attempted to help in the meantime. Although Mel did not ask the dean to visit his webliography, she finds there only fifteen links, all posted by students and not by Mel.

The dean, using the traditional rubric for evaluating instructor perfor-mance, gave high marks to Sal and wondered whether perhaps Mel might need a little help in getting his classroom back under control.

This is admittedly an extreme example, but one which highlights the need for administrators either to be online instructors themselves or to have online-specific questions and rubrics for evaluating the performance of online instruction. Sal, in his hypothetical food safety course, displays all of the outward signs of good classroom teaching: he has a syllabus that is tied to the academic calendar, he uses the glitter factor of multimedia to hold his students' interest, he is quick to respond to students questions, and he provides a wealth of resources to help students achieve. Mel, however, seems not to evince these traits, going so far as to let students questions sit for days at a time. It appears as though the students in Mel's class are having to teach themselves.

Just to be sure she had a complete picture of how things were going, The dean telephoned a few students in each class and was surprised to find that the students in Sal's course complained that he did not give students enough time to get a discussion going online before he gave the "right" answer. They also noted that his syllabus did not contain the URL for his class or instructions about how to log in or what to say in the class discussion. Some of Sal's students felt bored because they were just going through exercises in order to complete them; few things in Sal's course felt like learning challenges.

Students in Mel's class, conversely, felt that his assignments asked them to construct their own ways of learning, and they appreciated his allowing them to talk with each other and him. His style made them feel as though their learning was valued enough to become a part of the teaching materials for other students. When the dean asked them about the syllabus, many students said that having the initial heads up about how to be in an online class was helpful without being restrictive.

The dean had something of a quandary on her hands. Her evaluative instrument told her that Sal was the better instructor, but the students seemed to favor Mel. What has Sal done that allowed his performance to rank so high on the evaluative instrument? It seemed that quantity was the driving factor. Sal had a lot of discussion, posted a lot of documents, used a lot of flashy multimedia, and generated a lot of web links to outside resources. However, his students seemed to want not just the information but to know how to assess, use, and create more of it themselves—something that Mel seemed better able to provide.

Source: Adapted from Tobin (2004).

On Avoiding Quantity Bias

There is one factor in administrative evaluation of online teaching that is not typically encountered in observation of face-to-face classes and deserves separate consideration: quantity bias. The scenario presented in "How to Fool an Administrator" shows that an observer, particularly one who has not taught online himself or herself, can be tempted to equate several nonrelated factors with the quality of the online course experience for students. These factors include the amount of content in the online course environment, the amount of multimedia used in the course, or the number of communications from the instructor.

As has been emphasized in this chapter, the primary means of avoiding quantity bias is to focus exclusively on the interaction among the students and instructor. Items that get students to take actions, as opposed to items that are to be consumed passively by reading or watching them, are those that can be evaluated for administrative observations. It is safest to evaluate only the spontaneous aspects of the course and not the canned materials at all.

In the tale of Sal and Mel, the dean assumes that each instructor has created the entire collection of course materials. However, Mel might not have authored the content of the film history course and may not have had any control over the presentation of the entries in the course webliography. Likewise, Sal might have inherited the structural aspects of the course from someone else who authored the content. By focusing on just the interactions between students and instructor, as well as on the instructor's facilitation of student-to-student interactions, evaluators can get a true sense of how well online courses are being taught. This points to three take-away lessons:

- **Consider student interaction load.** Estimate the amount of effort being asked of learners in the unit or week under evaluation. In a three-credit course during a fifteen-week semester, the total effort asked of students typically ranges between six and ten hours per week, including in- and out-of-class work (Southern Association of Colleges and Schools Commission on Colleges [SACS COC], 2012). Give higher evaluative credit to instructors who interact more often with students as part of the student workload. For example, instructors may ask students to report on assignment progress, provide feedback on collaborative student work, and take an active part in guiding course discussion threads.
- **Evaluate required and optional elements.** Look at the structure of the communications between the instructor and students (e.g., discussions, news and announcements, stop-and-do exercises). Regardless

of whether they are required, must students stumble across them in order to move ahead? For example, are thought exercises and switch-your-thinking practice messages interspersed by the instructor among the discussion messages posted throughout a unit or week?

- **Look for a balance of planned and just-in-time communication.** Provide higher ratings to online courses in which the instructor posts regular communications, such as unit introductions, milestone-achievement messages, and roundup and review messages. In addition, look for just-in-time communications that respond to student requests for assistance and provide praise and correction for individual students. It's possible to have an entire online course in the can and post only prewritten messages—the equivalent of the same-lectures-every-semester prof who reads from fifteen-year-old notes. Evaluate the quality of instructor feedback on student work using Chickering and Gamson's (1987) principles (e.g., the instructor communicates high expectations, gives prompt and meaningful feedback, and respects diverse talents and ways of learning).

Especially in online courses, it can be tempting to equate greater quantities of interaction with better course experiences. Be sure to take into account the number of students in the course when evaluating the number of instances of interaction seen in the online course environment as well.

Looking Beyond the Administrator

This chapter has focused on best practices for converting the traditional face-to-face model of an administrator observing a classroom into a way for administrators to observe online teaching practices. There are many other models for observing online teaching practices, however; many move beyond the traditional participants:

- An administrator observes an instructor.
- The institution hires full-time teaching-practice evaluators.
- Administrators delegate the observation task to faculty peers or to department staff members.
- An instructor seeks out a peer or a professional staffer to observe his or her teaching practices.

In all of these cases except the first, the observer is not the department chair or dean and likely has a different level of access to—and authority over—the instructor being observed. The next chapter will focus on the tools and techniques best suited to peer review of online teaching practices.

Conclusion

At Northeastern Illinois University, when the technology coordinator finally met with the department chair to help prepare him to observe the faculty member's online course, the coordinator came with a proposed plan to help him to narrow down the work that they would need to do before, during, and after the observation. The plan included specific requests that the department chair would be able to make of the faculty member prior to the observation, such as getting a copy of the course syllabus and any supplemental materials.

The coordinator also suggested that the chair observe a single unit of material—one that had already been completed—so he could get a good feel for the overall experience of being a student in the course. Finally, the coordinator set up time to give the department chair a general introduction to the university's online learning environment so he would know what to expect and be better able to decide where to look within the environment to observe the various criteria in the department's observation rubric. The department chair left the consultation feeling better prepared and confident that the teaching center's staff would be there to support the observations.

A Thought Exercise

With a pen and paper, think for a few minutes about the administrative-observation situation at your own institution. Who currently observes classes from an administrative point of view and for what purposes? Some common purposes are as follows:

- To evaluate teaching practice regularly
- To address a reported issue or classroom concern
- To evaluate teaching performance toward an award or promotion

Also, write down the scope of the current observations that take place:

- How many class periods are covered?
- What communication, materials, and access are provided to the observer before, during, and after the observation?

Now that you have an outline of your current administrative-observation program, think of the observable criteria for evaluating good teaching practices (per Chickering & Gamson, 1987):

- How does your current system map onto those criteria?
- Would adopting an administrative-observation protocol for online courses entail a reexamination of your institution's current face-to-face observation protocol as well?

To wrap up this thought exercise, predict what resources you would need in place in order to make administrative observations consistent, no matter the modality in which they are performed. For example, if online-course observers get to ask for supplemental materials and a copy of the syllabus, the same should apply for face-to-face observations. Collect your notes into a list of core elements and begin the conversation with your colleagues.

CHAPTER SEVEN

ADMINISTRATIVE REVIEW TOOLS

Ann H. Taylor's Story

In 2009, I was the senior instructional designer for the John A. Dutton e-Education Institute within the College of Earth and Mineral Sciences at The Pennsylvania State University. The Dutton Institute was charged with supporting the college's entire portfolio of online courses and programs, from design and development of the individual online courses to overall program management and oversight. Although the college had been offering online programs for a decade at that point, there was still skepticism among some faculty members about the quality of online teaching and learning in comparison to the quality of teaching and learning taking place in the college's face-to-face classrooms. The Dutton Institute's director approached me with a challenge: to ensure that the evaluation of the college's online teaching and learning was at least on par with the level of evaluation conducted for its face-to-face offerings.

To this day, university policy for promotion and tenure requires that the evaluation of teaching effectiveness for these purposes be based on both formal student and peer (i.e., administrative) input. All academic units are required to use a standard student rating of teaching effectiveness (see chapter 5). By 2009, the Dutton Institute had already created a comparable survey instrument for use in the college's online courses.

The university's specific requirement for the formal administrative review component, however, has been left to the discretion of the individual academic units. The standard practice is for unit administrators or their designees (which often are faculty peers from the same unit) to attend one class meeting as official observers and to document those observations in a formal letter that is included in the observed faculty member's promotion and tenure dossier. No observation of this kind was being conducted in the college's online courses. This was clearly where I had to focus my efforts.

An informal review of practices taking place across the institution's academic units revealed unsurprising results: most administrative reviews were conducted without any formal guidance or rubric. One faculty member simply attended another's class meeting, took notes about whatever was observed, and then wrote up a summary of those observations in the form of a letter. Because the observer was typically not given any information on what to look for by way of evidence of effective teaching, the quality of observations varied widely. In the few cases where academic units did provide reviewers with formal guidance, such as a rubric, that guidance was not completely relevant to the online classroom. For example, one department's observation sheet included an entire section on "presentation skills." To make sure that the college's online teaching was evaluated effectively, I would need to create a tool and a process for conducting meaningful administrative reviews.

What Is Already Available?

As Ann discovered, rubrics and other guiding tools are often used when conducting formal administrative reviews of teaching, but a close look at these tools reveals that they don't lend themselves to the review of online teaching as is. We have already discussed the reasons behind this dissonance, and in this chapter, we will explore some of the tools and associated techniques that have been specifically developed for evaluating online teaching:

- Checklist for Online Interactive Learning (COIL)
- Quality Online Course Initiative (QOCI): Illinois Online Network

- Quality Matters (QM) Rubric
- Online Instructor Evaluation System (OIES): Park University
- Peer Review of Online Teaching: Penn State

We will discuss the origins of each tool as well as the considerations for using these in one's own institutional setting (see the next section for an overview of how one institution navigated this process). Figure 7.1 illustrates the general time line for these instruments and some of their historical antecedents.

The authors recently spoke with Steve McGahan, Christina Jackson, and Karen Premer at the University of Nebraska at Kearney about their experiences with developing and implementing a new evaluation of online teaching; they composed the following summary of their experiences with this process.

FIGURE 7.1. ONLINE-TEACHING EVALUATION INSTRUMENT "FAMILY TREE"

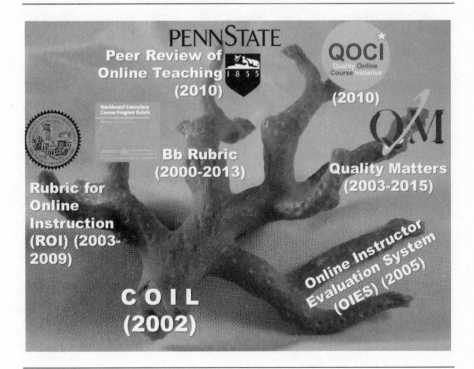

The Process of Adopting an Evaluation of Online Teaching

When tasked with creating an evaluation of online teaching, there are two primary approaches: adopt an existing evaluation tool or create a customized evaluation metric. The process to determine the most effective strategy for evaluating online teaching must include a number of considerations: time requirements, faculty buy in, ease-of-use, level of instructional design support, impact on student learning, and cost. Recognizing the complexity of the decision-making process and the time investment required to develop new evaluation tools, institutions may be tempted to simply adopt an existing evaluation instrument. But, as discovered by the University of Nebraska at Kearney (UNK), this approach may not be best suited for ensuring continued quality and growth in online education.

In 2006, increasing distance education enrollments at UNK mandated closer attention to the quality of instruction provided in online courses; as such, it was determined that online courses needed an evaluation instrument that could gauge effectiveness within the unique confines of the institutional LMS. Because evaluations are done independently under the purview of each department (with evaluators who may or may not have experience with online education), it was also determined that the evaluation tool needed to be simple enough to be used with minimal guidance or training.

A team of instructional designers from the eCampus Division was tasked with the project. The evaluation process began with a comparative evaluation of the numerous off-the-shelf instruments developed by other institutions (e.g., Maryland Online, Central Michigan University, and Illinois Online Network). Initial evaluation was based on three factors: ease-of-use (by both instructional designers and faculty), instructional design needs for UNK courses, and costs associated with the process. An initial field of five instruments (Quality Matters, Rubric for Online Instruction, Quality Online Course Initiative, CID Quality Assurance Checklist, and WebCT Exemplary Course Project) was reviewed during the first phase of the process. Of these metrics, two were eliminated because they did not align with the institutional structure and instructional expectations set forth by UNK. After reviewing the CID Quality Assurance Checklist, it was determined that there were several places where the objectives were tied to specific requirements for Central Michigan University, such as their use of a master course syllabus template that is targeted specifically to their resources and support structure, and thus not relevant in other contexts. The WebCT Exemplary Course

Project was rejected because of the complex nature of the rubric, which required both anecdotal and visual evidence to support the criteria being evaluated.

Three instruments advanced to further review and testing: MarylandOnline's Quality Matters (QM), Illinois Online Network's Quality Online Course Initiative (QOCI), and California State University Chico's Rubric for Online Instruction (ROI) (2009). The testing process included a review of several courses from different subject areas using the different metrics. Completed courses were subjected to the instruments to determine time and ease of use. The eCampus review team chose two courses of differing disciplines from each of the four colleges at UNK to test with each instrument. At the time, eCampus had two instructional designers, so each designer took a course from each college and tested the rubric in UNK courses.

QM and the QOCI were long and complex, so they were not seen as effective instruments for UNK. With only two instructional designers, the time necessary to apply these to the number of courses being reviewed each semester (usually twenty to thirty), the rubrics would have been time prohibitive. Additionally, the complexity would hinder its use by faculty as a self-evaluation tool. The ROI required less time but ultimately didn't cover the instructional design aspects that were needed for UNK. One such area was constant student feedback. Although feedback on the course is important, the focus of an entire section of the rubric on constant student feedback was deemed unnecessary. Additionally, the rubric also had metrics for course aesthetics. Again, although this can be useful, it was deemed as unnecessary for UNK online courses. Aesthetic design was not seen as necessary for an exemplary online course.

Recognizing that none of the off-the-shelf instruments were inclusively satisfactory for use at UNK, the instructional design team determined it was necessary to develop a customized instrument specific to the needs of UNK faculty. Specifically, because UNK has a large number of online courses and programs compared to the size of the instructional design team, it required an evaluation of teaching that was comprehensive and easy to use. To address these challenges and constraints, an instrument was developed that combined the ease of use in the ROI with the comprehensive nature of QM and the QOCI.

Creating a process to evaluate online teaching is daunting, but it is important to dedicate adequate time, resources, and attention to it. As highlighted in the experiences at UNK, the process can take up to a year and involves a range of stakeholders (e.g., faculty and instructional designers). Regardless of the quality, reputation, or value of an evaluation instrument, it is vital that each evaluation tool is reviewed and tested in light of the unique context of each institution. Existing instruments must be applied to multiple courses across various disciplines to determine their value, feasibility, and impact in relation to the needs of faculty and the campus. The key decision is *not* based simply on the quality of the evaluation tool but on the fit of the evaluation process to the institutional context and needs(McGahan, Jackson, & Premer, 2014b).

Checklist for Online Interactive Learning

The Checklist for Online Interactive Learning (Sunal & Sunal, 2002) is considered the granddaddy of online teaching evaluation instruments. Based on a meta-analysis of research in online instruction, the COIL consists of a checklist of best practices for developing and using online materials. The instrument focuses on measurable outcomes of online teaching and learning in four areas: student behavior, faculty-student interaction, technology support, and the completeness of the learning environment. Within each of these four areas, the reviewer uses a Likert scale to rate the quality of the online course. Sample items from each area are shown in the next section.

Sample Items from the COIL

Category 1: Student Behaviors Meet Criterion

- Students demonstrate that their prerequisite technology skills are adequate for hardware, software, and website use.
- Students seek opportunities to, and support for, interacting with instructor and other students.
- Students actively participate in all online activities.

Category 2: Faculty-Student Interactions

- Instructor provides clear and adequate guidance.
- Instructor actively evaluates the success and failure of the students in the course and reflects on how to meet student concerns.
- Instructor personalizes student-teacher communications.

Category 3: Technology Support

- Instructor troubleshoots technological difficulties in accessing website and communication.
- Instructor provides adequate, friendly, easy, continuous technical support.

Category 4: Learning Environment

- Instructor uses structured activities to provide an effective framework for online learning.
- Instructor uses flexible deadlines to motivate students, maintain communication, and allow for technical problems.
- Instructor creates social interaction through group collaboration to facilitate high achievement. (Sunal & Sunal, 2002)

Because of its design, the COIL instrument is considered to have a high degree of objectivity. Most of the items from the instrument are verifiable in terms of course output or content and correlate with actual instructor quality.

COIL Pros, Cons, and Considerations for Use

The COIL instrument most closely mimics the old bubble-sheet format from paper-based rating tools and may be easiest for administrators to use quickly. Likewise, the language and terminology used in the COIL instrument are generic enough that most evaluators will be able to understand and apply the statements in the instrument to specific instances within the online environment. Its language is, in other words, largely LMS or platform neutral.

One of the challenges for the COIL instrument is that it suffers from the assumption that the online instructor is also the course author, as discussed in chapter 5. Several COIL rating questions have to do with the design elements of online courses and could probably be discarded. Before coming to such a decision, however, readers should determine whether they wish to keep such elements. Berk (2013b) shows how ratings and evaluation of online teaching is still in its comparative infancy even today when he says that, "despite the similarity of ratings in f2f [face-to-face] and online courses with traditional f2f scales, the unique characteristics of online courses should be measured to furnish a more complete, as opposed to a biased, evaluation of those courses. The issue is how to do that efficiently and cost-effectively to produce psychometrically defensible scales" (p. 92).

Quality Online Course Initiative (QOCI)

A second tool was developed by the Illinois Online Network and the Illinois Virtual Campus in partnership with two-year and four-year public and private educational institutions in Illinois. Designed as a "tool to assist in the design, redesign, and/or evaluation of online courses" (Illinois Online Network and the Board of Trustees of the University of Illinois, 1998), the QOCI (pronounced "kwock-ee") is similar to the QM Rubric (discussed in the following section) in that it focuses primarily on the design of the online course. However, the rubric can also be used to evaluate some online teaching behaviors.

The full version of the rubric addresses eighty-one elements, each categorized into one of the following areas:

- Instructional design, communication, interaction, and collaboration
- Student ratings and assessment
- Learner support and resources
- Web design
- Course evaluation

For each of the eighty-one items, the reviewer rates how well the course and instructor addresses the item using a scale of nonexistent, developing, meets, exceeds, or not applicable. The rubric also includes spaces where the reviewer can add additional comments for each item.

Sample Items from the QOCI Instrument

Instructional Design

- **Sequence.** Content is sequenced and structured in a manner that enables learners to achieve the stated goals.
- **Multimodal instruction.** A variety of instructional delivery methods, accommodating multiple learning styles, are available throughout the course.

Communication, Interaction, and Collaboration

- **Student-instructor.** Learning activities and other opportunities are developed to foster student-instructor communication and collaboration.

Student Ratings and Assessment

- A statement explaining what type of feedback students will receive is provided.

Learner Support and Resources

- Links to tutorials and other CMS support sites are provided.

Web Design

- **Scrolling.** Scrolling is minimized or facilitated with anchors.

Course Evaluation

- **Instruction.** Opportunities for learner feedback throughout the course on issues surrounding the course's physical structure ... are provided. (Illinois Online Network and the Board of Trustees of the University of Illinois, 2014).

Because the QOCI address the full spectrum from course design to delivery and includes primarily aspects that may be beyond the control of the instructor (particularly if the instructor did not have a role in the course's design or development), institutions will need to adapt the QOCI in order to conduct administrative reviews that focuses on *online teaching* and not on *course design*. However, the QOCI still provides a valuable framework. Two versions of the instrument (with and without the checkboxes and comment areas) are freely available online for noncommercial use. Both are provided in rich text format to enable others to adapt them to their own institutional needs.

Quality Matters (QM) Rubric

QM has become an international leader in quality assurance for online teaching and learning. The QM program uses a faculty-centered, peer-review process to certify the quality of online courses. QM is a subscription service providing rubrics and tools to its members.

The QM Rubric was first developed in 2003 as part of a Fund for the Improvement of Postsecondary Education (FIPSE) grant awarded to MarylandOnline. The rubric is based on research, national standards of best practice in online education, and instructional design principles. The 2014 version of the QM Rubric includes a total of forty-three specific standards on which a course is rated, grouped into eight categories (MarylandOnline, 2014):

- **Course overview and introduction** (e.g., "Instructions make clear how to get started and where to find various course components.")
- **Learning objectives (competencies)** (e.g., "The course learning objectives, or course or program competencies, describe outcomes that are measurable.")
- **Assessment and measurement** (e.g., "The assessments measure the stated learning objectives or competencies.")
- **Instructional materials** (e.g., "The instructional materials contribute to the achievement of the stated course and module or unit learning objectives or competencies.")
- **Course activities and learner interaction** (e.g., "The learning activities promote the achievement of the stated learning objectives or competencies.")
- **Course technology** (e.g., "The tools used in the course support the learning objectives and competencies.")
- **Learner support** (e.g., "The course instructions articulate or link to a clear description of the technical support offered and how to obtain it.")
- **Accessibility and usability** (e.g., "The course navigation facilitates ease of use.")

(MarylandOnline, 2014). Quality Matters™ rubric standards fifth edition, 2014, with assigned point values. For more information, visit http://www.qualitymatters.org.

Each of the forty-three standards has an associated point value of between one and three points. If the course meets the standard, the associated points are awarded. If not, zero points are awarded. In this manner, each standard is weighted against the others.

Use of the rubric is intended as part of a peer-review process that is intended to be "diagnostic and collegial, not evaluative or judgmental." The rubric is used by the reviewer to provide the instructor with a "quality score," with a goal of achieving 85 percent or better. As stated on the

QM website, "courses do not have to be perfect, but better than good enough"(MarylandOnline, 2009).

Although intended as a collegial peer-review tool, many institutions use the QM Rubric in conducting formal administrative reviews. In response to institution-specific needs and concerns about the length of the QM Rubric, some institutions have adapted the QM Rubric for their own use. For example, Penn State University has created its "Penn State Quality Assurance e-Learning Design Standards" based on the QM Rubric. The Penn State rubric contains just twelve quality assurance standards. Each standard is described in detail and includes evidence of how that standard is met, suggested best practices, and resources for additional information. Following is a summary of the twelve standards used by Penn State. Note the mix of design and teaching skills to be evaluated.

A Summary of Penn State Quality Assurance e-Learning Design Standards

- **Navigation.** The course has a consistent and intuitive navigation system enabling students to quickly locate course information and materials.
- **Student orientation.** A course orientation is used to familiarize the students with the course.
- **Syllabus.** Students have easy access to a course syllabus that contains crucial course information and requirements they need to know about the course prior to starting.
- **Instructor response and availability.** Instructor response time and availability is clearly communicated to the students.
- **Course resource requirements.** Hardware, software, or specialized resources required are clearly communicated to the students.
- **Technical support.** Information regarding access to technical support is clearly communicated to the students.
- **Accessibility requirements.** The course adheres to university policies and guidelines regarding accessibility.
- **Learning objectives.** The course contains learning goals and objectives.
- **Learning activities and assessment.** The course learning activities and assessment serve to stimulate student interactions with the course content and determine how well student performance achieves the course goals and learning objectives.
- **Copyright requirements.** The online course adheres to the current university policies for the use of third-party copyrighted material or is able to provide evidence of appropriate copyright clearance.

- **Course functionality.** All aspects of the course perform properly and support student progress.
- **Student input for course improvements.** Opportunities are provided to gather input from students on an ongoing basis in order to inform course improvements. (Penn State Online, 2014). The instrument itself can be found in the companion website for this book (www.wiley.com/go/tobin).

When considering the QM Rubric for the purposes of a formal review of online teaching, it should be noted that the rubric actually focuses on the *design* of the online course and not its delivery (like the QOCI we discussed previously). Therefore, a comprehensive review of online teaching and learning should not rely on the QM Rubric alone. Additional information will need to be obtained in order to evaluate the quality of online teaching.

The Online Instructor Evaluation System (OIES)

Another tool for consideration is the OIES developed by Park University. You will recall that we first looked at the OIES in the case study in chapter 2. As described there, the OIES was developed specifically for use at Park and was based on a comprehensive review of the literature as well as generalized best practices in online teaching and learning.

The OIES is used to evaluate the online instructor at five points during the delivery of an eight-week online course: precourse, the end of week two, the end of week four, the end of week six, and at the end of the course. Each of these reviews focuses on a different aspect of course delivery.

A Summary of the Five OIES Reviews

- **The preterm review** is completed prior to the start of the term and focuses on the setup of the online course. While completing the preterm review, the evaluator ensures introductory items (e.g., course home page, home page content items, and syllabus) are updated, personalized, and reflect university requirements. These set-up activities are especially important in orienting learners in an accelerated format, whereby students often access their online classrooms prior to the start of the term to obtain textbook-ordering information and other preparatory materials. In addition, the evaluator provides targeted suggestions for enhancements related to course organization and the use of course tools and features.

- **Review 1**, which is completed at the end of the second week, examines community building and promotion of an interactive climate. The purpose of this review is to examine the use and implementation of discussion threads, including an overview of participation expectations, tips for grading discussion items, instructor availability, instructor presence, and student-to-student interaction.
- **Review 2** is completed during the fourth week and focuses on discussion facilitation, feedback, and grading. During this review, the evaluator provides guidance on instructor interactions, specifically addressing feedback and participation in the discussion threads as well as comments and use of the grade book. Reviews 1 and 2 emphasize discussion facilitation and feedback because meaningful, consistent instructor interaction is an ongoing essential of effective online learning.
- At the end of week six, **review 3** examines assessments and final exam preparation. The evaluator reviews the implementation of formative and summative assessments as well as preparation for final exam and the proctored exam process. In addition, interactions include an opportunity to share ideas about supplemental formative assessments that may be added to the course. Although instructors are expected to use the core curriculum provided, they are also encouraged to add supplemental content to their courses.
- Implemented during the final weeks of the term, **review 4** focuses on instructional materials and overall course climate and organization. As such, evaluators will review all supplemental information to ensure adherence to general instructional design principles and specific university curriculum standards and expectations.

As discussed in chapter 2, the first four OIES reviews are intended for peer mentoring and professional growth, and the final review is summative in nature and intended to inform not only the instructor but also the academic department as an administrative review. For a full review of the OIES, including how the reviews are implemented, see chapter 2. The instrument itself can be found in the companion website (www.wiley.com/go/tobin) for this book.

Peer Review Guide for Online Teaching at Penn State

The final tool we will review here comes from Penn State University and is the direct result of our story from the beginning of this chapter. Faced with the need to create a tool and a process for conducting meaningful administrative reviews, Ann Taylor first looked for existing tools that were in use in face-to-face classrooms because they had been specifically designed for the evaluation of online instruction (such as those we've examined already). Her work kept bringing her back to a basic philosophy: Good teaching is good teaching, regardless of the platform.

Returning to the seminal work of Chickering and Gamson (1987) described in "Seven Principles for Good Practice in Undergraduate Education," Ann found that the seven principles provided a useful framework to evaluate the effectiveness of online teaching, regardless of the level of study (i.e., undergraduate or graduate). The resulting "Peer Review Guide for Online Teaching at Penn State" was developed, implemented, and evaluated for use within the College of Earth and Mineral Sciences at Penn State. Subsequently, the tool has been vetted and revised with the help of colleagues from the Penn State Online Coordinating Council Subcommittee on Faculty/Staff Engagement and Professional Development. It is now available for use within the entire Penn State community and made available online to the entire higher education community for their use.

Designed initially for use in a formal administrative review process, the guide is structured around the seven principles. For each principle, a description of the intent of the principle is provided (adapted from Chickering and Gamson's original work), followed by examples of how that principle might be manifested in the online course environment. Reviewers are also provided with tips as to where one might look within the course to find such examples. Space is then provided where the reviewer can note what evidence was found, describe observed areas of strength, and note suggestions for improvement. The following section outlines principle 1 from the "Peer Review Guide for Online Teaching at Penn State."

Principle 1: Good Practice Encourages Contact between Students and Faculty

Frequent and timely student-faculty contact is the most important factor in student motivation and involvement, particularly in a distance education environment. Evidence of faculty concern helps students get through challenging situations and inspires them to persevere. Knowing a few faculty members well enhances students' intellectual commitment and encourages them to think about their own values and future plans.

Examples of evidence to look for:

- A welcome message is provided at the beginning of the course that encourages student-to-instructor contact for course-related discussions or concerns.
- The instructor encourages and fosters a healthy exchange of ideas and sharing of experiences among course participants.
- The instructor initiates contact with, or responds to, students on a regular basis in order to establish a consistent online presence in the course (and prior notice is given to students in the event that the instructor will be unavailable for more than a few days, such as might be the case during professional travel).
- A prominent announcement area is used to communicate important up-to-date course information to students, such as reminders of impending assignment due dates, curriculum changes, scheduled absences, and so on.
- The instructor holds regular office hours and is available for appointments that are mediated by technology (e.g., the telephone, chat areas, Adobe Connect Pro) to accommodate distance students.
- Student inquiries are responded to in a timely manner.
- The instructor provides students with interaction space for study groups, "hallway conversations," and so on.

Where to look:

- Discussion forums
- E-mail messages
- Posted announcements
- Course syllabus
- Chat space

Resources:

- "What to do when opening a course"—www.e-education.psu.edu/facdev/pg3
- "Using online icebreakers to promote student/teacher interaction"—www.southalabama.edu/oll/jobaidsfall03/Icebreakers%20Online/icebreakerjobaid.htm (Taylor, 2010)

An important component of the guide is the associated instructor input form. Designed to be completed by the course instructor for the reviewer, the instructor input form provides the reviewer with key contextual information about the course to inform the review. In addition to providing the reviewer with course name, title, and location of various online elements, the instructor also provides information about how the course relates to other courses in the curriculum, any synchronous or face-to-face components of the course, supplemental materials that may not be provided online, and any additional information that the instructor wishes to have the reviewer consider. Sharing this document with the reviewer is also intended as a way to open a line of communication between the instructor and the reviewer for the duration of the review. Because each online course can have unique features, establishing an open line of communication is valuable as questions arise.

A suggested review process is included in the guide (shown in the next section), culminating with the dossier letter that is common to the administrative review of face-to-face teaching. The "Peer Review Guide for Online Teaching at Penn State," the associated instructor input form, and sample dossier letters are all freely available online and can be found in the companion website for this book (www.wiley.com/go/tobin).

Recommended Process for Faculty-Peer Review

The following recommended process is provided in the introductory section of the "Peer Review Guide for Online Courses at Penn State." Note that in this process, a faculty peer conducts the formal administrative review.

1. The department or division head or school director or, when appropriate, campus chancellor and campus director of academic affairs, identifies a faculty peer ("peer reviewer") to conduct the peer review of teaching.
2. The course instructor completes the instructor input form and shares that document with the peer reviewer to convey contextual information about the course.
3. After reviewing the completed instructor input form, the peer reviewer uses the "Peer Review Guide for Online Teaching at Penn State" to work through the online course, observing how well the instructor addresses each of the seven principles. The reviewer notes the instructor's strengths and areas for improvement for each principle in the space provided.

Note: Reviewers should feel free to ask questions of the instructor any time clarification or information is needed during the review process.

4. The peer reviewer summarizes the feedback in the form of a letter to that instructor, which can be included in the instructor's dossier. The letter, as well as a copy of the completed peer review guide, is then shared with the instructor, the program manager (if the course is part of an online program), and the department or division head or school director or, when appropriate, campus chancellor and campus director of academic affairs.

For **provisional faculty** (not yet tenured), it is recommended that peer reviews should occur at least once per year and in a variety of courses. It is better to have a series of peer reviews over time for faculty members being **reviewed for promotion** rather than several in the fall immediately preceding the review (Taylor, 2010).

Ann Taylor's Story—Coming Full Circle

As I found, finding the right tool to support an institution's formal administrative review of online teaching can be challenging. We have also discussed the fact that, even when suitable tools are identified, rarely can they be used as is. Adaptations need to be made so that the tools can be used for institution-specific context and needs. Existing tools such as the ones shared in this chapter can provide a useful head start by illuminating collective knowledge acquired through research and an examination of best practices. Many tools can even be adapted for use beyond the formal administrative review process, as we will discuss in the upcoming chapters related to informal reviews of online teaching.

Conclusion

In this chapter, we examined five tools that can be used or adapted in order to conduct an administrative review of online teaching. The challenge for evaluation of online teaching at many institutions is that there is no instrument or rubric used consistently across campus, as in Ann Taylor's story from Penn State. The opposite problem can also be true: there may be existing solutions in place, none of which seem to fit the specific circumstances for the institution's online teaching program. We will explore in chapter 9 the details behind the assertion that "good teaching is good teaching," and discover how readers can best adapt existing student, peer, and administrative review instruments—or even design their own.

A Thought Exercise

In order to prepare for adoption of an administrative evaluation instrument on your campus, write down responses to the following concerns:

- What processes and instruments are currently used on your campus to help administrative evaluators observe teaching in the face-to-face classroom? If none, or if there are many, where does the authority rest for making employment decisions based on the information created?
- Roughly how many administrative evaluators have themselves taught online courses?
- Of all of the existing evaluation instruments provided in this chapter, which one(s) match most closely to your institution's needs and culture?
- Is the teaching of contingent faculty members evaluated by your institution using a different process or a different frequency than full-time or tenure-line faculty members?

Of all of the processes and best practices in this book, these have perhaps the greatest potential to create sustained dialogue among the stakeholders across campus because they deal directly with employment decisions, so be sure to share your responses with your colleagues as a way to begin or continue the discussions at your institution.

CHAPTER EIGHT

INTEGRATING DATA ANALYTICS IN THE EVALUATION OF ONLINE TEACHING

Ashford University's Story

The challenge at Ashford University is not unique to their institution: how do colleges and universities support a large, growing body of online faculty in a meaningful way that is simultaneously effective and efficient? Intensifying this issue are the associated practical factors:

- A high ratio of faculty members to support specialists (which, in some cases, may be more than one hundred faculty members per support staffer)
- Reliance on a contingent faculty population that may or may not teach on a continuous schedule
- Emphasis on faculty support to increase instructional quality rather than reliance on summative evaluation to penalize underperforming faculty members

Ashford University addressed these issues via the development of an integrated model of faculty evaluation that stressed the role of faculty support and ongoing professional development to improve the quality of online teaching (Cohen, Molnar, & Johnson, 2013). At the heart of the model is a clear set of instructional best practices that have been adopted by the university as the baseline expectation for teaching behavior in the online classroom. These instructional expectations provide an operationalized, measurable metric from which faculty performance can be compared.

Although it is theoretically feasible to compare online teaching behaviors against a list of prescribed requirements, the challenge for Ashford University rested in the practical constraints associated with manually completing the large number of individual course observations necessary to gauge each instructor's alignment with the standards. Thus, working in conjunction with their LMS provider, Ashford University created an instructional support (IS) dashboard that uses the digital footprints that faculty members leave in the online classroom to track key instructional activities.

The IS dashboard enables support specialists to have a one-click snapshot of specific instructional behaviors that relate to the prescribed best practice requirements; performance indicators include activities such as posts in discussion forum, timeliness of feedback, and time on task. The goal is not to simply rely on these metrics as indicators of performance but to use the IS dashboard information as a means of efficiently observing the online courses so that instructional support specialists can reallocate their time to more in-depth evaluations (such as the quality of interactions or feedback). As explained by Cohen, Molnar, and Johnson (2013), through the analysis of the IS dashboard information, support specialists can accomplish the following:

- Pinpoint struggling instructors to prioritize instructional coaching opportunities
- Target the development of professional materials to address issues that are widespread across all faculty
- Tailor personal communication with faculty based on their individual instructional behavior patterns
- Invest increased time on proactive interactions to foster increased instructional quality rather than reactive issues based on poor performance

Ashford University is a pioneer in the integration of data analysis for evaluating and supporting online teaching. Unique to their approach is the use of a faculty performance dashboard that provides an automated snapshot of faculty teaching behaviors in an online course. Key to their system is an integrated appreciation for the complementary roles of humans and data.

The limited human resources are simply unable to manually monitor the individualized clicks and movements in a course; likewise, the digitized analytic analysis can't gauge the validity or relevance of the instructional artifacts. But, together, these two systems provide an efficient—and effective—approach to evaluating online teaching in a dynamic, growing online program.

Data Analytics: Moving beyond Student Learning

Data analytics are quickly becoming an integral component of a comprehensive approach to effective online learning. Similar to Ashford University, a number of other institutions are beginning to integrate data analytics into a comprehensive approach to evaluating online teaching. For other examples of the application of data analytics for online faculty evaluation, see Fierro and Yankowy (2011), Ford (2012), and Shreckengost (2013). The value of analytics is tied directly to the ability of data to help institutions make smarter, faster decisions that result in better use of resources. Higher education as a whole is actively exploring the power of learning analytics to measure student learning progress, gauge effectiveness of educational approaches, and tailor learning experiences to the needs of individual students (Johnson, Adams, & Cummins, 2012). Although the application of data to create analytic models designed to foster increased student learning is on the rise, there has been less attention on the application of data analytics to maximize the efficiency and effectiveness of other aspects of higher education.

Online courses provide a vastly expanded set of potential evaluation data compared to their face-to-face counterparts. Most LMSs enable institutions to access a wide range of individual data points and a variety of "big data" collections of information. Online courses are increasingly equipped with every-click-tracked infrastructure that not only creates a plethora of student data but also gathers an equally impressive set of indicators regarding faculty behavior and performance. Beyond the formative data that can help individual faculty members with their teaching practices, there is now the potential to aggregate results at the department or institutional level in order to provide insight into faculty performance.

Although data from student and administrative evaluations is regularly included as a component of the evaluation process, less common is the inclusion of teaching artifacts that are present in the online classroom.

Within an online course, there are a number of evidence-based, behavioral indicators that provide insight into faculty effectiveness:

- Number of announcements posted per module
- Number of contributions to the asynchronous discussion boards
- Quality of contributions to asynchronous discussion boards
- Timeliness of posting student grades
- Timeliness of student feedback
- Quality of instructional supplements
- Quality of feedback on student work
- Frequency of log-ins to the online course environment

Represented in these classroom artifacts are two distinct forms of data: quality-based indicators (e.g., quality of contributions to asynchronous discussion board, feedback, or instructional supplements) and behavioral data (e.g., number of posts to discussion board, number of days logged into course, time spent in the online classroom). Although present limitations of most LMS analytic features currently require that quality-based indicators be evaluated by peers or administrators, the administrative analytic functions of most LMSs are able to provide descriptive statistics on faculty behavior quickly and easily.

The range, type, and availability of analytic data depends on the capabilities of the LMS used at each institution as well as the administrative settings established for that particular system. In some cases, instructors are able to directly access analytic data, whereas other setups require administrative rights to run analytic reports. Institutions should work with their LMS administrator to determine what data are currently available through the LMS and what options exist for future analytic reporting functions.

Also, it is important to note that as colleges and universities continue to integrate data analytics into their decision-making processes, the LMS providers are likely to respond with increasingly sophisticated analytic capabilities. The following provides an examination of the potential of data analytics for evaluating online teaching.

DATA ANALYTICS AND PREDICTIVE MODELING: THE FUTURE OF EVALUATING ONLINE TEACHING

When evaluating teaching effectiveness, online learning offers one distinct advantage over its face-to-face counterpart: tangible artifacts. [Although] the principles of effective teaching don't vary as a function of instructional mode, instructors in the online classroom create teaching footprints, concrete evidence of each and every interaction. Evaluating online teaching simply becomes a matter of identifying, operationalizing, and assessing the trail of instructional footprints.

Traditional evaluations of online teaching rely on an observer to review the compilation of instructional artifacts and make quality judgments based on the evidence. To ensure a valid and reliable evaluation, these observations generally follow a rubric, standards checklist, or some other pre-established criteria. Although these types of observer-based reviews are indeed effective, they require considerable time, effort, and resources to implement. Thus, despite the utility of observer reviews, practical factors often limit their effectiveness in large, scalable online programs.

But, with advances in learning management technology, evaluations of online teaching have a new weapon, a weapon that can quickly and easily examine countless teaching footprints with minimal time, effort, or resources: data analytics. The concept of data analytics isn't new. Since the emergence of learning management systems, analytics have allowed us to view basic artifacts such as log-in time, log-in frequency, and number of posts. Advances in the data analytics systems that underlie newer learning-management technology are taking the possibilities of data analytics to a new level.

At present, learning management systems can track every log-in, key stroke, date stamp, time stamp, and related indicators of instructor behavior. But, this is only the tip of what is possible; advances in educational technology, learning management systems, and predictive modeling may soon allow for more integrated, informative analytics. For example:

- **Word and thematic analysis.** Currently, technology exists to recognize key words and string them together to identify themes and patterns. As thematic analysis becomes more advanced, evaluations of teaching could integrate content analysis of instructional posts to determine the validity and relevance of instructor-student interactions. [Although] automated thematic analysis is not likely to serve as a stand-alone metric, the efficiency offered through this type of analytic provides an indicator to prompt attention toward those faculty [members] who may be struggling.
- **Predictive dashboards.** Much like the push for predictive analytics to analyze student demographic characteristics as a means of predicting student success, predictive analytics may be utilized to identify which faculty [members] are likely to need additional support and who would

be most likely to benefit from additional training or mentoring. Predictive dashboards (based on factors such as teaching experience, online experience, disciplinary background, age, etc.) allow for more tailored faculty development programming to target instructional resources and support to those faculty most likely to benefit from it.

- **Faculty quality and retention.** Complementing the information available via predictive dashboards, data analytics focusing on faculty behaviors in the classroom provide an efficient means of focusing evaluation efforts on the faculty [members] who are most in need. Rather than wasting resources to evaluate all faculty [members] on the same schedule or time line, data analytics on faculty teaching behavior (time in online classroom, number of discussion posts, length of discussion posts, length of feedback, timeliness of feedback, number and nature of announcements, patterns of classroom interaction, etc.) could pinpoint faculty [members] who need additional attention. The efficiency of this type of data [enables] evaluation (and mentoring) resources to be quickly aligned with those who need it most. Not only does this provide additional support for the struggling faculty member but it also fosters increased educational quality during the active course.

- **Disciplinary evaluations.** In most online programs, all instructors are evaluated on the same basic criteria to support best practices in online teaching. The integration of data analytics [enables] predictive modeling to determine if there are disciplinary differences in the value and effectiveness of various online instructional behaviors. It is possible that the online teaching activities that effectively support math are different than the instructional activities necessary in psychology. Data analytics and predictive modeling [enable] the development of more targeted evaluation criteria.

- **Student-instructor matching.** Likewise, if data analytics can tell us how a particular student can best learn then it is feasible that analytic data can also help pinpoint how a particular faculty [member] can best teach. At present, because all faculty [members] are evaluated in the same way, [those who] receive higher evaluations are more likely to be retained and given ongoing teaching assignments. But, what if the "lower performing" faculty [members] are no longer "lower performing" if they are allowed to adjust their teaching to conform to different expectations based on student needs that are more a match to the instructor's natural teaching style versus being forced to institutional expectations of "good teaching"? The use of data analytics to identify instructors' patterns of behavior in relation to the success (or failure) of particular types of students opens the door for targeted enrollment that maximizes the "fit" to promote success for both faculty and students.

Predictive analytics is seeing growing popularity as it applies to the promotion of student success; the future of analytics must also examine the role of learning management system artifacts and predictive modeling for maximizing the success of faculty [members] in the online classroom. This is not to suggest that institutions fully embrace data-driven decision making to guide faculty evaluations, but rather to prompt the inclusion of data analytics to [enable] efficient and effective targeting of faculty development and evaluation resources. (Palese & Mandernach, 2015, reprinted with permission)

Although one could argue that human evaluators are also capable of conducting data-driven evaluations, the value of analytic data lies in their efficiency. At the touch of a button, you can generate a host of analytics to determine the frequency and timing of a variety of instructional behaviors. But keep in mind that analytic data used in isolation can be deceiving; to maximize the value of analytic data, you should combine analytic data with other indicators of quality. For example:

- Combine analytic data on the number of instructor posts to the discussion board with student rating data highlighting students' perception of the value of instructor's posts to promoting learning; the combined information provides an efficient metric for assessing an instructor's active engagement in the online classroom.
- Combine analytic data on average instructor response time for grading students' assignments with a peer evaluation of the quality of feedback for a randomly selected sample of artifacts; the combined information provides a more holistic assessment of the instructor's ability to provide prompt and useful feedback.
- Combine analytic data on the number of instructor posts and number of student posts in an asynchronous discussion thread; the combined information provides insight into the ability of the instructor to foster students' active engagement and ongoing dialogue.

It is important that evaluations of online teaching integrate analytic data with an explicit awareness on the limits of this type of data. For example, best practices in online teaching highlight the importance of an instructor being actively engaged in the online classroom. Two possible ways of operationalizing "active engagement" using LMS analytics include assessing (1) the time an instructor spends logged into the online classroom or (2) the number of instructor posts to the asynchronous discussion board.

Although these indicators *might* be representative of an instructor's active engagement, they can be misleading. For example, an instructor may log into the online classroom and simply leave the application open; in this case, the analytics would report extensive time in the classroom, but this would not be an accurate reflection of the instructor's active engagement. Vice versa, an instructor may be working extensively one-on-one with students via e-mail, videoconference, or telephone; in this case, analytics would show very little time in the LMS classroom, yet the instructor's engagement would be very high. Using the number of instructor posts as another example, an instructor can post a very high number of comments to the threaded discussion but fail to actively engage (e.g., posts with comments such as "I agree" or "good work"). Or, an instructor may have only a few posts, but those posts may be engaging, insightful, and provoke ongoing discussion among students. In either case, a single analytic data point fails to adequately capture the teaching behavior of interest.

These examples do not suggest that evaluations of online teaching should avoid analytic data. Rather, analytic data should be examined within the confines and scope of what it can actually tell you. Depending on your specific LMS, there may be a plethora of relevant, useful analytic data that can be mined to inform a comprehensive evaluation of online teaching. Integration of analytic data provides an efficient means of capturing a snapshot of teaching behavior. Such data can even be valuable in suggesting aspects of teaching that should be examined more closely. However, it is important to combine these data with complementary information to make the analytics meaningful. The following provides an example of how analytic data can be used to create an efficient evaluative metric for online faculty.

AN ANALYTIC MODEL FOR EVALUATING ONLINE TEACHING

The faculty evaluation metric (Grand Canyon University, 2014) is a quantitative model that uses multiple LMS indicators to establish an average faculty performance score for each individual course. Key to the faculty performance metric is the need to devise a system that enables between-course variability. As such, the evaluation system is not an overall comparison system; rather, it provides a direct peer-to-peer comparison at the individual course level during the same time frame. The metric is based on a two-term moving average of performance; as such, it adjusts each term in light of the current learning conditions and faculty resources.

The faculty evaluation metric is conceptualized as a means to devise a metric that is based on a combination of peer observation and student performance factors with the following variables contributing to the quantitative score for each faculty member:

- **Faculty training rating** is used as an indicator of instructional quality. It is an annual quantitative rating based on observations received through the peer evaluation system focusing on participation, grading, feedback, and course facilitation.
- **Final student grades** are used as an indicator of student learning; the proposed quantitative value is based on the percentage of students passing the course with a grade of C-minus or higher.
- **Student completion** rates are used as an indicator of student satisfaction and retention; the proposed quantitative value is based on the percentage of students finishing the course.
- **Student persistence** is used as an indicator of student satisfaction and preparedness for advanced courses; the proposed quantitative value is based on the percentage of students enrolled in subsequent terms.
- **Grade variance** is used as a means of preventing instructor motivation for grade inflation; the proposed quantitative value is based on distribution across the grade spectrum.
- **Student end-of-course surveys** are used as student satisfaction measures; the proposed quantitative values are based on the summative total of selected items.
- **Student engagement factor**s are used as an indicator of the level of instructor-student activity and involvement in the course; the proposed quantitative value is based on interaction ratios.

The conceptual goal behind this multifaceted metric is a desire to create an efficient quantitative rank that enables timely identification of faculty members at both ends of the performance continuum. Key to the metric is a need for quick, easy-to-access data that accurately ranks faculty performance without negatively affecting faculty teaching and student learning (Grand Canyon University, 2014).

Data Analytics Requires Data

It is important to note that the use of data analytics and descriptive modeling of faculty effectiveness is not for everyone. In order for data analytics to produce valid, reliable, and effective indicators of faculty performance, there must be sufficient data. One of the drawbacks to using data analytic techniques in self- and peer observation scenarios of face-to-face classrooms is the scarcity of data points. As recently as 2007, Arreola includes a visual joke in *Developing a Comprehensive Faculty Evaluation System* about the perceived impossibility of "double-blind peer evaluation of teaching" (see Figure 8.1).

Within the humor, we can see that Arreola's model for peer evaluation is grounded firmly in the face-to-face classroom. In fact, he cautions his readers not to use peer observation "*if the data is [sic] to be used for anything other than personal feedback to the instructor for his or her use in teaching improvement efforts*" (p. 95, italics in the original), and encourages readers to schedule multiple visits to the classroom to "make certain that a sufficient sampling of the behavior" is obtained, recommending that evaluators "schedule at least 8 to 10 visits to the class" (p. 96).

Theall (2012b) recently observed that "research has indicated that peer observation of teaching the way it is usually done (i.e., in a single visit) is not very reliable. That existing research is based largely on

FIGURE 8.1. DOUBLE-BLIND PEER EVALUATION OF TEACHING

SOURCE: ARREOLA (2004, p. 23).

observations done in a familiar environment (the classroom). In the virtual environment, what are the bases for comparisons and judgments? What are the criteria to be applied?" Likewise, just as the validity of a single peer observation of teaching provides a questionable overall evaluation of quality, so do data artifacts that are analyzed in isolation or used beyond the scope of what they can tell us.

During the 2014 Distance Learning Administration (DLA) conference sponsored by the University of West Georgia, Baird and Piña facilitated a roundtable conversation on "Evaluating the Evaluation of Distance Learning," and several participants pointed to the fact that now not only can evaluators examine multiple data points when observing online teaching but also the pendulum seems to have swung the other way toward having too much data to examine and parse, as in Piña's case:

> Let's face it: in higher ed, we don't know how to judge faculty quality. There's no consistent measure of it. One-shot class observation gives a very small amount. Part of the reason why distance education is under a different standard is this general suspicion of something new that they don't fully understand and feel a little threatened by, and the other is the availability of the data.
>
> When the Department of Ed came to us to do its routine audit for Title IV federal funds, they asked us to generate 7,000 pages of student-activity data out of our LMS, because we could. They're trying to figure out the "last day of attendance" for online students, which is a rabbit chase. Now, in order to access Title IV funds for a face-to-face student, what does that student have to do? Show up in the class. The student can sleep! Because the idea is that they merely need to have the opportunity to engage in academic activities. However, the equivalent would be logging in to an online course. As of 2012, that cannot be counted as "attendance" any longer. They have to "academically engage"—they have to turn in something. (Baird and Piña, 2014)

Not only are these types of data-driven chases fraught with interpretation and comparability errors, but statistical analysis can be time-consuming and the decision about what behaviors to observe (and their comparative weights in summative decision making) can be fraught with political significance as well. There is opportunity for campus leaders to create clear, defensible, behavior-based criteria for the summative evaluation of online teaching. Research has made strides in this direction, at the quantitative level; Piña & Bohn (2013) cite the following specific behaviors as predictors of instructional quality in the online classroom:

- Frequency of instructor log-ins
- Length of instructor biography
- Frequency and size of course announcements
- Speed in responding to queries
- Participation in course discussions
- Performance of administrative tasks

Integrating Prescriptive Analytics for Evaluating Online Teaching

The value of data analytics rests not in its role as a stand-alone summative evaluation but in the ability to create prescriptive modeling that enables the most efficient investment of faculty evaluation resources. Prescriptive analytics use data-driven predictions to "prescribe recommendations or actions to influence what ends up happening in the future" (Schaffhauser, 2014, p. 11). As is evidenced throughout this book, it takes considerable time to conduct high-quality evaluations of online teaching geared toward the ultimate goal of fostering increased learning. The challenge is not simply in creating and conducting the evaluation, but rather in having sufficient time and resources in order to evaluate an increasing number of online faculty members on a limited budget.

But, the reality is that not all faculty members need to be evaluated equally; some faculty members continually excel and require less external validation of their teaching and others struggle more and demand increased attention to ensure they are providing students with a high-quality learning experience. Data analytics enable prescriptive models that can alert institutions when additional faculty evaluation, support, or mentoring intervention is needed.

For example, best practices in online learning have established the value of timely feedback for fostering student learning. On a basic level, prescriptive analytics can be applied to automatically trigger a reminder e-mail to faculty members who have failed to provide assignment feedback within the university's established time line for grading. These reminder e-mails can then be tracked to provide an overall metric that may indicate the need for more detailed evaluations of teaching (and the associated instructional support). In this fashion, those instructors who continually meet the university's expectations for established benchmarks of online teaching may be put on an evaluation time line with increased delays between evaluation periods, whereas those who receive warnings may be scheduled for more frequent evaluation intervention.

It is important to note that for the integration of a prescriptive analytic model to be effective, the data have to be used in a manner that meets the needs of the institution. The previous example of applying analytics to track faculty response times would only be valuable in an institution in which the number of faculty members teaching online is so large that more personalized means of monitoring is not feasible; by contrast, it would not be efficient or effective to integrate this type of analytic modeling at an institution offering only a handful of online courses. Analytics should not be used because the LMS system offers the capabilities; analytics as a component of the evaluation of online teaching should be integrated only when it adds to the efficiency or effectiveness of current evaluation strategies.

Bukralia (in Schaffhauser, 2014) offers twelve lessons for effective integration of prescriptive analytics; these lessons can be applied to the evaluation of online teaching to create more efficient (and effective) evaluation models:

- **Choose the problem to solve.** Although data analytics can be used to address a wide range of challenges, it is essential that there is a sufficient amount of data to address the target problem. The use of analytics may not be feasible or desirable for institutions offering a relatively small number of online courses. By contrast, prescriptive analytics provides an effective evaluation supplement to manage the evaluation of teaching for large numbers of contingent faculty or institutions that are building scalable models of faculty evaluation.
- **The model needs cross-validation.** Not only do you need to ensure that the data effectively captures the target dimension but also you must examine the value and relevance under a variety of conditions to ensure its efficiency and validity within the unique context of your institution. The data available from one LMS may or may not align with the data available from another, and the data from one faculty population may or may not be applicable to the other. It is important that you are able to clearly identify artifacts in the LMS that inform the target online teaching dimensions and then test these artifacts across disciplines, faculty populations, and teaching environments.
- **Business needs to drive the work.** The individuals most closely associated with the data need to lead the data analytic initiatives. Those individuals

who are responsible for the evaluation of online teaching must be intimately involved in the development of the analytic modeling that drives decisions. Decisions on how to use the data and what data to include should be made as a function of the needs of the evaluation system and not as a result of what data are easily available.

- **Have practitioners define business rules.** To maximize the value of the prescriptive analytics, you need to involve all relevant stakeholders in the formulation of the rules that underlie the model. In the context of evaluating online teaching, the rules underlying the evaluation structure should be made in consultation with full-time and contingent faculty members, department chairs, program directors, LMS administrators, and faculty development personnel.
- **Data can't be used indiscriminately.** Although unlimited amounts of data may be available (both traditional and more non-normative sources), it is important that the mining of data is balanced with the rights of the individuals involved. Faculty teaching online should be aware of the teaching artifacts that will be used for evaluation and understand the implications of how teaching behaviors will be integrated for formative and summative evaluation purposes.
- **Put data governance in place first.** The use of data analytics mandates that institutions establish a data governance strategy that clearly articulates data communication, oversight, and rights. Although this recommendation is not unique to the online environment, discussions concerning data governance should be made with an explicit awareness of how LMSs and other teaching data may be used for evaluation purposes.
- **Focus on project management.** The integration of data analytics can't simply be an add-in afterthought to an existing model; rather, the inclusion of analytics must be an integrated component that includes steps to ensure buy in, resource support, and feedback cycles. As such, when you are designing your overall strategy for evaluating online teaching, the availability, use of, and access to teaching indicator data must be part of the discussion. Not only does this include LMS data but also the use of student, administrative, and self-evaluations, as well.
- **Skills may be lacking.** To effectively use data analytics, you need personnel that understand the unique considerations of this type of information; be prepared to invest resources to find and train data scientists. Within each institution, different individuals are responsible for evaluation oversight of online teaching; online teaching evaluations may be the responsibility of department chairs, program coordinators,

or administrative units. It is important to ensure that the individuals responsible for conducting evaluations of online teaching understand the meaning (and limits) of analytic data.

- **Prepare for change management.** Institutions must be prepared to change in response to data; it is important to understand the impact of data decisions on policies, systems, and organizational structure. The integration of analytics for evaluating online teaching should not be done in isolation. The role of data for evaluation purposes should be integrated with faculty development, training, hiring, and related systems for ensuring instructional quality.

- **One size does not fit all.** The prescriptive models developed from data analytics must be designed in relation to the unique context of each institution. Although it may be an effective investment of resources for institutions with a large number of faculty teaching online to create an evaluation of online teaching that integrates prescriptive analytics into a comprehensive, automated system, this investment is not likely to see an equivalent return on investment at an institution with a much smaller online program.

- **Benefits come in two flavors.** There are both tangible and intangible benefits of effective prescriptive analytic models. Tangible benefits may include increased faculty performance (e.g., better feedback, more interaction in discussion threads, increased use of instructional supplements); intangible benefits might include the ability to coach or mentor struggling faculty members in a timelier manner. It is important that institutions consider both the tangible and intangible benefits when examining the potential of prescriptive analytics for evaluating online teaching.

- **Prescriptive analytics aren't always right.** Data analytics can provide valuable information about generalized behavior, but prescriptive models cannot effectively account for individual variability. As such, the information from analytics should not be used in isolation for making decisions; rather, prescriptive analytics can effectively pinpoint attention toward issues that require a more personalized analysis.

Making Data Meaningful

Analytic interpretation of trend data at the aggregate level is being made possible by the ability to enable formerly siloed campus data system to communicate. For example, at Northeastern Illinois University, the LMS, student-data system (Banner), student-service systems, and other sources of demographic, identifying, and performance data are being linked together in a secure operational data store in order to enable all campus systems to contribute to and query one source about the progress of students, courses, programs, departments, colleges, and the university as a whole.

The ability to drink deeply from a data source enables evaluators to see various dimensions of teaching; data analytics can offer greater breadth and depth about the teaching happening at an institution over time. Depending on the institutional agreements in place about the observation of teaching, administrators can compare faculty members against their own past experiences and against their peers. Data analytics offers the possibility for comparing and ranking faculty members across various dimensions within their departments, the institution, and among peer institutions. It is imperative, therefore, prior to implementing an online course evaluation program for summative decision making, to agree on any limits that faculty members and administrators wish to impose. For instance, administrators may be permitted to use aggregate teaching-analytics data at the level of the institution but are not allowed to create quantitative rankings of individual faculty members. Conversely, it may be agreed on that data analytics can be used to rank the effectiveness of contingent faculty members teaching online in order to determine scheduling priority, but that these rankings will not bear merit for tenure and promotion decisions of full-time faculty.

Integrating Analytics for Evaluation of Online Teaching

If you are interested in using data analytics as a component of your evaluation of online teaching, you should start by answering the following questions (adapted from Ikanow, 2014):

- **What problem or challenge are you hoping to solve with data analytics?** You must begin by clearly determining what challenge you have in your current evaluation of online teaching that may benefit from the integration of data analytics. Data analytics are not a silver bullet and should not be used simply because they exist. Your institutional needs, and not the availability of LMS data, should drive choices about the integration of data to help create a more effective and efficient evaluation of online teaching. In many cases, the use of data analytics is driven by a need for efficiency and scalability. In large online programs, it is not cost effective to manually oversee instructor activity in all online courses; thus, analytics provides a cost-effective, low-resource means of conducting surface-level evaluations of instructor activity in the LMS.

- **How is this challenge affecting your institution?** Once you have established the evaluation challenge, you need to understand how this challenge is affecting your institution. For example, is there a concern that faculty are not meeting university expectations for teaching in the online classroom? Are you losing students in your online programs because of issues with the quality of online teaching? Are limited personnel resources being wasted on low-level evaluative tasks that could be automated? It is essential that you clearly define what you hope to gain from integrating a data analytic model so that you have a baseline for gauging the value and impact of this shift.

- **How will you know if data analytics is meeting your goal?** Linked to your understanding of the impact of data analytics on your evaluation challenges is the establishment of clear success criteria. For example, if your challenge lies in a lack of resources to be able to consistently and effectively evaluate the quality of online teaching, indicators of success may be linked to increases in the rate of faculty members who receive an evaluation each academic year. Or, if the driving challenge is a concern about student satisfaction with the quality of online instruction, you may examine shifts in end-of-course student evaluations as an indicator of the success of your data analytic model in helping to monitor instructional effectiveness and target corrective instructional coaching.

- **What is the value for your institution if data analytics is able to solve your challenge?** You need to have an agreed-on understanding of the value, meaning, and implications for your institution if your data analytic model helps to address the target challenge. Not only is this type of *a priori* planning helpful for ensuring that you are using data analytics within the appropriate parameters but also it helps to determine the viability of the entire project and creates a context for making budget decisions. For example, let's assume that because of a rapid program growth, your institution is struggling to ensure that all online faculty members are providing a quality online learning experience and that because of limited resources, current evaluation processes provide only a summative evaluation of online teaching. The result is that a large number of students are leaving their online course dissatisfied with their learning experience and are unwilling to enroll in future online courses. Now, let's assume that you have planned an evaluation model that can pinpoint instructors who are struggling early in the course so that you

may provide additional instructional coaching prior to the completion
of the online learning experience. As such, if your model is successful,
you predict an increase in student satisfaction that results in ongoing
enrollments in the online program. The key question becomes, what is
the cost of declining enrollments in relation to the cost to implement
the data analytic evaluation model? If the return on investment is favor-
able, then it makes sense to budget accordingly and proceed with project
development. But, if the cost of implementing the data analytic evaluation model is not offset by the potential gains to the institution, then it
is advisable to look at other evaluation options.

You have likely noticed that none of the questions up to this point
have focused on the actual data or the associated technology that supports data analytics. It is worth reiterating that the integrations of analytics is seldom a viable solution for all evaluation needs (even if large
amounts of instructional data exist). If you are able to articulate clearly
the challenges, anticipated outcomes, indicators of success, and impact
for your institution, then you are ready to explore the more detailed
issues related to mining, analyzing, and using data analytics as a component of your evaluation of online teaching.

- **What system are you going to use to store, analyze, and access your data?**
  At this point, you will likely need to bring in the expertise and guidance
  of instructional technology directors, LMS administrators, and institutional research personnel. In order to integrate data analytics into your
  evaluation process, you must examine the technological infrastructure
  that will support your data. Although data concerning instructor
  behaviors may be mined from the LMS, you may also want to integrate
  larger institutional data on enrollments, enrollment persistence,
  withdrawals, grade distribution, or pass-fail rates. In addition, your data
  analytic model might take into consideration other data such as self,
  administrator, or student evaluations. While you are determining what
  data you would like to include in your analytic model, you will also need
  to decide where the data will be stored, how it will be accessed, and who
  is responsible for data management.
- **What data do you need to address your challenge?** As previously discussed, there is a plethora of data that you may want to consider for
  the evaluation of online teaching. Analytic models may include behavioral data from the online classroom (tracked via the LMS as a function
  of the quantity and quality of instructor activities), supplemental evaluation information obtained from other sources (peer, administration,

or student evaluations), and a virtually limitless list of associated indicators. But, unlike the growing body of research on learner analytics (in which extensive sets of big data are used to create robust statistical models for predicting student success based on preestablished demographics or behaviors), there is limited—if any—existing research that firmly establishes the link between specific instructional behaviors and target educational outcomes. As such, you must pay close attention to the selection of data and behavioral indicators to monitor their ongoing relevance for gauging the desired outcome. For example, although it is a natural leap to assume that the frequency and quality of an instructor's discussion posts represents "active engagement," ongoing data analysis should closely examine—and seek to empirically verify—this association. As institutions gain more experience with the use and application of analytic models for evaluating online teaching, we are likely to see the development of more standardized metrics to tie instructor data to specific teaching or learning outcomes. In the interim, it is essential that analytic models integrate valid, reliable data (see "Understanding Big Data," below, for more information) and ensure evaluation decisions are limited to what the data can actually tell us.

- **What resources, information, or technology do you need to implement your data analytics model?** Once you have a plan for your analytic model, you need to examine your model in relation to the institutional structure, resources, and staffing. Your goal at this stage is to identify gaps that will need to be addressed prior to implementation. This may include a review of technological considerations, an examination of current staffing in relation to staffing demands of implementing the analytic model, examination of training needs, and a predictive analysis of ongoing issues for ensuring sustainability. You will want to anticipate gaps so that you may plan accordingly as you move into implementation.

- **How will you implement your data analytic model?** As is the case with all new evaluation processes, it is advised that you begin with a pilot implementation of your analytic model. In most cases, you will want to start with a select number of online classes and integrate the model in a no-stakes evaluation context that provides for feedback, reflection, and revision but that does not put the instructor's performance record at risk. It is important at this stage to seek feedback from all relevant stakeholders (e.g., full-time faculty members, contingent faculty members, evaluators, department chairs, faculty development personnel, administrative directors, and data management administrators) to ensure holistic support prior to widespread implementation.

Understanding Big Data

The ever-advancing analytic features of LMSs are enabling the generation of big data that was previously only in the dreams of statisticians. Big data simply refers to data sets that are too large or too complex to analyze effectively with standard data-analysis tools (Picciano, 2012). It is commonly defined by the three Vs: the "volume, velocity, and variety of data the people and high-tech systems generate" (Kamin, 2014). LMSs can provide information in all three of the V dimensions. Compounding the complexity of the decision-making process is the eventual need for disparate streams of information (e.g., from student ratings, self-assessments, peer evaluations, and administrative observations) to be evaluated and reported across common behavior-based competencies (Varvel, 2007).

To decide what data streams should be included in campus-wide evaluation programs, you should consider three variables: reliability, validity, and factor structure. Keeley (2012) examines these variables in terms of student evaluation of instruction (SEI) instruments, and there is broader applicability of these variables to campus online-teaching evaluation programs.

Reliability

Reliability has to do with how consistently an instrument produces data under similar circumstances. Especially concerning variability within categories of raters (the same students, peers, and administrators will seldom rate or evaluate the same faculty member and course multiple times), internal instrument reliability enhances program reliability.

> [I]t can be quite difficult to establish the consistency over time of student ratings of their instructor because those ratings are designed to change.... [The] preferred metric of reliability for SEIs is internal consistency, or how consistent individuals are across items within the same administration. In the case where SEIs accurately reflect differences in teacher characteristics across items (i.e., the variance we want to measure), internal consistency values will drop. Therefore, perfect

> internal consistency values would be an undesirable characteristic; instead medium to high values are ideal ($\alpha \approx .60-.80$). Despite these limitations to measuring reliability within SEIs, nonetheless it is possible to compare various SEIs in terms of their test-retest and internal consistency values because they all face the same measurement issues. (Keeley, 2012, pp. 13–14)

For online teaching evaluation, this means that multiple, related questions should be asked in clusters around key teaching practices. The responses of students, peers, self-evaluators, and administrative evaluators can be compared between individual respondents within clusters (how consistent an individual rater is across a single response session) and across respondents within clusters (how comparable ratings are from each group).

Validity

The adage that we measure what we want to measure holds true for evaluation of teaching practices and rings doubly true in the case of online teaching because there is often so much documentation to look through that a case can be made to support multiple interpretations, depending on the goals, knowledge, skills, and training of the evaluator.

> The validity of SEIs is similarly fraught with pitfalls .... [A]ll validity evidence can be reduced to construct validity, or the accuracy of the measurement relative to the hypothetical construct it is designed to emulate. In this case, the hypothetical construct might be "good teaching," which could have a very multifaceted definition. Instead, we might focus upon lower level constructs of good teaching like communication skills or fairness in grading. It is important to note that the validity of an instrument is always tied to its purpose. A particular SEI might be valid for one purpose but not for another, depending upon its construction. For example, if the developers of an SEI did not consider interpersonal factors like rapport or immediacy to be important in their definition of "good teaching," then those constructs would be poorly represented in their measure. (Keeley, 2012, p. 214)

For these reasons, Berk (2006) suggests that no peer or administrative evaluation be conducted without "adequate training on observation procedures with the scale" (p. 20), and Keeley (2012) strongly cautions that

"SEIs should never be one's only strategy for gathering information about one's teaching" (p. 215).

Factor Structure

Keeley (2012) suggests a final variable that is not often considered in the use of an instrument in an overall evaluation program—*factor structure*—in which different questions in an instrument cluster around an underlying concept that is not explicitly stated in the instrument.

> In traditional psychometrics, a factor is a latent (that is, not observable) variable that represents the communality between a set of items. For example, if an instrument has 10 different items that all assess some aspect of the relationship between the student and instructor, and those items all correlate amongst themselves more so than with other items on the scale, there might be an underlying factor (e.g., rapport) that influences students' ratings across those items.... Interestingly, many SEIs have evidenced similar factor structures regardless of whether they were intentionally developed or not. Two general factors that represent the procedural skills of teaching (e.g., being an effective communicator, constructing fair assignments) and the interpersonal aspects of teaching (e.g., being approachable, warm, considerate) appear to emerge consistently in the literature. (p. 215)

It is interesting to note that Keeley's two general latent factors in student-rating instruments match up well against the seven principles of good teaching from Chickering and Gamson that we examined previously. In order to incorporate various online-teaching evaluation methods into a holistic program of evaluation at the instructor and program levels, readers can examine the various instruments used to make sure they assess all of the key behavioral criteria from a source such as Chickering and Gamson.

Conclusion

As highlighted by Picciano (2012, p. 1), "While big data and analytics are not panaceas for addressing all of the issues and decisions faced by higher education administrators, they can become part of the solutions integrated into administrative and instructional functions." Data analytics offers a means of leveraging the vast amounts of behavioral data created via online teaching to more effectively understand, assess, and monitor quality online education. As demonstrated by Ashford University, the integration did not alleviate the need (or desire) for human evaluations; rather, the integration of analytics enabled limited human resources to be more effectively distributed to support online faculty members.

The integration of data analytics enables efficient and effective evaluations of teaching that begin to blur the distinctions among evaluation, mentoring, and professional development. No longer do limited resources require that evaluations occur at the conclusion of a course; the integration of prescriptive analytic models enables continual evaluation—and continual improvement—throughout an active course. Whether used in a formative fashion to provide individual instructors guidance on their online instructional behaviors or to provide administrators with an evaluative snapshot of an instructor's effectiveness in the online classroom, the information obtained through data analytics complements more individualized evaluation information to produce a more comprehensive, complete picture of instructional behavior.

In reference to the use of learning analytics to promote student success, Wagner (2014) asserts that "simply knowing who might be at risk really isn't enough. If you don't know what to do to mitigate that risk or to respond to the needs of that student you are really only halfway there." The same logic applies to data analytics in the evaluation of online teaching. Simply knowing which instructors are struggling really isn't enough. If you don't know what to do to mitigate that struggle or to respond to the needs of the instructor, you are really only halfway there. Integrating data analytics into your evaluation model doesn't ensure instructional quality in the online classroom but it is a first step in the timely identification of instructors who may not be performing in ways that maximize the online learning experience for students.

A Thought Exercise

While data analytics may not currently be an integral component of your faculty evaluation model, awareness of the potential of data analytics as a supplemental information source provides a host of opportunities for making evaluations more efficient and scalable. Reflect on the learning management system (LMS) utilized at your institution to answer the following questions:

- What faculty behavior data does your LMS currently collect?
- Who has access to LMS analytic data?
- How can you utilize analytic data to inform established expectations for best practices in online teaching?

PART FOUR

SUSTAINING A CULTURE OF EVALUATION

CHAPTER NINE

FROM TOOLS TO PROCESSES

Creating a Holistic Evaluation Plan

Parts 2 and 3 of this book have demonstrated ways to conduct formative and summative evaluations of online teaching, with examinations of various tools that help faculty members to collect data about their online teaching practices. Individual faculty members can use such ratings and evaluations to evolve their teaching practices, customize their course materials, and incorporate changes in response to feedback gleaned from a number of sources and methods.

Administrators and faculty members should move beyond the individual tools and think about the place of online-teaching evaluation in the institution's overall evaluation program. Lattuca and Donagal-Goldman (2007) call for institutions to adopt holistic views of students' overall educational experiences within "online courses [that] allow the implementation of new forms of peer review and interaction" (p. 85).

A holistic evaluation plan should include both formative evaluation, in which observations and ratings are undertaken with the purpose of improving teaching and learning, and summative evaluation, in which observation and ratings are used in order to make personnel decisions, such as granting promotion or tenure, remediation, and asking contingent faculty to teach again. A holistic evaluation program should collect information at both the individual faculty and program levels. For example, Berk (2006) outlines how various types of evidence of teaching performance inform formative, summative, and program decisions.

Formative Decisions

- Student ratings
- Peer and external expert ratings
- Self-ratings
- Videos
- Student interviews
- Exit and alumni ratings

Summative Decisions

Annual Review for Retention and Merit Pay

- Student ratings
- Self-ratings
- Teaching scholarship
- Administrator ratings

Promotion and Tenure

- Administrator ratings
- Teaching portfolio

Program Decisions

- Student ratings
- Exit and alumni ratings
- Employer ratings

Note that although Berk's categorization is not specific to evaluation of online teaching practices, he places many of the individual measures discussed in parts 1 and 2 of this book into multiple categories. Ideally, an institutional program of evaluation will include several streams of information to be used for various related purposes, including the improvement of teaching, assessment of teaching quality, personnel retention decisions, and accreditation reporting. Online teaching provides two significant advantages in terms of campus-wide evaluation plans.

Scope and Scale of Data Recording

First, the online medium records more data related to teaching behaviors, enabling aggregation and analysis on a scale far greater than is possible for evaluation of face-to-face teaching. Examinations of online teaching can be based on a greater scope of information, both in terms of types of information collected and the time frame observed. The challenge associated with the collection of vast quantities of data is determining what data are relevant to the evaluation being performed, and by extension, the decision being made. There is typically a high noise-to-signal ratio in LMSs where every faculty and student click is recorded. If the traditional observation of face-to-face class sessions provides too few data points to be able to make an informed judgment, then the opposite problem arises in online courses. The "noise" is being able to observe every discussion post, feedback item, course announcement, and interaction that faculty members have with learners throughout the entire course. The "signal" equates to a more representative sample of the core interactions between faculty members and students, as outlined in chapters 6 and 7.

Theall (2102b) provides some perspective on why the distinction between design elements and teaching behaviors matters in collecting data from individual instruments, especially when trying to define peer and administrative observations of online teaching:

> "Observe" is probably not the best word to use in this case, since there may be limited opportunities to actually do that (e.g., one way might be a chance to sit in on a synchronous session as a student). However, peers or others involved in evaluating online teaching/courses can and should be able to review documents per se (e.g., see the syllabus, assignments, materials) and also review the ways in which the course is run online (e.g., see what is delivered and how it is done; review chats/groups/other communications; look at students' work; investigate how the LMS or whatever system employed is used). To do this with some reliability and accuracy, though, would require specific information about institutional or other online policies [and] practices, as well as knowledge of the capabilities and limitations of the external (e.g., LMS) and internal (e.g., institutional) systems used . . . .
>
> In sum, I think that peer review of online teaching for summative purposes is best if restricted to matters like
>
> - content currency/accuracy,
> - compliance with institutional and department requirements,
> - review of materials such as assignments or assessments, and
> - review of student work . . .
>
> . . . all within a framework that clearly specifies criteria for judgment, characteristics and limitations of the systems used, any factors that can

affect the teacher's opportunities to access, provide, and use t[eaching] and l[earning] resources, and the nature and extent of user (faculty and student) resources and support. As well, one-time evaluations should not be used for summative purposes unless there is no other choice. Effective and accurate and fair evaluation requires a series of activities over time and comparison (if that is done) against data gathered in similar situations and under similar conditions. (Theall, 2012b)

Theall's (2012b) comments show how data from individual summative evaluation instruments (e.g., student-rating forms, peer- and self-evaluation tools, and administrative-evaluation rubrics) can overcontribute to campus-wide evaluation programs if the content collected in each process is too broadly defined. The other side of this coin is when an instrument's sample rate is too brief to be reliable. Having too few data points risks collection of ratings or observation of behaviors that are not typical of the overall experience in the course.

Online teaching offers a possible remedy for Theall's (2012b) concern: there can be many more data points in each instrument used. To avoid reviewer and rater oversampling (not to mention reviewer fatigue), a comprehensive and specific overall evaluation program is a requirement.

Ability to Compare Performance Statistics

The need to evaluate online teaching often forces institutions to examine their existing overall evaluation processes. In many cases, the greater granularity of online-teaching data affords faculty members and administrators the opportunity to compare student ratings, formal peer reviews, and administrative observations in more targeted ways, such as being able to move beyond the crude benchmark of "I need a four on the five-point scale to be safe" and into domain-based peer-group comparisons. Online-teaching data can be analyzed to show who in a department, college, or institution are the comparative leaders and laggards on many criteria—and whether a 4.3 rating is a leading or a trailing score. Admittedly, it is possible in evaluating face-to-face teaching to encounter similar "must get a four out of five" analysis, but the ease of performing analytical queries on quantitative data in online courses (e.g., number of instructor log-ins, number of discussion postings, time spent in the LMS) enables evaluators and faculty members to draw more detailed distinctions with less effort than needed to produce similar types of face-to-face evaluation statistics.

For example, as of this writing, Dee Fabry, Colin Marlaire, and their colleagues at National University are designing an evaluation system for their online faculty members that balances the need to improve teaching practices based on formative student- and peer-review processes against more formal ratings and evaluation by students and campus administrators.

The National University Story

Dee Fabry: We have a robust system right now for a program annual review process. Every program leader works very collaboratively on the program annual review, looking at the program learning outcomes to clearly determine whether the program is serving our students. The School of Education spent the last year deeply mired in going up for NCATE [now CAEP] accreditation, which is the huge national recognition of the program and how well they serve students. We thought we were doing a stellar job with those program learning outcomes, looking at those signature assignments and getting down in and saying "oh, this doesn't work really well. You'll need to change that because your students aren't understanding it." Lo and behold, we learned—painfully so—that we need another level in our forms of assessment. What evidence do we have of the impact of what we're doing with our students on *their* students? In teacher education, that's where the rubber meets the road.

Colin Marlaire: In our current form, the majority of those types of scalable institutional solutions are pretty much retroactive, backward looking. So, it's only in the time period of "before you teach your next course," we might have a conversation. With the additional improvements in analytics, we'll have more of an opportunity to look at in-course real-time behaviors and see if there are opportunities for remediation there. That's something that we're very excited about. We don't know which metrics we're going to use, but the ability to take a look at, frankly, seeing a course that proves successful for a larger number of students, and those students identify strong teaching part of the success, and being able to play back the behavior for faculty members in that context and see what it is that they're doing as the faculty presence in the course. That is something that we can turn to other faculty members and say "here's a model that we know is successful, that improves student success in the course." That's what we're all about as an institution.

We do a review, if you teach an on-site course. Faculty avail themselves of the opportunity of having their peers actually attend a course to review a session. We do that also for online courses, but it's a much less formal process. In several different disciplines, we're talking about the notion of an onboarding faculty getting a shadow with a lead faculty member for the first time that they teach an online course. We currently use surveys, but with the additional analytics, I think we're going to be able to go to that next level and talk less about student assessment and more about the details of faculty behavior, and tying that to increased student success. I think that's the important thing: saying to a faculty member "you need to do this in your course" just because—that seems arbitrary and capricious and doesn't build the sort of positive relationship that you would like. But if you can turn around with the data and say "you should do this, that, or the other thing," and give them three different ways of doing it. "You should do that in your course" because when faculty members do that in the course, students are more successful. Then, that's the best way to talk about faculty training.

As part of the reappointment and promotion process, our faculty members do peer, self, and administrative analysis of their course work. If they teach on-site, it looks one way. But if they teach online, then a peer and yourself and an administrator will actually go with you into one of your past courses that you've taught. I think one of the opportunities with the analytics is not to be prescriptive and say, "this is the one way" or "this number is what we need to hit." That's not really the role of analytics in this context. It's more of a way to offer a spectrum of faculty activities. We tend to see some strong data and saying that they're having an impact. Faculty member A is present in this way in the course, and faculty member B is present in this way in the course. Those can look like two very different things, but those faculty members who choose to be present at that increased level (in whatever form), that's showing as having a positive impact on the students.

Dee Fabry: I'm going to make this very specific. I teach online. I haven't taught on-ground for at least six years. In the School of Education, we have a form that we use, and I think it's a university-blessed form, that guides your evaluation of online teaching performance. It contains multiple sections, and guides one through the process of evaluating an online course. You're not willy-nilly going into a course and clicking here and there.

We realize that time in the course is important for an instructor, and there the analytics are readily available: "you spent 4,628 minutes in the course during the month." Big deal. I could turn on my computer, go in, and walk away and watch *Downton Abbey*. Our instructors don't do that, but we can't know that for sure.

More valuable are the items in which you go in and say "please go into the discussion threads. What we're looking for in the discussion threads is the instructor's ability to increase critical thinking in the conversation that's taking place. Please provide evidence that this took place." I've done this for my peers. So, I will go in, and I will completely read through a discussion thread. Yes, I understand that when you've got thirty-five students, and they are responding, you're reading a lot of responses. When you follow through those threads, and you get how that instructor is using the art of teaching to connect students to each other, to encourage higher-level thinking, that piece is evaluated in that process.

The evaluation form: I personally found both my peer's and my supervisor's feedback on that online-course evaluation extremely helpful because it went far, far beyond knowledge and comprehension. It was "what's going on with the sense of information? How are concepts integrated? How were the tools in the course utilized to increase engagement among students? What kind of feedback was provided?" So, you open an assignment, and you look at (we in the School of Education use Microsoft's Track Changes feature) what kind of feedback was provided to the students, the level of detail. We use grading rubrics, so in addition to the Track Changes [feedback], the student receives back the paper with the Tracked Changes, with the feedback, with the grading rubric, with what they did well highlighted, what they need to improve on highlighted, with an explanation of all of that.

On the assessment-evaluation end of our online courses, in the School of Education, the kind of feedback I provide when I evaluate a peer, we provide a really in-depth level of feedback and areas for improvement. We always identify areas for improvement, and I have found that while people praise what I do well, they have absolutely no problem saying, "if you would do these three things, you would increase your effectiveness as a teacher." No one seems to be shy about saying, "let me really share with you how you want to improve this." It's less an exercise in "let's just do this and get it over with" than a very thorough process, and they take a lot of time. So it's very valuable.

Department chairs receive course-load reductions for their responsibilities, and peer evaluation is part of their responsibility. That's how they're compensated. For those of us who do peer-to-peers, we do it out of the kindness of our hearts. It's part of the expectation, especially once you've moved through the ranks. We don't have tenure here, but we do move through assistant, associate, and full professorships. As you move up those ranks, mentorship and coaching of faculty is part of the expectation as you rise in rank, for those of us who take that peer-evaluation process seriously.

I personally only take on one per year. At the beginning of the year, I send an e-mail out, as the program lead, to my instructors and say "you know my practice. I will evaluate one of you this year. Please let me know who would like an evaluation this year." Because I want to do it mindfully, thoughtfully, and completely, taking on more than one person is like taking on more than one doctoral student.

Colin Marlaire: I would love to see more space given for peer mentoring. That's, frankly, the best way to do it. But that's also the most challenging, because it's time-intensive, and it's a lot of work for those willing to do it. I think the point about contrasting to an on-site course is exactly right, in the sense that, since there are a lot of different educational technologies, and there are a lot of different ways to be successful in an online course. Now, there are a million different ways to be successful in an on-site course, too. The difference is that if I go to that on-site course, it all sort of happens to me if I'm the peer reviewer. Your commitment to the time frame is exactly right. When we go to online, there's whole different ways of using technology to help you teach. To be an effective peer reviewer, you have to understand how those technologies deliver additional content and interactions. It's an interesting challenge. To be a peer reviewer online, you have to get some training or have some understanding of the specific tools that the faculty member is employing as part of that teaching experience.

The other thing I'll mention is that we've talked about formal processes—the yearly review and things like that. I think for online, of tremendous importance is a more voluntary asynchronous capacity. What I mean by that is we have a virtual community where we really encourage our faculty members. It's behind walls—only our faculty members are there. It's really a place for our faculty members to share best practices and to share things that didn't work so well. We've created an environment that establishes trust. It's a place where I can ask questions about what's not working, and I can also talk about the things that, from my perspective, are working. Only through that process do we continue to foster peer relationships. If there's an opportunity for one to acknowledge "I'm having an issue in this area of my online course," I can go look and see somebody who seems to be more confident and more successful in that exact area. Maybe there's some opportunities for a voluntary peer-review based on that, so I can get some one-on-one mentoring and coaching.

That's definitely a process that we would like to help make easier for faculty members and reward it even more than it already is. That's the best way for those conversations to happen: for somebody to feel that they're in an environment that's comfortable to acknowledge their own weaknesses, to see others who are successful, to feel that success, and feel enough trust (and, frankly, enough equal ego) to be able to have a conversation about how you might help me get a little better at this. If we can create that context, that would be very successful. (Fabry & Marlaire, 2014)

Although all of National University's methods are designed to help instructors improve their teaching practices, the formal review mechanisms also provide data relevant to decision making at the university, which we examined in chapter 2, such as which contingent instructors will be invited to teach more courses and which full-time faculty members will achieve promotion. The informal and formal evaluation instruments used at any institution, therefore, are the core determinant of the quality and utility of results obtained.

Readers who are responsible for the implementation of the evaluation process (which we will examine next in chapter 10) should ask four key questions when selecting or creating the instruments to be used in the evaluation of online teaching:

- What teaching behaviors do we wish to measure or evaluate?
- Whose observations should be part of the evaluation outputs?
- How will the results of evaluation be used on campus?
- Should evaluations of face-to-face and online teaching use different instruments?

The answers to these questions help evaluation planners to decide on the structure, content, and approach to be used in the evaluation instruments to be adopted.

Separating Teaching Behaviors from Content Design

As we have seen in part 1 of this book, the best evaluations are those designed to observe and assess specific behaviors (e.g., Achtemeier, Morris,

& Finnegan, 2003; Chickering & Gamson, 1987). Part of the challenge in evaluation of online teaching, from whatever viewpoint (student, peer, administrative), is that it is easy to confuse course-design elements with teaching behaviors. For example, in face-to-face courses, the instructor's presentation of information and content—what we typically call *lecturing*—is often considered a key teaching behavior. However, in online courses, the lecture content may or may not have been created by the person facilitating the course, and even when the creator of course content is also the course facilitator, student consumption of course content (e.g., watching video clips, reading lecture content, interacting with online learning objects) is difficult, if not impossible, to tie back to specific teaching behaviors undertaken directly by the faculty member. Yes, the faculty member may have created the lecture content and video snippets, but is the faculty member "teaching" when students read the lecture materials or watch the videos on their own time? This becomes a slippery slope for evaluators who are looking for specific teaching behaviors to observe in online classes.

Thinking along these lines, we would never include the quality of the textbook as a factor in evaluating the teaching of face-to-face instructors; online-course content materials occupy a space that is uncomfortably not exactly like a textbook and not exactly like teaching, either, so it is easy to see why there has been confusion even among experts about whether to include the designed elements of online courses in the evaluation of teaching practices. We argue that course-design elements should not be included in evaluation of online teaching practices, despite a significant history of their inclusion in assessment rubrics (see chapter 11 for a more detailed examination of this history).

A timely example is Palloff and Pratt's (2011) book, *The Excellent Online Instructor*. They examine many models for evaluation of online teaching, and they put forward nuanced suggestions for how institutions can develop their own evaluation processes for online teaching, at both the course and program levels. Palloff and Pratt include course-design elements as suggested criteria for evaluating online teaching (p. 96), and say that "[e]valuation should be focused on the main activities involved in online teaching—course facilitation and course development" (p. 102). We agree that, in a comprehensive evaluation plan, course-design elements do need to be evaluated. We argue only that course-design elements should be evaluated in a process separate from the evaluation of teaching.

Palloff and Pratt are not alone in including course design as an element to be considered in evaluations of online teaching. They base their recommendations on Fink's "Model of Good Teaching," which contains four core areas for evaluation:

- *Course design*
- Instructor-student interactions
- Quality of student learning
- Instructor improvement of practice over time (Fink, 2008, p. 11, italics added)

Palloff and Pratt construct a faculty-evaluation rubric based on these criteria, which include observations of "development of social presence," "evidence of learner interaction," "evidence of instructor interaction," and "instructional design for interaction" (pp. 155–158). This last category is problematic, given that previously in their book, they remind readers that "it is important to remember, however, that many instructors do not write or design the courses they teach" (p. 93).

Likewise, many previous theorists include course content or course design as areas to be observed in evaluation of online teaching. Drouin (2012) includes "lecture-delivery quality" and "course content" as evaluation criteria (pp. 62–63). Peltier, Schibrowski, and Drago (2007) note six criteria for student ratings of online-teaching effectiveness, including "course content" and "course structure" (p. 142). DiStefano and Witt (2010) privilege online courses as being better able to provide better data for evaluation than face-to-face courses: "[t]he online environment provides unusually rich documentation of course design and delivery" (p. 412).

None of these theorists is intentionally trying to mislead readers by including course content or course design elements in their recommendations for what to observe in online courses. In fact, they are following a well-established pattern. Many of the earliest online-teaching evaluation instruments assume that the designer of the course materials is also the instructor (e.g., the Checklist for Online Interactive Learning [Sunal & Sunal, 2002]; the Rubric for Online Instruction [2003]; the Blackboard Exemplary Course Program Rubric [Blackboard, 2003]; and the original Quality Matters rubric [MarylandOnline, 2004]). Because of this assumption, the design of the course content was seen as a key teaching behavior—one that most often happens to occur before the actual course takes place. Thus, the design choices of the course constructor have been included as observable "behaviors" in many evaluation instruments. Three examples may serves to demonstrate how widespread this inclusion is.

Online Course Assessment Tool (OCAT), Western Carolina University

The OCAT focuses on five areas:

- Course overview and organization
- Learner objectives and competencies
- Resources and materials
- Learner interaction
- Learner assessment

Each of the five areas is further subdivided into evaluation questions on "elements of course design" and "elements of teaching" (DeCristofaro et al., 2007).

Student Assessment of Their Learning Gains (SALG)

The SALG is highly customizable, but the question sets evince a design bias toward face-to-face interactions, such as including questions about specific actions such as "attending class lectures" and asking learners to evaluate "any notes of presentations the instructor may have posted online" (Seymour, Carroll, & Weston, 2007).

Guide for Evaluating Online Instruction, Santa Rosa Junior College

The authors of this evaluation rubric advise observers to look at course content as part of their evaluation of teaching. "In an online class the instructor will provide online learning units containing reading assignments (on the [w]eb, in textbooks, or both), explanatory 'lecture notes,' discussion, answers to questions, and an online exercise or quiz." Further, the instrument includes an unanswered question about a category of communication not observable in face-to-face courses: "Pending: what about instructor comments from Gradebook? For some online classes that may be a large component of student interaction" (All-Faculty Association, 2012, p. 2).

Only interactions between instructors and learners should be included in the teaching behaviors measured or observed in evaluation instruments. Indeed, even before online courses existed, theorists from the early days of technology-assisted teaching called for a separation of the evaluation of design tasks from the evaluation of teaching practices.

Online-course design and online-course teaching must be evaluated separately, even in institutions where online course designers own the intellectual property in the designed content and are always the instructors for their online courses. Most institutions already have their own intellectual property and copyright policies in place. Such general policies are often not a good fit, however, for the situations that commonly hold for online courses, which have more fixed-format content than is typically used to support face-to-face courses.

For example, in face-to-face classes at Northeastern Illinois University, observers look for how faculty members use the materials that they have adopted (e.g., textbooks), adapted (e.g., publisher-created PowerPoint slides), or created themselves (e.g., study guides). It can be easy for face-to-face observers to conflate "the faculty member made this resource" with "this resource is, by itself, an indication of teaching quality." Faculty members use such resources, regardless of whether they themselves created them, in order to interact with their students, and it is such interactions that comprise the teaching behaviors for which observers should look.

Observing online teaching has a similar goal: to separate the observation and evaluation of the materials in the course environment (design evaluation) from the observation and evaluation of how faculty members use course materials when interacting with learners (teaching evaluation). Both types of evaluation are necessary, but they should be performed separately for online courses, especially because the person or team who designs an online-course environment may not be the same people who teach from those materials.

In 1978, Bogen warned of a coming wave of adult learners who "want considerably greater control of their learning environment" (p. 52), and advocated for increased "informal student-faculty contact" (p. 57) away from formal classroom time and apart from discussion of materials and course content per se. Bogen also called for establishing holistic feedback systems to advise faculty members about how they can change and adapt their own teaching behaviors (p. 62), again separate from the materials they produced and used to support course delivery. A few years later, Marsh (1982) wondered whether it was necessary to include materials-development processes in the Students' Evaluations of Educational Quality (SEEQ) evaluation instrument.

By 2002, McInnis examined the "Impact of Technology on Faculty Performance and Its Evaluation" and concluded that several tasks formerly undertaken exclusively by faculty members could be performed by others through an "unbundling of academic work" (p. 55), including "designing and coordinating units and courses of study; [and] designing and developing resources used in learning, including textbooks, videos, and computer packages" (p. 55).

This is not to say that course design is unimportant to the quality of teaching behaviors. For instance, imagine an online course without any built-in forum for asynchronous or real-time communication. However, the quality or existence of course-design elements should be evaluated separately from teaching; this is accomplished most often as part of institutions' existing curriculum-review processes, whereby courses are reexamined on a regular basis to make sure they reflect the current state of the field of knowledge.

Moving from Instruments to a Holistic Evaluation Program

Before we can discuss a campus-wide evaluation program, however, we must confront the relative quantities of data available to evaluators of face-to-face and online teaching. McInnis predicted in 2002 that "new technologies are suggesting new ways to measure performance that had not been considered previously. It is now possible to monitor Web-site use, level of student participation, availability of faculty, and the timeliness of faculty response to students" (p. 59). McInnis thought it "hard to imagine that faculty could be faced with detailed analyses like those currently used to monitor the performance of other workers operating in on-line environments" (p. 59). It has come to pass, especially with recent advances in the analytics packages of LMSs, that faculty members teaching online and their administrators have access to an every-click record of their teaching behaviors—a level of detail unavailable to face-to-face faculty members.

Most campuses have a program in place for evaluating face-to-face teaching, usually as part of the promotion-and-tenure process. The introduction of online teaching can force campuses to reexamine their face-to-face teaching-evaluation processes, as Rob Kelly found out recently about Kennesaw State University:

> The problem with faculty performance reviews is that many institutions have "fuzzy" performance expectations. "We expect faculty to be active in teaching, service, and research but most universities, colleges, and departments have not done a good job of defining what constitutes acceptable performance in those areas," says Teresa Joyce, dean of

graduate studies and professor of management at Kennesaw State University in Georgia.... Proper documentation of review criteria and results [are] essential to help faculty find ways to improve performance and to provide detailed evidence should a promotion or tenure dispute arise. (Kelly, 2012)

But what is "proper documentation," and should one's campus adopt evaluation methods and instruments for each delivery modality? Especially when online courses are relatively new to the institution, the campus must consider whether to adopt a single evaluation instrument for all course-delivery methods or whether to use separate instruments for each delivery modality. In other words, what's so special about online teaching behaviors?

The core teaching behaviors and interactions that constitute good teaching are similar, regardless of how courses are offered. Ron Berk has performed years of analyses and meta-analyses. In his article, "Face-to-Face versus Online Course Evaluations: A 'Consumer's Guide' to Seven Strategies" (2013b), Berk outlines the pros and cons among seven ways of developing student-evaluation instruments for online courses:

1. **Instructor-developed scale.** Although the technology exists with free online survey providers, ... it is not recommended ... [because of] the complexity of multiple measures, such as student, self, peer, administrator, and mentor rating scales.

2. **Traditional F2F student rating scale.** Studies ... yield comparable ratings on ... course and instructor global items, ... similar item means, internal consistency reliabilities, and factor structures, and nearly identical overall ratings of the instructor. [This method] will not capture elements that are unique to each type of course.

3. **[Ten] optional items added to F2F scale.** [T]he most efficient and cost-effective approach to retain those items in common to both F2F and online courses, but also add items to address the uses of technology and other aspects of teaching that are different for online courses.... A major advantage of this option is the norms available for various score comparisons.

4. **Revision of F2F scale.** Adapt or revise the current scales to fit the online courses. This is an extension of the preceding strategy when the 10-item add-on subscale is not adequate. If more items are required to cover online teaching, then this may be your option.

5. **New rating scale.** This "throw-the-baby-out" approach may be the most time-consuming and costly option.

6. **Commercially developed student rating scale.** [O]nly two vendors market scales that are designed expressly for online courses: (1) e-SIR, which is a 41-item scale with half of the items from the SIR II by Educational Testing Service; and (2) a 31-item distance learning form from the IAS Online at the Office of Educational Assessment, University of Washington.

7. **Published student rating scale.** There are three published student rating scales identified by Drouin (2012) that were designed expressly for online courses, which are worthy of review:

- Student Evaluation of Online Teaching Effectiveness (SEOTE) (Bangert, 2008)
- Student Evaluation of Web-Based Instruction (SEWBI) (Stewart, Hong, & Strudler, 2004)
- Students' Perceptions of Online Courses (SPOC) (Rothman et al., 2011).

Source: **Berk (2013), reprinted with permission.**

In *Considerations in Online Course Design,* Creasman (2012) notes seven key differences between online and face-to-face courses. In online courses, Creasman finds the following unique characteristics:

- Asynchronous activity, in which students can interact with each other and course materials anytime, 24/7
- Nonlinear discussions on message boards and forums, in which students can participate in multiple conversations simultaneously
- Communication primarily via written text
- Slower communication between instructor and students, primarily via e-mail
- Greater social contact and time spent by instructor with students on the website
- Greater volume of information and resources available
- The instructor's role as a facilitator, guide on the side, and also co-learner

To help make the decision about how to select or design evaluation instruments for online teaching, then, we can note that the differences in online courses identified by Creasman are qualitative and not categorical: communication may be slower in online courses, but it is still a key component of the course experience. Instructors may have increased contact with learners in online courses, but contact is not absent in face-to-face environments. We can also easily confuse specific actions with the broader teaching behaviors they represent. For example, some face-to-face evaluation instruments ask learners, peer evaluators, and administrative observers to rate instructors on their voice tone, body language, and eye contact: all specific actions that fall under the teaching behavior of establishing instructor presence in the course environment. By dissociating the teaching behavior from specific physical actions and recouching the definition in terms of desired outcomes, we can begin to better judge or create evaluation instruments that are delivery-mode neutral.

This would seem to argue for creating or adopting a single evaluation instrument for all modalities (Culver, 2012). However, Creasman's larger point in listing all seven methods of adoption, creation, and adaptation is to suggest that there may be strategic reasons to treat online teaching separately from, or at least in more detail than, face-to-face instruction. Likewise, a holistic evaluation program should examine teaching behaviors from several vantage points.

What Observations Count?

As we have seen in previous chapters on formative and summative ratings and evaluations, the most pressing need for campus-wide programs is to define what measures count toward the evaluation program—and, perhaps more important, what measures fall outside the program's scope. Because online courses offer exponentially more (and more frequent) sources of information about faculty members' teaching behaviors and their students' experiences of the courses, institutions might be tempted to see "collect everything" as the best strategy. Two factors argue against this assumption: collective program development and the need for extra-institutional comparisons. Some recent postings to the Professional and Organizational Development (POD) Network Listserv demonstrate both concerns:

- We are in the midst of this process as well. We collected many sample forms from other peer colleges and found most inadequate and not helpful, based on the principles of effective student rating forms.... Are they to be used to evaluate instructors or just give instructors formative information from the students' point of view to assist in course redesign? (Baker, 2014)

- We [Western Carolina University] developed our own instruments and criteria, drawn from our university-wide tenure standards for excellence in teaching, which are strongly influenced by Lee Shulman's pedagogical content knowledge concept. (Cruz, 2014)
- The great danger to reliability in such evaluations would be a lack of clear guidelines about the process, the expectations, the requirements, and the intended outcomes (the teacher's and the institution's). Without these guidelines, there could be a lot of judgments based on whether or not a course appears to be done "the way I would do it" or whether and how certain approaches, resources, technologies are used. Materials from Quality Matters, for example, can help by providing specific tools (e.g., rubrics), but generic tools may not reflect the particular expectations of an institution, a college, or a department. (Theall, 2012b)

This gets faculty members and administrators in a pickle. One approach for campus-wide evaluation programs for online teaching is to use a standard set of expectations, to define the measures to be used in making decisions, and to be able to compare face-to-face and online learning outcomes. The opposite approach can also be used: look at other institutions' models in order to customize instruments and outcomes for one's own campus, to adopt the decision-making tools created by others, and to compare apples to apples with data about one's own institution's online teaching versus results from comparable peer institutions.

Fortunately, there is a middle way. Institutions should define first for themselves the required data elements they will collect for summative evaluation. Then, using those criteria and examples from other institutions, they should create an overall program that provides those summative data, plus methods for collecting formative information as well. Two perspectives help to support this conclusion:

It is recommended that an institution should employ several different [student rating] forms, one for each major type of course. However, the two modes of teaching—in class and online—do not require different forms. A study of more than 5,000 courses compared SRI ratings of in-class and online classes using the same SRI instrument (IDEA). No meaningful differences showed in most aspects of ratings. (Hativa, 2013, p. 56)

Increasingly, the use of information technologies is a part of course design. Most courses now use a course management system such as Blackboard ... to store the syllabus, calendar, handouts, and other instructional materials of the course. Some use these systems to conduct online discussions, perform assessments, or host group projects . . . . To the extent that peers may access these course environments, [they are] more open to review. (Chism, 2007, p. 125).

Hativa and Chism see the core behaviors of online teaching and face-to-face teaching as equivalent, and both acknowledge that the data trail for online teaching practices is much richer than that available for evaluating face-to-face teaching. It is tempting to want to wait until all teaching methods have similar levels of supporting data for the evaluation of teaching practices in order to avoid the possibility of making personnel decisions and program-level decisions based on fundamentally variant (and thus differently reliable) data sets—a poorer stream from face-to-face teaching evaluations and a richer stream from online ones. However, as Berk states with tongue in cheek, "even in the absence of data, administrators will still make staffing and program decisions, so it's imperative to design our rating and evaluation programs effectively" (2006, pp. 212–213). Such holistic programs must start with an examination of the applications to which results will be put.

Applications of Evaluation Results

Results from all three types of evaluation (student, peer, and administrative) can be put to three common uses: teaching improvement, employment and promotion decisions, and programmatic assessment (support for accreditation and strategic planning). Thus, evaluation instruments should support all three outputs. Questions in each type of instrument should directly address at least one of the three outputs. Theall's approach neatly encapsulates the needs statement for a campus-wide evaluation program:

> Committee decisions made by choosing "favorite" items from other forms often results in long debates about the wording and merits of individual items and eventually, a least offensive compromise instrument that may not serve any purpose very well. If you have the luxury of stepping back, try to guide the discussion to issues such as
>
> - the purposes of the ratings process,
> - the commonly understood and accepted definitions and criteria applied to "effective teaching,"

FIGURE 9.1. DATA SOURCES FOR ONLINE-COURSE EVALUATION

Data Source	Concern	Application
Student Course Ratings	• Students can rate their experience, but not faculty-member skills or knowledge. • Students may not differentiate between content and teaching behaviors in online courses.	• Count responses to scaled questions toward summative evaluation. • Open-ended comments should be used for formative purposes only.
Self Evaluation	• Use of standardized review instrument can assume a cookie-cutter instructional approach.	• Self-evaluation should never be used for summative evaluation.
Peer Evaluation	• Open-ended peer evaluations can vary widely in scope and rigor. • This is the one instrument that should be the same across all units of campus; expect resistance.	• Don't automatically count peer evaluations toward promotion, tenure, or retention. • Allow faculty members to cite results as evidence of teaching-practice improvement.
Administrative Evaluation	• This should not be the same as the peer-review instrument: "Peer evaluation and administrative evaluation are separate functions that work alongside one another but are not the same process" (Palloff & Pratt, p. 102).	• Administrative observations can be used for summative and formative uses: promotion and awards as well as teaching improvement. • Hanz and Nigro (2005) are especially insightful for details on developing programs that include administrative observation of online courses.

- the performance expectations for faculty,
- the kinds of information you need,
- the sources (students and others) of that information,
- the weight assigned to each kind of information, and
- how all these issues fit together to guide the choice of the instrument(s) you need. (Theall, 2012a, bullets added)

Each campus should determine what data sources from online courses respond best to the categories that Theall lays out. For example, figure 9.1 illustrates one possible configuration.

Further, campuses with faculty unions should also note where contractual obligations or established practices require the collection of certain types of data about online teaching. For example, no one can teach online at Northeastern Illinois University without demonstrating core teaching skills, either through reports from other institutions, certification from a recognized source (such as the Illinois Online Network [ION] Master Online Teacher program), or completion of an online-teaching professional-development curriculum from the campus Center for Teaching and Learning. The development of core online-teaching skills is necessary as the university develops online teaching and learning opportunities. The gatekeeper policies protect the faculty, students, and institution and also set a baseline against which administrators then evaluate faculty online-teaching practices.

Conclusion

Fabry, Marlaire, and their colleagues at National University are grappling with the selection of evaluation instruments that will help them to accomplish both teaching-improvement and administrative-decision outcomes. The strategic direction for their curriculum and programs helps them to conclude that they want to evaluate core teaching behaviors in the same fashion regardless of delivery modality.

National University's questions about their online-teaching evaluation processes led them to reexamine their face to face teaching-evaluation instrument. They are now updating their student, peer, and administrative evaluation instruments to reflect delivery mode neutral language, moving away from naming specific actions (e.g., asking about eye contact) in favor of asking about categories of teaching behaviors to which the actions might belong (e.g., establishment of instructor presence).

Further, Linse (2012) cautions us to try to see through some of the internal politics that get in the way of defining, observing, and evaluating good online teaching:

> I don't think that Penn State's policies or the departmental questions lead to our faculty liking or seeing the ratings as any more valuable than they do at any other institution. Before we moved online, very few units had made any changes to the departmental selection of questions since the inception of the student ratings in 1987. Sadly, all too often I hear from other faculty [members], chairs, and committees that they pay attention only to the two overall questions because they are what promotion-and-tenure committees look at. Some good news is that the move to online has prompted a number of departments to re-examine their question choices. It is nice to see the current faculty wanting to take ownership, and perhaps these faculty voices will prompt other units to do likewise. And, by the way, our student ratings were initiated by the university Faculty Senate for the express purpose of use in promotion and tenure and annual review; they were *not* a formative instrument co-opted by the administration. Honestly, that doesn't seem to matter much, but I can (and frequently do) refer faculty [members] to the senate legislation when they complain about some aspects of the ratings.

The lesson to take away from this chapter is that good teaching is good teaching, regardless of how it is accomplished, and the fact that many institutions are just now beginning to treat evaluation of their courses in a delivery-neutral way does not mean that there is some special teaching behavior that online instructors do that is different from the behaviors of good classroom instructors. The challenge for evaluating online teaching, then, is operational rather than essential, and that means we can attack such a challenge with programmatic and strategic thinking. In chapter 10, we will establish strategies for implementing online-teaching evaluation processes and explore ways to align online-teaching evaluation with existing evaluation efforts on campus.

A Thought Exercise

Look at a copy of your institution's evaluation instrument(s) for face-to-face courses and answer the following questions. If you have instruments for online courses, repeat the process and compare the results from the two examinations.

- Are there separate instruments for student, peer, and administrative evaluation purposes?
- What teaching behaviors are measured or evaluated in each instrument?
- Do the questions in the instrument(s) refer to specific actions or to general behaviors and their desired outcomes?
- How would evaluators using the instrument(s) apply the questions to the teaching that happens in various delivery modes?
- What elements of face-to-face or online courses that go beyond teaching behaviors are still useful to track for purposes of teaching improvement?
- What method is best for your institution's purposes: creating or adopting one evaluation instrument that is delivery-modality neutral, adding online-specific questions to the face-to-face instrument, or creating or adopting separate instruments, depending on delivery modality? *Note:* This answer can differ depending on the type and audience of instrument (e.g., one answer for student ratings and different answers for peer- and administrative-evaluation purposes).

Once you have examined your existing evaluation instruments and determined how you wish to adopt, adapt, or create instruments for online-teaching evaluation, it is time to start thinking about how such instruments form a part of your institution's overall assessment-and-evaluation program.

CHAPTER TEN

IMPLEMENTING THE EVALUATION PROCESS

Roadblocks to change are unavoidable. Naysayers will abound, key power holders will put their feet down to slow or even halt progress, and inevitably there will be extremely vocal individuals who feel left out of the entire process. These obstacles have to be overcome, however, if change is to occur and be successful. Creating an evaluation process for online teaching is no different, and the challenges can be even greater. For example, some administrators may bring a healthy skepticism about online teaching and learning, faculty stakeholders may be difficult to involve fully in the deliberations if they are geographically dispersed, and online student input might be difficult to obtain if students are not physically present on campus.

Ann H. Taylor's Story

Anyone who has been part of a large decision-making body or involved in a high-impact decision-making process knows that there are many roadblocks and land mines along the way. Several recent examples immediately come to mind from my own community. There was the desperately needed high school renovation project that failed to be funded when my children were

---

in elementary school (one is now in college and there still haven't been improvements to the high school), the public backlash against a proposed new park in our neighborhood incorporating public lands that neighboring private homeowners had come to consider their own, and proposed changes to long-term care when a new vendor took over the retirement community where my own parents are living.

Although each of these examples was very different in its settings, their history, the people involved, the roadblocks, and the land mines were surprisingly similar. In each case, there were stakeholders who felt the following:

- They had unique needs.
- They were not being adequately consulted.
- Their concerns were not being heard.
- Financial implications were not getting sufficient consideration.
- Implementation would be too challenging to warrant the proposed changes.

When trying to create and implement an evaluation plan for online teaching, roadblocks such as these are no less commonplace. On my own campus at Penn State, at times they seemed insurmountable. I encountered a perfect example when I was asked to assist another college within our university with the development of their own online-teaching evaluation plan. I brought with me my own college's successfully implemented instruments and plan, but quickly realized that the context and stakeholders in the new setting were quite different.

The college's stakeholder committee was charged with creating a single online-teaching evaluation plan that would be adopted across all of the college's departments and programs so that the resulting data could inform college-wide decision making. The stakeholders, who represented each of the college's academic departments, were quickly skeptical about the proposed one-size-fits-all approach. They each wanted to make seemingly small changes that would, unwittingly, have made it extremely difficult to implement a single plan and almost impossible for administrators to use the resulting data to make comparisons across the college. Even specific instruments that were proposed proved problematic because various administrators wanted to swap in department- and program-specific questions. Their faculty members became sidetracked with tinkering with the carefully crafted and already validated evaluation questions.

As all of these tweaks and changes were being proposed, the information technology folks on the committee became increasingly concerned with how they would manage all of these requests and produce needed reports for the leadership. The financial folks in the room grew worried about how much time and effort the plan—which was getting quite complicated—would take to put into place. They wondered if it was even going to be worth it, from a return-on-investment standpoint, in the long run. The faculty senate representative wondered if and how the plan would need to be ratified by the entire faculty body of the college. There were a number of meetings in which it seemed that developing and implementing a plan that would satisfy everybody in the room was impossible.

Step 1: Identify the Barriers

Whether perceived or real, barriers will be in the way. The first step toward creating and implementing an evaluation process is to determine which barriers exist and how they might be overcome. A few simple questions are helpful here:

- Who are your key stakeholders?
- What objections or problems might each stakeholder group have with implementing a program evaluation process?
- Which of these are the biggest hurdles to adoption?
- What can be done to address each of these concerns?

Who are your key stakeholders? Certainly students come to mind first because they are the ultimate beneficiaries of our educational systems. The faculty members who teach those students are also an obvious stakeholder group, as are the administrators (program leads, department heads, deans) who oversee their work. The number of stakeholders, however, can far exceed these typical players, though, as we discussed in chapter 2 (see "Stakeholders for the Evaluation of Online Teaching"), bringing technical support staff, instructional designers, librarians, and other important members of the online teaching team to the discussion.

Stakeholders for online education can also bring special concerns to the table. For example, some administrators may see online education as a potential cash cow that will generate new revenue and may seem focused only on program efficiencies. Likewise, some faculty may bring concerns about how they perceive that their administrators care only about the financial bottom line and not the quality of their online teaching. Employers will want to know that the institution is producing high-quality graduates. Parents who support their child's education will want to be sure the expense, which seems to rise daily, is worth their investment. Each of these stakeholder's interests and potential objections and concerns will need to be considered in the evaluation of online teaching.

So how do you find out what those objections and concerns might be? It is often fairly easy to make an educated guess as to what objections and concerns various stakeholder groups will have when considering the implementation of something new, whether that is the construction of a new park or the formation of a new plan to evaluate your institution's online programming. But to uncover the full scope of questions and concerns, one must ask and listen. Conducting focus groups, surveys, and listening sessions are an excellent way to gather input from your key stakeholder groups. A document in the companion website (www.wiley .com/go/tobin) for this book, "How to Use Focus Groups to Solicit Ideas and Feedback" (Pennsylvania State University, 2007), provides helpful tips to get you started.

Because we are discussing the evaluation of online teaching, faculty members and students are key starting points. When listening to these groups, consider the following:

- How do *they* define "good teaching"?
- What criteria do *they* think should be measured in order to provide evidence of good teaching?
- What methods do *they* suggest for gathering that evidence?
- What do *they* think are the most difficult aspects of good teaching to measure?
- What are *their* suggestions for ways those aspects could be measured?

Step 2: Bring Together Key Stakeholders

With this important information about stakeholder objections and concerns in hand, you will next need to analyze these findings to create an evaluation plan for online teaching that will provide the evidence you seek while avoiding roadblocks and barriers. This is not a task that should be done in isolation. Forming a steering committee made up of representatives from each of your key stakeholder groups will ensure that you review the data and create an evaluation plan that has the best chance of success. As you form your steering committee, be sure to include representatives from your central administration and bargaining units (if applicable) to ensure your plans have institutional support as well.

Creating an evaluation plan is not a process that can be completed in just a few short meetings, so these individuals will need to make a sufficient time commitment to the process. How much time will be needed varies depending on the context of the plan itself (e.g., a program-specific plan will likely take far less time to develop than an institution-wide one). Whether you hope to complete your steering committee's work in three months or three years, you will want to communicate your expectations for the level of commitment upfront so you have the best likelihood of having a stable steering committee. Let them know your anticipated time frame (from first meeting through pilot testing and full implementation) and anticipated meeting schedule so they can make an informed decision about whether or not they can participate.

This committee will also be important to create buy in for the evaluation plan, a critical aspect if success is to be realized. Reflecting back on experiences such as those shared in the beginning of this chapter, a common criticism that emerges from failed initiatives is lack of involvement. If stakeholders are not actively involved in creating a solution, they will certainly find problems.

Making sure your steering committee has a strong level of involvement can be particularly challenging given the nature of the subject—online teaching and learning. As we have discussed previously, your stakeholder steering committee membership may not all be physically located on the same campus and may even be located in a number of different time zones. Conducting regular meetings and making sure all parties are given the same opportunities for input is challenging when even a handful of individuals are geographically dispersed. You will need to take special care to coordinate schedules across time zones and to use meeting tools skillfully to ensure that every participant has sufficient input to the deliberations.

TIPS FOR BETTER VIRTUAL MEETINGS

Whether you incorporate remote participants through a conference call, a videoconferencing tool such as Skype or a Google Hangout, or a web conferencing tool such as WebEx or Adobe Connect, there are several things you can do to help ensure that your meeting participants are all equally engaged.

1. **Keep meetings short (30–60 minutes).** It is even more difficult to keep attention spans going when not physically present. When participating remotely, it is even easier to become distracted and tune out.
2. **Create and disseminate a detailed agenda ahead of time.** All meeting participants will want to know what will be covered in the upcoming meeting, but having that document in hand is particularly useful for remote participants so they can more easily follow along.
3. **Distribute handouts and visual aids in advance of each meeting.** There is nothing more frustrating to the remote participant than not being able to see a document that has been physically distributed to those who are in the central meeting room or not being able to see something that is being projected only on a screen in the physical meeting room. Send out all documents and visual aids ahead of time and be prepared to quickly e-mail or fax last-minute resources during the meeting.
4. **Make time for housekeeping at the beginning of each meeting:**
   a. Quick introductions at the start of each meeting will help remote participants know who is in attendance and also reminds those who are physically present that there are remote participants, too.
   b. Reminding everyone of any technology ground rules at the beginning of the meeting is also a good way to reduce the chance of unnecessary interruptions that can be caused when participants do things such as shuffle papers near microphones, have side conversations that make it difficult to hear the main speaker, or forget to mute their phone or microphone when not speaking.
   c. Finally, remind participants to state their name when speaking so remote participants can more easily follow along.
5. **Frequently give remote participants a chance to weigh in.** It is difficult to jump into a discussion if you are not physically present in the room. Make sure to offer remote participants a chance to speak throughout the meeting by periodically calling on them or using technology to enable them to raise their hand (e.g., many web conferencing tools enable participants to click on a "raise hand" icon that lets others see that they would like to speak).
6. **Use an online whiteboard to record meeting notes as you go.** Whether you use a simple Google Doc that all participants have access to or the notes tool within a web conferencing tool, keeping visible notes of the discussion as you go will help ensure that nothing is getting lost or miscommunicated through the airwaves.
7. **Record meetings for those who cannot attend.** One great benefit of using technology to enable remote participants to join meetings is that those same technologies often provide the ability to record the session.

Not only are those recordings helpful for those who might not be able to make it but also they provide a valuable record of the meeting that can be referred to if needed.

8. **Ask for feedback**. Reach out to remote participants periodically, off-line, to ask them how the meetings are going for them. Are they feeling involved? Are there things you could do to help them feel more connected?

Step 3: The Small-Step Approach

Whether your task is to build a plan for evaluating online teaching within a single program or department or to build one that will be used across the entire institution, taking small steps toward your ultimate goals will help you work kinks out along the way. It is much easier to adjust and adapt in this manner than it would be if an entire master plan is put into place all at once.

So where might you begin? In this text we have discussed a variety of evaluation methods including formative reviews of online teaching, student reviews, faculty peer reviews, and administrative reviews. We suggest starting with just one or two of these methods, depending on your needs and circumstances. Pilot your efforts with a small number of courses or a single program, modify your instruments and methods as needed, then build on your successes by expanding your evaluation efforts to more courses and programs. We often don't realize that a given question isn't stated clearly enough or that a certain procedure is too cumbersome until we test it. As we have said throughout this text, one size does not fit all. Once your initial efforts have been fully implemented, consider adding additional evaluation components in a similar fashion.

Throughout the process, measure the impact of your efforts. Are students completing instruments at a high enough rate to provide meaningful feedback? Are faculty members feeling that they are receiving the feedback they desire and need? Are modifications needed to the instruments being used or the evaluation processes? Are you seeing improvements in the quality of teaching over time? The evaluation process is truly one of continuous quality improvement. Adjustments *should* be made along the way. In fact, a revision cycle should be built into the process to ensure that the process is successful over time. The steering committee is a logical body to provide ongoing oversight and stakeholder involvement.

What Can Administrators Do?

Unless instructors truly believe that good teaching is highly valued at their institution and that professional growth is expected of them, most will not embrace the opportunity to evaluate and improve their online classrooms. One of the most important things that an administrator can do is to communicate the importance of high-quality teaching to the institution's mission and then reinforce that communication through the recognition and rewarding of good teaching at all levels. In the world of online education, high-quality teaching is paramount to student retention. Unlike the captured audience we have on our campuses who might dismiss a single, poorly instructed course as an anomaly and would simply avoid taking a class from that same instructor again, online learners are more likely to dismiss the entire institution altogether, knowing well that the next institution is just a click away.

The larger the institution and the more broad its mission, the more difficult it can be for faculty members to feel that their teaching efforts are valued by the institution. This can be particularly true for geographically dispersed and adjunct faculty populations who, as research has indicated, tend to feel less connected to their institution (Dolan, 2011; West, 2010). Research, service, and outreach efforts may seem to be more highly valued and rewarded at some institutions, making it challenging to devote much of one's limited time and resources to teaching. This can be particularly challenging at larger research institutions, where often the institution's online courses and programs often are already seen as second-class entities.

Administrators are well advised to communicate to faculty members, staff, and also students the importance of good teaching and how the evaluation process will benefit them personally (Nulty, 2008). This communication from administrators about the importance of evaluation feedback should be repeated every semester or term as end-of-semester student surveys are distributed, administrative and peer reviews are conducted, or any other formal or informal evaluation method is used to reinforce their message. This can easily be done in the online environment through direct, mass e-mails, postings on program websites and discussion forums, and in electronic newsletters.

Administrators can also affect the improvement of teaching by encouraging faculty members to experiment through a process of trial and error. The business world has long recognized that a key to increasing creativity and improving performance is to encourage risk taking. Administrators can support safe risk taking by allowing faculty to try new things in their online classroom while temporarily looking the other way (e.g., not counting a given semester's student evaluation scores in that year's performance review).

Providing adequate and accessible faculty development tools and resources is another important aspect of administrative support. Faculty members should not be expected to figure out how to improve their performance alone. In the United States, we insist that our public school educators receive training and certification not only in the subjects they teach but also in the related pedagogy. In other words, we teach them how to teach. In higher education, however, we are more apt to put faculty members in the classroom without any such training or preparation. In the online classroom, this is no different. In fact, despite the fact that teaching online is very different from teaching in the face-to-face classroom, it is not unusual for institutions to provide no additional support when assigning faculty members to teach online. Administrators who are serious about improving the quality of online teaching should prepare to assist faculty members who need support by providing faculty development resources that are clearly aligned with teaching evaluation criteria. Such alignment will help not only prepare faculty to teach in the online environment but also will make it easier to provide remedial support for those faculty members whose evaluations indicate a need for additional guidance and professional development in a specific area.

Faculty development resources range from institutional offices dedicated to working with faculty members one-on-one to improve teaching performance to self-help resources that are widely available online (www .wiley.com/go/tobin). As has often been our message throughout this text, institutional needs will vary widely. Some institutions may already have resources in place to support face-to-face teaching that can be expanded to support online teaching, yet others may be starting from scratch. Benchmarking with similar institutions to one's own can yield faculty development models that can be adapted locally.

What Can Faculty Members Do?

Individually, faculty members can be proactive in the improvement of their teaching by using a wide array of strategies to self-assess and to collect feedback from their students, peers, and administrators about their teaching performance, even when their institution does not readily provide these mechanisms. We have discussed many different approaches in this text and countless more can be found online in print resources and in discussions with others involved in teaching. Sometimes the challenge is just to get started. Explore, experiment, and learn from both failures and successes until you are getting the feedback you desire.

Documenting and sharing evidence of good teaching with supervisors and requesting faculty development resources and programming when help is needed are also important components of the process. Don't be afraid to speak up. Busy administrators may be unaware of our successes if we don't make them known. This can be particularly true with online teaching and learning, and with geographically dispersed students and faculty members, because supervisors are not as likely to witness good teaching in our physical classrooms. Likewise, they may not know when we need assistance. Particularly when online instructors themselves are geographically dispersed, and don't have access to office or hallway conversations with faculty members about their resource needs, they may think "no news is good news." Work within governance councils, faculty senates, unions, and other faculty bodies to strengthen faculty development support and to create opportunities for reward and recognition related to online teaching.

Finally, faculty members, similar to administrators, should convey to their students, peers, and administrators who are helping review their online teaching the importance receiving the feedback, how it will be used, and how the evaluation process will benefit those individuals personally. Helping evaluators understand how important their role in the quality improvement process is and convincing them that the feedback really will make a difference will help all parties involved take the matter seriously, resulting in meaningful feedback. It will also help demonstrate the concern that the entire institution has for high-quality teaching. This can go a long way toward student retention.

Conclusion

As we stated at the beginning of this chapter, encountering roadblocks to adoption are inevitable. By listening to and closely involving stakeholders in the development and implementation of an evaluation plan for online teaching, many of these roadblocks can be overcome or even avoided. Both administrators and faculty members have important roles to play in ensuring that the evaluation process is successful. The process itself will ultimately vary widely, depending on the size and scope of the initiative. We end this chapter with a look at how one department within an institution tackled its own evaluation needs to illustrate one of many ways the evaluation of online teaching might be accomplished. As you read this case study, consider how this model may inform work in your own situation.

Case Study: Maximizing the Benefits of the Peer Review of Teaching

The motivation for engaging in peer review of teaching vacillates between providing opportunities to improve teaching and to evaluate teaching performance. The first is an exercise that is formative in nature when improvement of teaching is the purpose. The latter is a summative report used for accountability purposes. Both purposes for peer review of teaching have the potential to create productive opportunities for faculty members to focus on quality teaching and learning, but when conducted in isolation it is less likely to create a culture of learning and continuous quality improvement. For this reason it is important to find ways to maximize the benefits of peer review of teaching so valuable opportunities for peer collaboration and curricular coordination are supported, regardless of which purpose is targeted. To remedy this, our graduate online program in applied statistics asks faculty members to participate in a range of information-gathering activities, including mid semester and instructor/student surveys, concept mapping, curricular reviews, and faculty development events, in order to maximize the benefits of our peer review of teaching process. And, while individually each of these mechanisms has their own singular purpose, as a whole, they can also be effectively leveraged to involve online faculty members in thinking critically about the quality of online instruction, that is, to set the stage for peer review of teaching. Once set, our peer review of teaching process promotes synergistic thinking about teaching and learning and creates a rich collaborative context for ongoing faculty discussions about the quality of online learning and our overall program goals.

Peer Review of Teaching: What Do We Want to Accomplish?

Our online program includes two instructors who are both tenure-track faculty and for whom teaching evaluations are important. In addition, there are also other instructors who do not have a research directive and for whom focusing attention on teaching strategies that are effective with online learners is a higher priority. As with other higher education faculty, our instructors rarely have certifications related to teaching and while teaching as they were taught might work for face-to-face instruction on campus, these same strategies are not always successful in an online learning environment.

Both purposes for peer review of teaching, formative and summative, are important for helping to ensure quality teaching. However, whether arguments are made to use peer review of teaching to support either purpose (or both), the reality of how this exercise is typically implemented diminishes the success of either goal. Bernstein's (2008) report highlights this lamentable circumstance: "Historically, the peer review of teaching has typically meant only that a faculty member has watched a colleague lead a class. An observation of an hour in the life of the course yields a letter describing the performance of a teacher, and that letter becomes the peer-review component of the professors teaching evaluation" (p. 48). If faculty members are required to spend time visiting classrooms and reviewing class interaction, how can we make better use of this time?

Hutchings (1996) provides a comprehensive review of the research and practices of peer review of teaching. Though this article was published a while ago her characterization of the challenges that all teachers face has not changed: "teaching is exceedingly difficult to learn alone. Recent research on what good teachers know and can do indicates that teaching is a highly complex, situated activity which is learned largely and necessarily through experience" (p. 225). Hutchings's recommendations should also be heeded today, especially as they relate to online learning environments: "What is needed, rather, is thoughtful, ongoing discussion by relevant groups of peers, attempting to say ever more clearly what constitutes good teaching, putting forward powerful images and examples of it, and working toward definitions that can guide and be guided by concrete acts of judgment" (p. 227). This is our challenge. How do we establish a culture of inquiry that centers on the practices of effective online teaching?

Setting Up Peer Review of Teaching

Initially, our online program replicated the peer review of teaching process that is in place in many of the academic departments in our institution but we found this snapshot perspective lacking when a more comprehensive assessment of teaching was desired. In looking for ways to improve the peer review of teaching process we found that engaging our faculty in a range of information-gathering activities that relate to what they might see in an online course made sense. What follows are short descriptions of the various information-gathering activities faculty members engage in before they participate in our peer review of teaching process. In essence, the following activities set up the peer review of teaching process.

Overall Program Goals: The Foundation

Although each of our online courses has articulated learning goals and objectives for what students should know and be able to do, the foundation of our program evaluation is the establishment of overall program goals. These broad program goals involve higher-level learning objectives that span the student's experience throughout their entire program of study. For example, in our masters of applied statistics program, "drawing conclusions from data in the presence of uncertainty," "developing confidence in applying statistical analysis," and "being a proficient user of statistical software" are examples of overarching goals that are supported throughout the program. Although course objectives are often assessed in exams, these overall program goals are often overlooked; however, they provide a cohesiveness to the program and are considered in conversations between colleagues involved in peer review of teaching.

Mid Semester Surveys

At the halfway point in the semester, each of our online courses administers a midsemester survey that collects information and feedback from students about their course experience. Information about the number of courses students are taking, the number that are online, and how much time they are spending on the course materials is important for our instructors to find out about their students. Questions about the students' perceptions of the timeliness and quality of the communication that takes place in the course are flags that alert instructors about their responsiveness to student needs. And finally, input from students about what they would change and what they would *not* change about the course is collected. Although the primary purpose of these surveys is to provide instructors with information so that they might better support student learning as the course progresses, these results are also combined across all of the courses in the program. In this way instructors can compare their results with the program averages. This cross-program tally gives the program a broader view of the characteristics of its students, and instructors can compare their course results with those of the program. For example, if students are spending much more time on one course than is typical in the program or if students are reporting that response time or the quality of feedback is lower in one course than what is found in the program overall, these become areas that are now open for discussion in the peer-review process.

Instructor Satisfaction Survey

Each fall semester an anonymous survey is distributed to all instructors asking for feedback about departmental, instructional design, and university support structures as well as inquiring into their overall satisfaction with teaching online. Instructors provide feedback regarding the support they feel they need or resources that may be lacking. Is teaching online developing their professional skills? Are they satisfied with the learning that their students are able to achieve? Are they able to use the available online tools to adapt or enhance the online materials to support the learning needs of their students? These are all questions that get the instructors to think about what it is they do as teachers and the impact they have on student learning. As with all of our surveys, these submissions are tallied across the program so that everyone can review the perceived status of support and the comments for improving the program.

Student Ratings of Teaching Effectiveness

Each semester a Penn State survey is distributed by the university's central administration to all courses that gathers student input on teaching effectiveness. Students are asked to provide feedback on the teaching and learning process from their perspective as learners. These results are accessible only by the instructor and the director of online programs who requests a copy. Although there is no mechanism in place to combine these comments across the program in order to provide an additional comparison point, the results are another opportunity for an instructor to gain feedback about his or her teaching and may serve as a talking point during instructor review meetings with the director of online programs or the department head.

Other Opportunities for Discussing Program Curriculum

There are several other less formal ways that we generate discussions about our online curriculum and teaching online among online instructors.

Create a Concept Map. We printed out the syllabi from all of the courses in the masters of applied statistics program and literally cut out the topics that were listed as being covered in each of these courses. With topics on small slips of paper we were able to mix these up on a table and then ask faculty members and instructors to answer the question, "How do all of these go together?" Groups of related topics appeared that were then transferred to concept-mapping software so that all of the linkages could be made explicit. It was then easier to ask questions, such as "What nodes of the concept map are covered in the course you teach?" "Where is there overlap?" "Are there any gaps in what should be covered?" This concept map made it relatively easy to address these questions and provided the program with another opportunity to talk about what we are doing and why.

Establish a Process for Course and Curriculum Review. Each semester a few courses are selected for a comprehensive review that involves an examination of all of the instructional aspects of the course. This review includes the course content, the approaches to content presentation, and the plan for interaction with students, and assessment. An instructional designer facilitates regular discussion throughout the semester between faculty members who are currently teaching the course or have recently taught the course and are assigned as reviewers. Ideally, one of these faculty members might also be teaching this same course in residence. At some point in the semester additional faculty are also assigned as outside reviewers. These faculty members look for gaps in the curriculum, topics that initially were to be covered in prerequisite courses or topics that extend into the courses that follow.

Recommendations about where these topics exist or should exist in the curriculum and the degree to which these links are supported are added to the recommendations for the course. These recommendations from the course reviewers and the outside reviewers are used to generate a list of development and revision tasks for the course content. Whenever possible, these tasks are implemented immediately. However, when the amount of revision required is beyond the usual expectation of teaching faculty, supplemental contracts for faculty development of these items are offered. In addition, a list of concepts, methods, and procedures are developed that articulate what a student must know or be able to do as a result of participating successfully in the course. Consequently, these concept lists become the basis of coverage for the problems that are given on the final exam. Involving a group of faculty and current instructors in generating these course changes lends coherence and promotes consistency throughout the curriculum.

Engage in Faculty Development Events. Throughout the academic year we either host or participate in events related to teaching and learning online beyond our online instructor meetings. These events cover everything from reviews of new technologies related to teaching and learning to topics of mutual concern related to quality of teaching and learning. The last three sessions included "Cheating in the Online Classroom," "Pushing Students to go Beyond without Shooting Yourself in the Foot," and "Getting to Know Piazza [the university's question-and-survey tool]." In general, our professional development focus over the past year has focused specifically on interaction between students and instructors. We then examined instructor performance on this topic using our midcourse survey. Results indicated that 81 percent of students responded "agree" or "strongly agree" to the statement: "The e-mail replies I have received from my instructor are of high quality and helpful," and 71 percent of students responded "agree" or "strongly agree" to the statement, "The activity and engagement between students and between students and the instructor in the course's online discussion forum(s) are of high quality and helpful" ($n = 186$).

The Stage Is Set

Having been engaged in thoughtful and ongoing discussions with their peers up to this point makes the peer review of teaching activity much more meaningful and worthwhile. And thus, it is against this backdrop of activities that we situate the activity of peer review of teaching. In essence, we have set the stage by building on an array of information-gathering activities that keep instructors continually involved in discussions about quality of online instruction and overall program goals. Furthermore, within our peer review of teaching process there are assignment decisions and support structures that are put into place to guide this process. Whereas in resident courses, you might watch a lesson, look at a syllabus, and write a snapshot assessment of what you saw, in an online classroom you can see so much more, from the content presented to the day-to-day interactions that occur online. Helping faculty members make sense of and evaluate the massive volume of information that is available in online learning environments is a necessary part of the peer review of teaching process and a big part of the reason why setting the stage in this manner is important.

Peer Review of Teaching: A Guided Process

The process begins with the director of online programs assigning instructors a course to review. There are many strategies the director uses in making these assignments. Instructors may be assigned to review another section of the same course they teach, a course that they have not taught but are interested in teaching, or a course that precedes or follows the one that they teach. In each of these scenarios, the idea is to motivate instructors to see connections between courses. Similarly, a weak instructor may be assigned to review a strong instructor, a good communicator assigned to review a good user of technologies, or resident faculty members may be invited to review an online course. All of these arrangements bring with them strategies that benefit the individual instructors being reviewed and the reviewers, plus the program in general.

Before a reviewer goes online to the assigned course to review, the instructor fills out and shares a short form that provides the reviewer with information about the course. This includes the locations where materials and interactions may be found as well as a place for instructors to add notes to highlight items that may be of interest to the reviewer or areas where they are looking for suggestions.

With input from the instructor the reviewer begins a note-taking stage using a version of the "Peer Review Guide for Online Courses at Penn State" document that has been adapted to meet the needs of the Department of Statistics online courses. This guides instructors through the review process. Initially, there is a short checklist that targets "Penn State's Quality Standards for Online Learning" in which the reviewer checks for evidence of consistent navigation, a proper syllabus, and other items that would help flag basic deficiencies within an online course. Beyond this, the bulk of the "Peer Review Guide for Online Courses at Penn State" is structured to feature the "Seven Principles for Good Practice in Undergraduate Education" (Chickering & Gamson, 1987), a summary of fifty years of higher education research that addresses good teaching and learning practices. Several of these principles have been topics of discussion in activities that led up to the peer review and during the review. Using the document that has a page devoted to each principle, the reviewers can add comments where appropriate. To assist the reviewer, possible course locations are suggested in the document about where to find material related to each principle.

On completion of this note-taking stage, both the peer reviewer and the course instructor find a time to discuss the instructor's involvement in the course using the notes from the "Peer Review Guide for Online Courses at Penn State" as the basis for this conversation. Most agree that this conversation is the most beneficial stage of the process because it is at this time that topics of interest emerge and are discussed between the paired colleagues.

Additional questions are asked, suggestions made, and advice is given. The peer reviewer summarizes this conversation in a single document that, along with a copy of the completed "Peer Review Guide for Online Courses at Penn State" form, is submitted to the director of online programs.

A Simple Conclusion

Peer review is one component of a comprehensive program to help faculty members enhance their understanding of teaching and learning. Our goal is to ensure that peer review of teaching does not take place in isolation. We have been intentional in making sure that there are ample opportunities for instructors to be immersed in activities and discussions that focus on the quality online teaching. And, through this increased level of engagement within this richer context about teaching and learning online, it is our hope that the peer review of teaching experience builds and capitalizes on the continued professional development of our instructional faculty and the quality of our online program before, during, and after the peer review of teaching. In coming full circle, our peer review process has provided our instructors with a rich source of topics for future investigation. The ideas and strategies that have been generated out of our peer review conversations often serve as the grounds for implementing changes in what we do.

Source: Johnson, Rosenberger, & Chow (2014). Reprinted with permission.

A Thought Exercise

Chapter 10 is, by itself, one big thought exercise. Project planning goes most smoothly when obstacles are envisioned and planned for. Even though we cannot predict every roadblock, doing a premortem exercise can be instructive.

Imagine the following scenario: it is five years in the future, and, with your guidance and input, your campus has implemented an evaluation program for online teaching. The program is a failure.

Write for about fifteen minutes about why the program failed. Do not limit yourself to any causes. Ask questions such as the following (and come up with your own, as well):

- What technological concerns caused the program to fail?
- Who was needed for the program but was not involved (or actively worked against it)?

- What factors outside your control caused problems to arise?
- What rare long-shot occurrence could have caused things to go wrong?

Once you have a sufficient list of what-ifs, turn the questions around. Rank the possible causes of failure according to two factors: how likely it is to occur (e.g., needed people not involved is pretty likely but an extended power outage is rarer) and how much control your campus has over the inputs to the failure (e.g., backup power for technology is within the scope of most IT departments but a faculty strike is not). Encourage your colleagues to perform similar premortem predictions as well. Line up those possible problems that are both more likely to happen and are within your scope of control and use those as springboards for conversation at your institution that will help you and your colleagues to think through the planning process with open eyes.

CHAPTER ELEVEN

THE ONLINE-TEACHING EVALUATION LIFE CYCLE

B. Jean Mandernach's Story

During a department committee meeting to consider faculty applications for promotion, a debate emerged concerning the role of online teaching within a faculty member's academic portfolio. On one side of the debate was the belief that the online teaching experience—and its resultant artifacts of effectiveness—should be given equal weight to other teaching indicators. On the other side was the argument that the role of online teaching was not sufficiently established within the university to weigh equally into promotion recommendations.

As the debate continued, several pertinent issues arose:

- Most faculty members were not hired explicitly to teach in an online format; thus, evaluations focused on this role may not align with the scope of their job requirements.
- Promotion and tenure guidelines were developed and worded in a manner geared toward traditional face-to-face instruction.
- Faculty members received minimal guidance or training on effective online pedagogy so it may be unfair to evaluate their performance in the online classroom.

- The university lacked clear expectations for online teaching; thus, determining effectiveness in a reliable fashion from one promotion application to the next proved challenging.

Although all committee members acknowledged these challenges, many felt that it was unfair not to consider the quality work that individual faculty members had contributed to the online programs. Despite wanting to give credit in the promotion decision to faculty members who had done well in the online classroom, the committee was unsure of what to do when evidence suggested that a faculty member was not effective in the online environment. Compounding the debate even further was a recognition that not all faculty members were engaging in online teaching, so there were concerns about penalizing faculty members who had unsuccessfully attempted to teach online—but not penalizing faculty members who had avoided this challenge altogether.

Central to the issue was concern over how to handle inconsistent indicators of teaching effectiveness. If a faculty member showed clear evidence of teaching effectiveness both online and face-to-face, then committee support was unanimous. Likewise, if a faculty member was unable to show teaching effectiveness in either instructional format, the committee's recommendation was clear. The debate rested in how to respond to inconsistent indicators. How do you evaluate faculty members for promotion if they are effective in one mode of teaching but not the other?

More troubling yet, there seemed to be inconsistencies in the perceived value, role, and worth of each mode of teaching. The majority of the committee felt that if an instructor was effective in the face-to-face classroom but not in an online environment, then that individual should not be penalized for his or her lack of online-teaching effectiveness; rather, that instructor simply should not teach future courses online. But, if a faculty member was a good online instructor and a poor face-to-face instructor, there was concern about recommending promotion and continuation at the university.

Although the committee members were aware of the inconsistencies in their logic, continued discussion was unable to resolve the dissonance. Without standards, expectations, and support for online teaching that were equivalent to the associated dimensions for the face-to-face classroom, they lacked the necessary structure to make an informed decision.

Integration of Evaluation

Inherent in the challenges discussed in the opening scenario is a discrepancy in the extent that each mode of teaching is integrated within the institutional structure. Although face-to-face teaching has an established history, the role of online teaching is often less clear. Creating an evaluation system to gauge the effectiveness of online instruction is a laudable first step, but for the evaluation to be valid and sustainable, the expectations and standards underlying the process need to be aligned with the larger hiring, training, professional development, and decision-making processes. To begin integrating the online evaluation within the larger institutional structure, consider the following questions.

What is the institutional structure that oversees the hiring and evaluation of faculty teaching online?

One of the challenges with the evaluation of online teaching is that online education may—or may not—be organized, structured, and managed differently than face-to-face teaching. There are two primary institutional approaches for overseeing online education: departmental or centralized. In a structure with departmental authority, the hiring and evaluation of faculty members (whether teaching online or face-to-face) is under the sole discretion of the academic department. In institutions with a centralized online learning administrative unit, faculty members who teach strictly online may be hired and evaluated by the centralized administrative unit. Complicating the issue further, there are various combinations of oversight in which one of the following could occur:

- A centralized administrative unit makes recommendations to the department for final authority.
- The department makes recommendations to the centralized administrative unit for final authority.
- The department hires all faculty members, but the centralized administrative unit is responsible for evaluation.
- Hiring is conducted solely by either the department or a centralized administrative unit, but both provide evaluations for faculty members teaching online.
- Some other combination of shared oversight and decision making is done.

Regardless of your institutional structure, you will need to examine the extent to which the qualifications and expectations used to hire faculty members to teach online align with the components of the online teaching evaluation. For example, the following sections highlight skill sets necessary for effective online teaching.

Sample Job Description for Faculty Members Teaching Online

Essential duties and responsibilities include the following:

- Stimulating asynchronous class discussions via regular engagement in the online classroom
- Providing substantive one-to-one and one-to-many feedback to foster student learning
- Teaching material from approved curriculum in accordance with assigned schedule to ensure student satisfaction
- Providing regular and timely feedback to students via the LMS
- Assisting students in achieving completion of objectives and learning outcomes; responding to all student inquiries within forty-eight hours
- Proactively advising students in matters related to academics, attendance, and behaviors
- Motivating students to actively participate in all aspect of the educational process; demonstrating active engagement in the online classroom
- Maintaining and reporting student grades and attendance in accordance with university policies

Requirements:

- Qualified candidates must have a terminal degree in a related field from a regionally accredited college or university.
- Experience teaching using an online platform and asynchronous simulation-based teaching or experience with other experientially based, innovative teaching techniques is highly desirable.
- Skills such as outstanding written communication skills, excellent motivational and instructional skills, and ability to facilitate diverse groups are needed.

Guidelines for Selecting an Instructor for an Online Course

Similar to a course that is taught in a traditional classroom environment, the online instructor is responsible for providing an educational atmosphere in which students have the opportunity to achieve academic success in accordance with university, college, and departmental policies. Teaching in an online environment, however, can be considerably different in nature than teaching face-to-face. Most important, course content is typically developed in advance of the course's start date. In effect, the lecturing has already been done. This leaves the role of the online instructor to shift focus from the sage on the stage to the guide on the side.

Similar to instructors who teach in the face-to-face classroom, online instructors are expected to be highly knowledgeable about the subject matter for the specific course that she or he is assigned to teach and to maintain expertise in the subject area. When selecting an online instructor, one should also consider faculty members who they feel would thrive in the online classroom.

Online instructors should demonstrate mastery of the following characteristics within the context of the online classroom environment:

- Being aware of the unique learning needs and situations of both traditional age and adult learners, providing an educational experience that is appropriate for both
- Demonstrating sensitivity to disabilities and diversities including aspects of cultural, cognitive, emotional, and physical differences
- Attending to the unique challenges of distance learning in which learners are separated by time and geographic proximity and interactions are primarily asynchronous in nature
- Promoting and encouraging a learning environment that is safe, inviting, and mutually respectful
- Supporting student success by promoting active and frequent dialogue and interaction among all members of the class
- Possessing excellent written and verbal skills (requesting writing samples is highly recommended)
- Managing time efficiently while handling a continuous workflow that includes responding to student inquiries and providing feedback on student work in a timely manner
- Monitoring each student's progress toward course goals through active tracking, providing mediation and direction as needed
- Attending to student feedback and making adjustments to teaching style and course expectations when necessary
- Effectively mediating course-related student conflicts
- Being comfortable and competent with computer-based technology, including having mastery of basic computer operations and the teaching and administrative aspects of the course's LMS

As part of the hiring process, one may want to consider requesting a portfolio of an individual's work to provide evidence of these competencies. These items could also serve well as the basis for interview questions. In addition, it may be helpful to the interviewee to see copies of any contractual agreements that would ultimately govern the position as well as examples of the type and quality of courses that they would be expected to teach (Penn State Online Faculty Engagement Subcommittee, 2011).

If both hiring and evaluation are conducted by the same institutional unit, it is important to ensure that job descriptions and hiring guidelines are aligned with outcome expectations. If hiring and evaluation are conducted by separate institutional units, it is essential that all stakeholders coordinate to discuss—and agree on—the dimensions used for both processes.

What faculty population is primarily responsible for teaching online courses?

The issue of hiring and evaluating becomes even more complicated when you factor in the primary role of faculty teaching online. Depending on the institutional structure, online courses may be as diverse as the following:

- Supplemental or add-ons to traditional campus programs
- A component of an independent online program operating in tandem with the campus-based curriculum
- The sole program mode for that department

As a function of these various structures, faculty members who teach online courses may belong to one of these groups:

- Full-time campus faculty teaching both online and face-to-face courses
- Full-time campus faculty teaching only online courses
- Full-time remote faculty teaching only online courses
- Contingent faculty teaching only online courses

Although evaluation standards for effective online teaching should not vary as a function of a faculty member's role within the university, it is important to consider how online teaching fits within other expectations for faculty performance. If a faculty member's sole obligation is teaching online, then institutions may want to prioritize hiring individuals with established credentials in online education. But, if online teaching is only a portion of a faculty member's role, then it may be more important to prioritize other credentials in the hiring process and invest additional resources to train faculty members in online pedagogy.

In addition, depending on the institutional structure, there may be different oversight for faculty members teaching online as a function of whether they are full-time or contingent. In large online programs, there is increased reliance on contingent faculty members to teach online course offerings; as such, it is more likely that the hiring and evaluation of contingent faculty members is conducted by a centralized administrative unit, whereas full-time faculty members, regardless of program size, may be more likely to be hired and evaluated by the academic department. Although there is no overarching preference for either mode of oversight, it is essential that hiring and evaluating online teaching is done as a coordinated process that takes into consideration the institutional structure and the role of individual faculty members.

Who is responsible for training faculty to teach online?

Regardless of whether online teaching is the purview of the department or of a centralized administrative unit, faculty training is typically conducted as a centralized process. Not only is centralized faculty training an efficient means of preparing faculty members to teach online but also it ensures that all faculty members are uniformly exposed to consistent information about best practices, standards, and expectations.

Following principles of backward design, faculty training materials should be based on the standards set forth in the evaluation of online teaching. Once an institution has an agreed-on process for evaluating online instruction, training materials should be developed or revised to align with each component of the evaluation. Likewise, in the initial training process, faculty members should be provided with all evaluation tools so that they are clearly aware of expectations for performance and best practice standards for online teaching.

For some faculty members, the training they receive prior to teaching online may be their only exposure to online education. Thus, it is essential that training designed to prepare faculty members to teach online goes beyond instruction on how to use the LMS to provide guidance on best practices in online pedagogy. The next section will provide a sample of topics that you may want to include in a faculty training for online teaching. Institutions will also need to determine whether or not faculty members should be required to participate in formal training prior to teaching online or whether training is an optional resource used at the discretion of each faculty member (Bates, 2014).

Outline for Faculty Training for Initial Online Teaching Experience: Northeastern Illinois University

The online teaching course is a forty-hour noncredit training course designed to provide faculty with the basic tools, techniques, and theories needed to be able to create and conduct online courses. On completion of this four-week online course, faculty members are certified as by the NEIU Center for Teaching and Learning (CTL) to teach online courses. Course topics include the following:

- Building learning communities
- Distance-education models
- Online learning theory and learner profiles
- Interactivity and collaboration
- Online instructional design
- Media selection
- Online facilitation, assessment, and evaluation
- Asynchronous and synchronous tools
- Online-course syllabus development
- Effective course-management techniques. (Center for Teaching and Learning, Northeastern Illinois University, 2014)

Who is responsible for faculty development in online pedagogy?

In some institutions, faculty development and training are coordinated by a single department; in others, training and development are independent initiatives. Likewise, faculty development may be supported by a centralized department handling faculty development for all modes of teaching (face-to-face and online) or faculty development specific to online instruction may be supported by the distance education administrative unit. Whichever approach is used, it is essential to ensure that faculty training and development are coordinated efforts that align with evaluation standards and that follow up processes are in place to gauge effectiveness of faculty development initiatives. Research (Ebert-May, Derting, Hodder, Momsen, Long, & Jardeleza, 2011) finds that 89 percent of faculty members attending a faculty development event indicated their intent to adopt techniques learned, yet observers noted only 25 percent of faculty members actually did (and, worse, 20 percent thought they had implemented the technique but hadn't).

In addition, it is important that ongoing faculty development is an integral component of the overall evaluation process. Rather than viewing faculty development initiatives as isolated events offered as optional activities for interested faculty members, faculty development programming should be developed in response to challenges and issues that arise in the evaluation of online teaching. In this type of coordinated approach, instructors that do not perform at the standards outlined in the online teaching evaluation should be directed to the relevant faculty development resources that address their specific needs.

Not only should the focus of faculty development resources be aligned with the evaluation of online teaching but also the scheduling and format of faculty development initiatives targeting online pedagogy needs to be uniquely relevant to those working in the online classroom. Recognizing that online teaching is often performed by remote or contingent faculty members, it is essential that the university provide options for faculty development programming in an asynchronous format that is amenable to a range of schedules. Citing scheduling as one of the key barriers preventing participation in professional development activities, research finds that online contingent instructors prefer independent, static, multimedia resources over other forms of professional development (Dailey-Hebert, Mandernach, Donnelli-Sallee, & Norris, 2014). See Table 11.1 for a ranking of the initiatives most desired by contingent faculty members teaching online.

TABLE 11.1. ONLINE ADJUNCT FACULTY MEMBERS' PREFERENCE FOR FACULTY DEVELOPMENT INITIATIVES

Rank	Faculty Development Initiative
1	Self-paced online modules (short courses) with lectures and interactive components but no threaded discussions
2	Static best practices examples
3	Static multimedia presentations
4	Archived recordings of webinars
5 (tie)	Moderated threaded discussions you can participate in over a specified time period
5 (tie)	Facilitator-led, asynchronous online modules with lectures, interactive components, and threaded discussions for a cohort of faculty
5 (tie)	Static web pages
6	Individual consultations on teaching via e-mail or online communication
7	Static white papers
8	Moderated threaded discussions that are open with no specified beginning or ending time period
9	Peer review of teaching materials via e-mail or online communication
10	Live webinars
11	Individual consultations on teaching via live interaction
12	Videoconferencing seminars
13	Peer review of teaching via observation
14	Conference calls with multiple participants
15	Virtual assistants (i.e., avatar-led webquests)
16	Live chat sessions
17	Professional communities networked via Facebook, LinkedIn, and so on
18	Archived recordings of chats

Source: Dailey-Hebert, Mandernach, Donnelli-Sallee, & Norris (2014, p. 81).

Topic Ideas for Faculty Development in Online Teaching

Although initial training to teach online should provide a basic overview of the essential knowledge and skills necessary to be effective in the online classroom, there is a wide range of topics that can support enhanced pedagogical strategies for those with more experience in the online classroom. Possible topics for ongoing faculty development related to online teaching include the following.

Enhanced Pedagogical Strategies

- Promoting critical thinking via online discussions
- Questioning strategies to foster an engaged discussion
- Integrating announcements to foster student engagement
- Creating tips for getting more from your online discussions
- Generating strategies to increase student satisfaction

Web 2.0 Tools

- Creating course overviews using Screencast-o-Matic
- Using Jing to create a syllabus overview
- Using more than text: using EyeJots for asynchronous video discussions
- Creating visual summaries with Wordle
- Personalizing your introduction via Animoto

Personalizing the Online Learning Experience

- Connecting with your students via video
- Making the most out of the micro-lecture
- Using strategies to personalize the online classroom
- Gathering tips for connecting with your students
- Using one-to-many instructional strategies

Feedback and Grading

- Learning how to create and use feedback banks
- Providing automated feedback
- Using one-on-one versus one-on-many feedback strategies
- Integrating feed-forward strategies in the online classroom
- Using audio and video feedback

Managing Work-Life Balance

- Teaching more in less time
- Managing the ubiquity of the online classroom
- Creating a teaching schedule
- Learning how to use discussion boards more efficiently
- Coming up with strategies for maximizing time investment in the online classroom
- Maximizing your time and resources in the online classroom

Resources to Enhance the Online Classroom

- Offering tips for teaching with YouTube
- Integrating TedTalks in the online classroom
- Finding multimedia with MERLOT
- Finding resources on MindGate media

The Life Cycle of Evaluation of Online Teaching

Many begin the process of developing an evaluation of online teaching with an isolated focus on the tool or rubric that will be used to conduct the evaluation. But development of the evaluation instrument is not the end of the process; it is the beginning. With an ultimate goal of ensuring that students receive a high-quality online learning experience, the evaluation is just a checkpoint to monitor progress toward this larger goal.

For the evaluation process to successfully support effective online teaching and learning, it is essential that evaluation is integrated with associated services and processes. You not only need to assess online teaching effectiveness but also you need to use the information from the evaluation to foster better teaching. This cyclical process mandates ongoing collaboration among all stakeholders involved with online course offerings.

To integrate the evaluation of online teaching with associated institutional processes, you should start with the end goal—the evaluation—and work backward. Figure 11.1 shows the cyclical nature of this process. The evaluation of online teaching is based on the core competencies that underlie effective online learning. From this, you operationalize the

FIGURE 11.1. THE ONLINE-TEACHING EVALUATION LIFE CYCLE

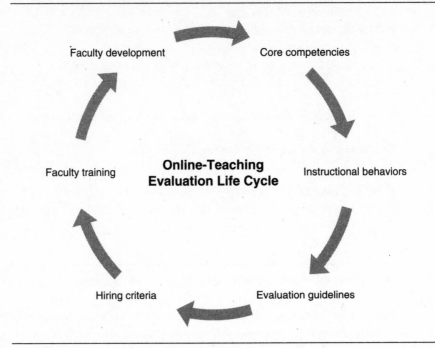

core competencies into measurable instructional behavior and develop guidelines to gauge effective teaching in the online classroom. Once the evaluation instrument is complete, you are able to identify essential teaching characteristics and criteria to drive hiring decisions. Likewise, faculty training and development programming should target the same set of core competencies to foster enhanced teaching.

Each of the following dimensions should be continuously reviewed and revised in relation to one another:

Core competencies. Ongoing research continues to explore best practices and essential instructor competencies that support effective online education. As technology and our understanding of its impact on student learning evolves, research is likely to uncover new competencies that facilitate the online learning experience. It is essential to monitor research to ensure that institutional expectations are current, relevant, and aligned with research findings.

Instructional behaviors. Core competencies must then be operationalized to highlight the range of instructor behaviors that support each goal. For example, research highlights teaching presence as a core competency that effectively supports online learning. Teaching presence can be achieved via a number of instructional strategies including (but not limited to) the following:

- Posting announcements in the online classroom to guide learning
- Regular and frequent participation in the online discussion forums
- Timely posting of feedback to students
- Inclusion of multimedia to personalize the learning experience

Each institution must articulate its expectations for how faculty members will demonstrate effective teaching in relation to the selected competencies.

Evaluation guidelines. Once the competencies and instructional behaviors have been identified, the guidelines for evaluating faculty member performance can be developed. Evaluation guidelines will specify how each expectation will be assessed and the dimensions of the evaluation process. For example, the instructional strategy of "regular and frequent participation in the online discussion forum" can be evaluated in a number of different ways.

- Dichotomous criteria:
  - Instructor participated in the online discussion forum with a minimum of ten posts per discussion question. (yes/no)
  - Instructor participated in the online discussion forum on a minimum of four days per week. (yes/no)
  - Instructor's posts in the discussion forum stimulated ongoing discussion. (yes/no)
- Polytomous criteria:
  - Instructor participated in the discussion forum: (a) less than 3 posts; (b) 4–6 posts; (c) 7–9 posts; (d) 10+ posts
  - Instructor participated in the discussion forum: (a) not at all; (b) 1 day; (c) 2–3 days; (d) 4+ days
- Rating scale:
  - Instructor's posts in the discussion forum stimulated ongoing discussion. (1=strongly disagree; 2=disagree; 3=neutral; 4=agree; 5=strongly agree)

- Instructor's posts in the discussion forum fostered a sense of instructor presence. (1=strongly disagree; 2=disagree; 3=neutral; 4=agree; 5=strongly agree)
- Qualitative evaluation:
  - What did the instructor do in the discussion forums to establish instructor presence?
  - The selection of evaluation strategies must be done in relation to the practical considerations (i.e., staffing, resources, funding, use of data, expertise of evaluators, etc.) that underlie implementation of the evaluation process. As the institution evolves and the practical considerations change, it is important to revisit the evaluation guidelines. Likewise, evaluation guidelines must be continually updated to reflect changes in institutional adoption of core competencies and associated instructional behaviors.

Hiring criteria. The identification of the core competencies and associated instructional behaviors can then be used to determine the faculty skills, abilities, and background to be included in the hiring criteria for those teaching online. Once the institution selects and prioritizes their core competencies, faculty applicants can provide evidence of expertise or experience in relation to each dimension.

Faculty training. Although some components of a program to prepare faculty to teach online will include issues related to the LMS and institutional context, it is essential to also include training materials directly related to each dimension of the online teaching evaluation system.

Faculty development. Faculty development initiatives should be planned, conducted, and used as an integrated component of the evaluation process. The evaluation dimensions should provide the impetus for programming topics; and faculty members who are not performing at satisfactory levels (as indicated by the evaluation of online teaching) should be referred to faculty development programming to foster their online teaching skills.

To support and sustain quality online teaching, it is essential that instructional expectations, evaluation guidelines, hiring criteria, faculty training, and faculty development are all aligned to support the same core competencies. Equally important is an awareness that the evaluation of online teaching life cycle is a dynamic process. As research continues to explore online pedagogy, we are likely to gain new insights into competencies and instructional strategies that are effective in the online classroom.

The evaluation life cycle must be monitored and updated to ensure its continued relevance in supporting online teaching and learning.

Conclusion

As indicated by the challenges shared at the beginning of this chapter, without an integrated understanding of the value and utility of online teaching evaluations, it is difficult—if not impossible—to use the resultant data in a meaningful fashion. For online teaching evaluations to effectively foster quality student learning, it is imperative that they are not conducted as stand-alone events used in isolation to assess faculty performance. Online teaching evaluations must be couched within a larger system that identifies and supports effective online teaching. From the initial hiring of faculty members through training, evaluation of effectiveness, and necessary follow-up remediation, the evaluation becomes a component of a cohesive system that simultaneously assesses and fosters instructional behaviors that have an impact on student learning experience in the online classroom.

A Thought Exercise

Review your responses to the thought exercises from the earlier chapters of this book in which you identified the goals for the online-teaching evaluation program on your campus. Chances are pretty good that you did not include hiring criteria, faculty training, and professional development in those earlier exercises.

Take a few minutes and predict how your campus would create its own version of the life cycle loop proposed in this chapter. Many institutions, for example, have clear visions of what competencies they wish their faculty members to demonstrate (see Varvel, 2007).

Write down the people on your campus who are responsible for the major areas of the online-teaching evaluation life cycle:

- **Teaching competencies.** What background skills do good teachers possess?
- **Instructional behaviors.** What do good online teachers do when interacting with students?

- **Evaluation guidelines.** Who decides how faculty members are evaluated?
- **Hiring criteria.** Who has input into the design of job descriptions so they reflect good online-teaching requirements?
- **Faculty training.** Who shows faculty members how to use the technology and productivity tools available on your campus?
- **Faculty development.** Who teaches faculty members about teaching techniques and theories?

How much overlap is there among the people and offices at your institution who perform these functions? Do they currently communicate regularly? Try to identify opportunities to bring some new stakeholders into the conversation on your campus.

CHAPTER TWELVE

NEXT STEPS

The conclusions we offer in this book bring us largely full circle, as the SCARF loop model predicts. We began by asking what is special or different about teaching online. Reassuringly, the differences appear in the methods used by online teachers. By becoming more familiar with best practices in online teaching, evaluators can map specific practices back to the teaching behaviors that all good instructional situations have in common. Using the existing models provided in the companion website (www.wiley.com/go/tobin) for this book, readers can use the following six-step process in order to build a campus program for evaluating online teaching.

Step 1: Establish Context

One of the greatest challenges for institutions when introducing new methods and practices is to achieve transparency. A transparent change is one in which all affected stakeholders feel that three critical elements have been obtained:

- They have had enough time to examine the change in advance.
- The scope of the change can be understood and its effects predicted.
- The stewards of the change listen to and adapt the implementation based on stakeholder feedback.

Especially when introducing changes to the method, frequency, and criteria used to evaluate teaching practices, it is important to form a widely representative committee, identify all stakeholder groups, open a dialogue about the changes well in advance, define the changes with stakeholder input, listen to (and address) obstacles, measure the impact of the implementation, and anticipate various phases of adoption or resistance.

Before any of these elements can be implemented, however, establish the context in which the evaluation program will operate. One of the most important contextual elements is what part of the institution will drive the program.

- **Administration driven.** Institutions in the for-profit and nonunionized categories typically adopt changes based on direction from the central administration of the institution. Such institutions need to focus on strong communication plans and strong stakeholder-identification processes in order to ensure that everyone on campus knows about and has input into the evaluation program.
- **Faculty driven.** Unionized institutions and those with a strong shared-governance model typically have a faculty-driven context for campus changes. Adoption of online-teaching evaluation on such campuses requires careful identification of faculty thought leaders who will champion the process.

Other contextual areas to define include institution size, student demographics, faculty demographics, and expected size and growth of online teaching. These details will feed into the next step, establishing foundations for the program.

Step 2: Establish Foundations

Foundational elements of the online-teaching evaluation program include knowing whether departments or a central unit oversee the evaluation process, whether course design is performed by the same people who teach courses (it often isn't), stating an overall purpose for evaluation, and identifying the broadly defined sources of data to be used in the evaluation process. Also, consider the "three I" foundations: institution, implementation, and impact.

Institutional considerations. How do institutional considerations and factors affect the evaluation process?

- What are the current attitudes and opinions surrounding online education at your institution?
- How will your organizational structure affect the evaluation process?
- What is the role of faculty governance in approving evaluation systems?
- To what extent will funding influence evaluation decisions?
- What institutional, organizational, or programmatic barriers do you face in designing or implementing an evaluation structure?

Implementation considerations. What are the key considerations in implementing an evaluation process for online teaching?

- Who will be responsible for conducting evaluations?
- Will evaluation stakeholders have relevant expertise in online learning?
- What dimensions (teaching, course design, other) will be included in the evaluation process?
- Who will be the target of evaluation (contingent, full-time)?
- How frequently will evaluations be conducted?
- What data are included or collected via the existing evaluation process? What additional data will be needed?

Impact considerations. How will data from the evaluation of online teaching be used?

- How will you balance the use of student, peer, and supervisor evaluation data?
- How will the timing of evaluations affect the value of the information provided?
- Will evaluation data be a component of hiring, promotion, or continuance decisions?
- Will evaluations of online teaching be separated from generalized evaluations of teaching?
- To what extent will evaluation of online teaching be separated from evaluation of course design?

Closely examine core teaching competencies. It is easy to focus the evaluating of online teaching directly on the tools within an institution's LMS and build evaluation processes based on faculty members' use of those tools. After all, most of these systems can generate nice, neat data sets that report things such as number of log-ins and duration of page visits. Instead, we prefer to match online-teaching methods and tool use to their corresponding categories of good teaching practice. See Varvel (2007) for a comprehensive list of online teaching competencies.

For instance, in examining faculty member interactions in asynchronous course discussions, whether faculty members use the course management system tool or some other means of communicating (such as wiki updating or voice-recording threads), we prefer to evaluate the interactions based on the quality, timeliness, and breadth of faculty members' participation. In the context of Chickering and Gamson's seven principles, doing so enables us to evaluate how well the instructor "encourages contact between students and faculty," "develops reciprocity and cooperation among students," "encourages active learning," "communicates high expectations," or even "respects diverse talents and ways of learning" in a way that is not possible with nice, neat LMS reports.

Open a dialogue about changes. Identify potential stakeholder groups and work with them to craft a results-based statement of proposed changes. By focusing on results, administrators effectively state the case backward in order to show the reason for adopting the proposed changes.

For example, for an institution adopting online electronic student surveys at midterm (in addition to the student surveys performed at the end of the semester), such a statement might read like this draft, proposed recently at Northeastern Illinois University:

> In order to show students that faculty are responsive to student feedback during the semester, and in order to help increase student satisfaction and faculty members' end-of-term student-survey scores, the university proposes adopting "information only" mid-term electronic surveys.
>
> The results of mid-term e-surveys would be reported only to the individual faculty member, and would not be used for promotion-and-tenure purposes. Studies show that faculty who demonstrate direct responses to student feedback during the semester receive higher end-of-semester rating scores.
>
> The university community is invited to examine the proposed 6-question mid-term survey instrument at (www.wiley.com/go/tobin) until the end of the month—your feedback on it is important and will be used to tailor the tool to the needs of the university.

Enabling conversation to happen within the scope of the proposed change is important for creating formative and summative processes to support the end goals of the evaluation program.

Step 3: Design Formative Processes

It is a best practice to design formative evaluation processes first. Because formative evaluations are aimed at the improvement of teaching, and because they are not tied to employment decisions such as hiring, retention, tenure, and promotion, stakeholders are more likely to try out different approaches, create broad goal statements, and experiment with various instruments and methods: all good experiences in preparation for designing summative processes afterward. To create formative processes, use the SCARF design model and create self-review, peer-review, and student-feedback systems.

By adopting the **S**olicit, **C**ollect data, **A**djust, and **R**eturn **F**eedback design model for the creation of all of your institution's formative evaluation processes, you help to ensure that the various groups on campus who will take part in the implementation have a say in the development of the instruments and methods to be used.

- For formative peer reviews, ensure that the process and instruments are focused on observable behaviors, offer opportunities for "here's how I did it" feedback, and elicit actionable steps for behavioral changes.
- The design of self-review instruments should largely mirror the peer-review instrument, with elements that ask instructors to think through the effectiveness of their online teaching behaviors.
- Formative student feedback differs markedly from the typical end-of-semester student rating scheme. Design instruments ask for student opinions throughout the course period about course pace, instructor presence, and communication, and issues that are confusing or unclear to the learners.

Step 4: Design Summative Processes

When designing summative processes and instruments, keep in mind that they should all be measurable, repeatable, and there should be multiple sources of data used in order to make employment-related decisions. This is as needed for disciplinary decisions as for deciding who gets the online-teaching award. Include at least student ratings of online teaching effectiveness, administrative evaluation of online teaching, and analytic data (when possible). Student ratings of online teaching are best designed by considering what students are qualified to rate, as we have seen in chapter 5:

- Course organization and structure
- Communication skills
- Teacher-student interactions
- Course difficulty and student workload
- Assessments and grading
- Student learning

Administrative evaluation should consider the possible administrative biases toward face-to-face teaching methods: the belief that good teaching is embodied, intuitive, happens in real time, and appears effortless. Consider how much of the online environment to observe, how long to spend in the observation, and what elements of online teaching are available to observers that might not be available to face-to-face observers. Define what assistance observers can have, such as technical staff to drive the computer used for the observation.

Use analytic data only when they provide information that cannot be obtained in other ways, such as instructor time spent in discussion areas of the LMS. Ensure that the analytic data measure behaviors that must take place in the system being logged (e.g., time in online classroom, number of discussion posts, length of discussion posts, length of feedback, timeliness of feedback, number and nature of announcements, and patterns of classroom interaction). For instance, time spent reading student work cannot be measured via an analytic report from an LMS because instructors do not uniformly read student work in the LMS. Many, if not most, online teachers download student files for reading and comment offline. A final word about analytics can help online and face-to-face evaluations: analysis of student completion and persistence is a useful and valid indicator of instructional quality when corroborated by other metrics.

Step 5: Create a Holistic Campus Plan

Decide how to make program decisions. Pay attention to the impact that learning online has on learners and on faculty members. Although the "no significant difference" movement has demonstrated that online courses are on the whole as effective as face-to-face courses, we should pay attention to the changes in teaching approach, methods, and execution that online teaching necessitate. Just as our online students receive a very different experience of the class, program, and campus when they are online learners, our faculty members also perceive their roles in those structures differently when they are teaching online. Readers who implement campus-wide evaluation programs for their institutions have an opportunity to track both the performance-based and perceived differences between face-to-face and online iterations of courses and programs.

Decide how to use the results (and which results to use). Online teaching enables greater granularity of recorded data for both formative and summative decisions, and online-teaching evaluation requires significant effort to do well. The greater availability of recorded data about online teaching is useful only if there is a commensurate increase in the time and effort spent in decoding, summarizing, and evaluating the digital trail left by online teaching interactions. The definition of "faculty work" should be broadened to recognize the amount of time and effort that peers will need to put into the evaluation process in order to come up with meaningful and actionable results. In a recent *New Yorker* article, Schulz (2014) interviewed the director of the Centers for Disease Control and Prevention (CDC), an institution that relies in life-and-death ways on the comprehensiveness of its data collection and the efficiency of its evaluation methods:

> There is an inherent trade-off to adding more fields to any form. Thomas Frieden, the director of the CDC, puts it concisely: "The quality of the data you collect is inversely proportional to the amount of data you collect from each reporter." (Schulz, 2014, p. 37)

One area where future researchers can productively focus is the extent to which observing more kinds of teaching evidence (and observing more units within each kind) may be counterproductive. One intuits that there is a limit beyond which more data points merely reinforce already-observed patterns, rather than add meaningful information to the evaluation process.

Plan for the rollout and adoption of evaluation processes and practices. Draft a plan for which online courses will be evaluated and in what fashion. For example, the following scheme can align with an institution's existing policies related to face-to-face course teaching:

- All courses being offered for the first time online must be evaluated via student ratings, peer review, and self-review (for formative data collection only—no summative evaluation is performed for the initial online offering).

- Second offerings of new online courses must be evaluated via self, peer, and administrative review for summative decision-making purposes.
- All online courses taught by contingent faculty members must employ student ratings every time they are offered and undergo administrative review at least once every two years.
- All online courses taught by tenure-track faculty members must employ student ratings at least once every three years.

The suggestion to evaluate the first semester of online delivery as a formative-only process enables faculty members to have a low-consequences opportunity to teach a course, receive feedback, and retool their teaching behaviors before they are observed for summative decision making.

The other part of the time equation is to set expectations for how long self, peer, and administrative evaluation processes should take. Which elements within the course management environment are to be observed? How many and how often?

Step 6: Implement and Cycle the Program

Use a small-steps approach. The core takeaway about implementing a new evaluation process for online teaching is to follow a phased approach. By creating a core committee, assessing stakeholders, opening communication, setting the scope, and then measuring and adapting as the new strategy is rolled out, one stands a much better chance of gaining buy in and quicker adoption from faculty members, students, and administrators. A large part of gaining widespread adoption of online-teaching evaluation methods is simply opening the process and demonstrating that the goals are useful, clear, and well-defined.

Listen to (and address) barriers. As the conversation continues, administrators will likely compile a list of possible objections and obstacles. Some examples to anticipate include those in Patrick's "Six Layers of Resistance to Change" (2010):

- *Layer 1: We don't agree on the problem.* Identification and confirmation of the current constraint is needed.
- *Layer 2: We don't agree on a direction for a solution.* A breakthrough idea is needed for dealing with the root cause of identified symptoms.
- *Layer 3: We don't have an effective solution.* Clear vision is needed of the system-wide solution, its desired outcomes, and its implications.

- *Layer 4: "Yes, but" (reservations about undesirable side effects).* Identification and consideration are needed regarding concerns, reservations, and risks that may be encountered in implementing the proposed solution.
- *Layer 5: We can't do it because* … Planning is needed to overcome obstacles to implementing the solution.
- *Layer 6: Unverbalized fear.* Comprehensive change management is needed to create personal buy in of all key players. (Patrick, 2010, italics added)

Remember, too, that potential obstacles can also be individuals; make time to identify and talk with the naysayers and ask open-ended questions about how they might help to achieve the desired results. When they overlap with the proposed changes, ask them to become vocal champions for those elements of the changes.

Build the campus culture. An early phase of implementing a new evaluation method is to form a widely representative core committee (including administrators, full- and part-time faculty members, and students) to design the draft evaluation plan. The committee should consider the foundational criteria for the evaluative methods to be adopted, including details such as these:

- What is the institutional context and organizational structure (e.g., a small institution with a relatively flat organizational chart will approach new evaluation methods different from a large hierarchical institution)?
- What criteria define good online teaching? How do the local faculty members define good teaching (regardless of offering mode)?
- What methods can be used to measure these criteria?
- How often will these methods need to be conducted?
- Who is responsible for requesting the evaluations, setting them up, and running them? Whom can people contact if something doesn't go right?
- Who will have access to the results of the evaluations? For how long? Where and how will results be stored?
- Will each method of evaluation be performed for every faculty member? If not, can they opt in or opt out?
- Will tenure-line, full-time, and part-time faculty members be evaluated using identical or audience-specific methods?
- If low scores or ratings are observed, how can faculty members remedy them? Is remediation optional or required?
- Will there be penalties for receiving low scores or for not using remediative processes?

After a detailed plan has been drafted, it will be time to start the conversation with a fuller steering committee of stakeholders.

Bring together key stakeholders. Although it may be tempting to begin by crafting the messages by which new evaluation methods will be communicated, the first step is to identify all affected stakeholder groups who will be involved in the process. In addition to the ones who come immediately to mind—faculty members, students, other administrators—it may be useful to think of other groups who create, use, or consume the information created in a teaching-evaluation setting:

- Faculty support staff who actually administer the online evaluation instruments
- Departmental office staffers who tabulate results
- The larger student community, who often share informal rating instruments on sites such as RateMyProfessor.com
- Faculty members in their role as peers, who may be called on to provide informal assessment or who may be compared against their peer groups
- Accrediting bodies, who may wish to have access to data sets beyond the formal end-of-semester numbers
- Bargaining-unit representatives, who will want to know how results will be used and that results are relatively equivalent across evaluation and teaching media
- Alumni, who are a rich source of feedback about what they wished had been asked about their experiences and who, now that they are in the workplace, can provide insights to employers' needs from recent graduates

Although this is not an exhaustive list, it suggests that there may need to be several kinds of communications created and opportunities developed for separate stakeholder groups to examine and respond to any proposed teaching-evaluation methods. It also helps to overcome the silo effect by bringing many stakeholders into conversation with each other.

Create guidelines for evaluation processes. During the conversation with the stakeholder groups regarding the adoption of online-teaching evaluation methods, be sure to define the scope of the change. Some key questions to answer relate to the impact of the changes on various groups:

- What types of evaluation are performed and by whom (e.g., peer, administrative "visit," student ratings)?
- Are evaluations performed for every faculty member? If not, are they able to opt in or opt out?

- Who is responsible for requesting the evaluations, setting them up, and running them?
- Who has access to the results of the evaluations, for how long, and where and how are they stored?
- Whom can people contact if something doesn't go right?
- What process is in place for improvement and continued conversation about the new methods?

These kinds of questions and many more are likely to come up during the pre-implementation conversations, and administrators are wise to note and respond to them. Keeping a publicly accessible FAQ file (on the university's website, for example) helps to keep the boundaries of the change clear.

Also part of defining the scope is differentiating between online-teaching practices and online-course design. Just as the syllabus and textbook are not usually evaluated during a face-to-face teaching evaluation, make clear which observable teaching behaviors are part of the evaluation of online teaching.

Measure and compare. When you are actually implementing the evaluation program, remember to compare results against baselines and against competencies or other goal-oriented metrics. By basing evaluation outcomes on categories of teaching behaviors that are shared across course-delivery modes, it becomes more likely that comparative patterns can be discerned. First, comparisons can be made across the teaching life cycle of a single faculty member. We already compare faculty members against themselves over time for face-to-face courses.

Adding modality as a comparison factor adds to formative information that can be gleaned by faculty members to help show them their strengths and areas of opportunity for teaching improvement. Second, the outcomes and ratings of online teaching can be compared, over all, against similar measures for face-to-face learning across the institution. Significant opportunity exists for what we might call *intermodal cross-pollination*, in which demonstrated best practices in one delivery modality can cross over and be adapted for use in the other.

During the implementation, be sure to measure the process and outcomes using two different lenses: compare the results obtained using the new methods against the results obtained using the existing methods (if available), and—perhaps more important—compare the rate of adoption for the new methods against the current rate of usage for the existing methods. Using both sets of data gives a clearer picture of how much work is needed and where in order to maximize adoption and buy in among all stakeholders.

Plan for the future, as well. Include proposals about what kinds of training your institution will offer to faculty members as well as what support will be offered for off-campus professional development opportunities in the area of online teaching. Also create guidance for hiring new staff and faculty members who are skilled in online teaching techniques. It's great to support and train existing people, but moving toward a faculty composed of already-skilled online teachers helps to put a cap on the recurring training needs of the institution.

The Last Word

Our book ends where we began: with a focus on the core teaching behaviors that indicate quality instruction. Online teaching is a different endeavor than teaching in the face-to-face classroom. However, we can identify quantitative and qualitative evidence of good teaching in the online environment, and we can define how we will evaluate that teaching through several methods that together paint a rich and meaningful picture of what it means to be a good online teacher. Some day soon we expect that the evaluation practices we have shared here will lead to national standards for online teaching quality, much like our colleagues in the K–12 educational world have already adopted. We hope that readers will take the approaches we have outlined and test, refine, and share them back with the ever-growing community of online-education practitioners. Quality online teaching is a challenge to define, measure, and assess in a meaningful way. It is a challenge we should all be ready to meet.

Toward this end, we have condensed the lessons of this book even further into a single figure (Figure 12.1) that online-program administrators, staff, and faculty members can use to work through the evaluation setup, implementation, and review processes at a high level.

Online teaching has been happening in one form or another for more than twenty years now. Learners whom we would otherwise serve poorly—or perhaps not at all—can now avail themselves of a college education by shifting their interactions away from campus and freeing them from the clock. The cost of doing so is significant, both for our students and for us as teachers. We have to work harder to ensure that we communicate our ideas clearly. We are often obliged to tighten our own

FIGURE 12.1. ONLINE-TEACHING EVALUATION PROGRAM SEQUENCE

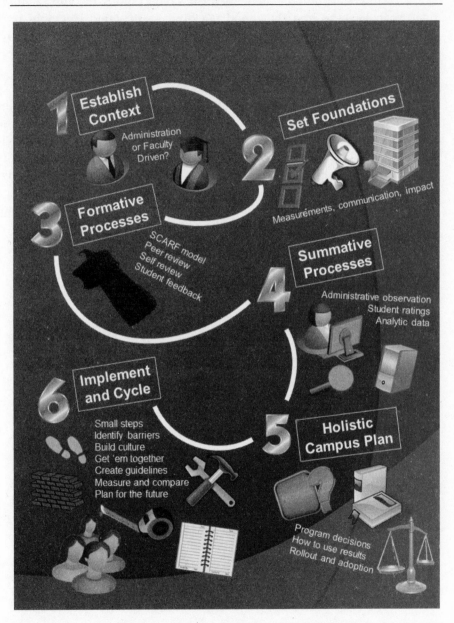

Note: All images public domain under CC0 license from pixabay.com.

time-management skills, and we, too, must reset our expectations about what it means to be in class (and when, and where, and how it takes place).

Even with all of the shifts in mind-set, approach, and technique, we can be reassured that good teaching is still good teaching, regardless of the medium in which it happens. We can take heart in knowing that more and more faculty members come into the profession having already taught online, and more and more campus leaders are making time to teach online, too. We hope that some of the cautions we have explored in this book (e.g., department chairs who need guides when they are evaluating online courses) will become less necessary over time and that they will eventually disappear, when online teaching is seen, rightly, as merely one more way to teach. Until then, however, we hope that readers will continue to advocate for greater knowledge and understanding about online teaching across their campuses, because the best way to share the quality work that we do in our online courses is to evaluate it and share the best practices with each other.

REFERENCES

Achtemeier, S. D., Morris, L. V., & Finnegan, C. L. (2003). Considerations for developing evaluations of online courses. *JALN: The Journal of Asynchronous Learning Networks, 7*(1). www.edtechpolicy.org/ArchivedWebsites/Articles/ConsiderationsDeveloping Evaluations.pdf

Allen, I. E., & Seaman, J. (2008). Staying the course: Online education in the United States. The Sloan Consortium and Babson Survey Research Group. www .sloan-c.org/publications/survey/pdf/staying_the_course.pdf

All-Faculty Association. (2012). Guide for evaluating online instruction at Santa Rosa Junior College. www.santarosa.edu/afa/Misc/guide_for_evaluating_online_ instruction.pdf

Arreola, R. A. (2007). *Developing a comprehensive faculty evaluation system* (3rd ed.). Bolton, MA: Anker Publishing.

Astin, A. W., Banta, T. W., Cross, K. P., El-Khawas, E., Ewell, P. T., Hutchings, P., Wright, B. D. (1996). 9 principles of good practice for assessing student learning. American Association for Higher Education (AAHE). www.academicprograms .calpoly.edu/pdfs/assess/nine_principles_good_practice.pdf

Baird, C., & Piña, A. [facilitators] (2014, June 11). Evaluating the evaluation of distance learning. Roundtable discussion session. Distance Learning Administration (DLA) annual conference. Jekyll Island, GA.

Baker, M. (2014, January 15). Re: course evaluations. *POD Listserv.* https://listserv.nd .edu/cgi-bin/wa?A2=ind1401andL=PODandF=andS=andP=87831

Bangert, A. W. (2008). The development and validation of the student evaluation of online teaching effectiveness. *Computers in the Schools, 25*(1–2), 25–47.

Bates, T. (2014). Online learning, faculty development and academic freedom. Online Learning and Distance Education Resources. www.tonybates.ca/2014/05/05/online-learning-faculty-development-and-academic-freedom/

Benton, S. L., & Cashin, W. E. (2011). Student ratings of teaching: A summary of research and literature. *IDEA Paper series, 1*(50). Manhattan: Kansas State University, Center for Faculty Evaluation and Development. www.theideacenter.org/sites/default/files/idea-paper_50.pdf

Berk, R. A. (2006). *Thirteen strategies to measure college teaching*. Sterling, VA: Stylus.

Berk, R. A. (2013b). Face-to-face versus online course evaluations: A "consumer's guide" to seven strategies. *MERLOT Journal of Online Learning and Teaching, 9*(1). http://jolt.merlot.org/vol9no1/berk_0313.htm

Berk, R. A. (2013a). *Top 10 flashpoints in student ratings and the evaluation of teaching*. Sterling, VA: Stylus Press. Bernstein, D. (2008, March/April). The review and evaluation of the intellectual work of teaching. *Change*, pp. 48–51.

Berquist, W. H., & Phillips, S. R. (1975). *A handbook for faculty development*. Dansville, NY: The Council for the Advancement of Small Colleges.

Betts, K. (2013). Lost in translation: Importance of effective communication in online education. *Online Journal of Distance Learning Administration, 16*(2). www.westga.edu/~distance/ojdla/summer122/betts122.html

Blackboard. (2003). *Blackboard exemplary course program rubric*. www.blackboard.com/getdoc/7deaf501–4674–41b9-b2f2–554441ba099b/2012-Blackboard-Exemplary-Course-Rubric.aspx

Bloom, B. S., Engelhart, M. D., Furst, E. J., Hill, W. H., & Krathwohl, D. R. (1956). *Taxonomy of educational objectives: The classification of educational goals. Handbook I: Cognitive domain*. New York: David McKay.

Bogen, G. K. (1978). Performance and vitality as a function of student-faculty fit. *New Directions for Institutional Research, 1*(20), 51–68.

Braskamp, L., & Ory, J. (1994). *Assessing faculty work: Enhancing individual and institutional performance*. San Francisco: Jossey-Bass.

Buller, J. (2012). *Best practices in faculty evaluation*. San Francisco: Jossey-Bass.

California State University Chico. (2009). The rubric for online instruction (ROI). www.csuchico.edu/roi/

Castley, A. J. (2005). Strengthening your reflective commentary. http://www2.warwick.ac.uk/services/ldc/resource/evaluation/tools/self/reflective.pdf

Center for Enhancement of Learning and Teaching. (2014). Formative peer review. Indiana University/Purdue University Fort Wayne. www.ipfw.edu/offices/celt/teaching-resources/formative-peer-review.html

Center for Teaching and Learning, Northeastern Illinois University. (2014). CTL online teaching course. http://homepages.neiu.edu/~ctl/workshops.html

Chatterji, M. (2003). *Designing and using tools for educational assessment*. Boston: Allyn & Bacon.

Chen, Y., & Hoshower, L. B. (2003). Student evaluation of teaching effectiveness: An assessment of student perception and motivation. *Assessment and Evaluation in Higher Education, 28*(1), 71–88.

Chickering, A., & Ehrmann, S. C. (1996). Implementing the seven principles: Technology as lever. *AAHE Bulletin, 49*, 3–6. www.tltgroup.org/programs/seven.html

Chickering, A., & Gamson, Z. (1987, June). Seven principles for good practice in undergraduate education. *The Wingspread Journal* (Special insert). Racine, WI: Johnson Foundation.

Chism, N. V. N. (2007). *Peer review of teaching: A sourcebook* (2nd ed.). Bolton, MA: Anker Publishing.

Cohen, J., Molnar, M., & Johnson, M. (2013, November 21). The 100 instructor dash: Leading the race towards meaningful faculty support and development. Presentation at the Sloan-C International Conference on Online Learning, Orlando, FL.

Columbus State Community College. (2009). Appendix F: Faculty online observation report. *Faculty Promotion and Tenure Handbook*, pp. 53–59. www.cscc.edu/about/faculty-staff/PDF/Faculty_Promotion and Tenure Handbook.pdf

Creasman, P. A. (2012). *Considerations in online course design.* Manhattan, KS: The IDEA Center. www.theideacenter.org/sites/default/files/idea_paper_52.pdf

Cruz, L. (2014, January 15). Re: course evaluations. *POD Listserv.* https://listserv.nd.edu/cgi-bin/wa?A2=ind1401andL=PODandF=andS=andP=94146

Culver, M. K. (2012). Analyzing the effectiveness of using a university course evaluation instrument to assess on-line course instruction. *JEP: eJournal of Educational Policy, 13*(2). http://nau.edu/uploadedFiles/Academic/COE/About/Projects/Analyzing the Effectiveness of Using a University Course Evaluation Instrument to Assess On.pdf

Dailey-Hebert, A., Mandernach, B. J., Donnelli-Sallee, E., & Norris, V. R. (2014). Expectations, motivations, and barriers to professional development: Perspectives from adjunct instructors teaching online. *Journal of Faculty Development, 28*, 67–82.

DeCristofaro, C., LeBaron, J., McGinty, D., Teslow, M., Crow, R., Sheffield, B., & Sisson, K. (2007). Online course assessment tool (OCAT) and peer assessment process. Version 2.0. eLearning Faculty Fellows. Western Carolina University. www.wcu.edu/WebFiles/PDFs/facultycenter_OCAT_v2.0_25apr07.pdf

DeVry University. (2009). Managing threaded discussions. www.nj.devry.edu/PDFs/Managing_Discussions_Tutorial.pdf

DiStefano, A., & Witt, J. (2010). Leadership and management of online learning environments in universities. In K. E. Rudestam & J. Schoenholtz-Read (Eds.), *Handbook of online learning* (2nd ed., pp. 404–422). Los Angeles: SAGE Publications.

Dobbins, K. (2011). Reflections on SoTL by a casual lecturer: Personal benefits, long-term challenges. *International Journal for the Scholarship of Teaching and Learning, 5*(2), 1–4.

Dolan, V. L. B. (2011). The isolation of online adjunct faculty and its impact on their performance. *International Review of Research in Open and Distance Learning, 12*(2), 62.

Dommeyer, C. J., Baum, P., Hanna, R. W., & Chapman, K. (2004). Gathering faculty teaching evaluations by in-class and online surveys: Their effects on response rates and evaluations. *Assessment and Evaluation in Higher Education, 29*(5), 611–623.

Drouin, M. (2012). What's the story on evaluations of online teaching? In M. E. Kite (Ed.), *Effective evaluation of teaching: A guide for faculty and administrators* (pp. 60–70). Washington, DC: Society for the Teaching of Psychology. www.teachpsych.org/Resources/Documents/ebooks/evals2012.pdf

Ebert-May, D., Derting, T., Hodder, J., Momsen, J., Long, T., & Jardeleza, S. (2011). What we say is not what we do: Effective evaluation of faculty professional development programs. *BioScience, 61*(7). www.msu.edu/~ebertmay/Website Images/Publications/EbertMay et al_2011.pdf

Ellis, D. (2012). *Peer review of teaching: A holistic approach to the review of teaching.* Waterloo, ON: University of Waterloo, Centre for Teaching Excellence. https:// uwaterloo.ca/centre-for-teaching-excellence/teaching-resources/teaching-tips/ professional-development/reviewing-teaching/peer-review-teaching

Erickson, B. L., & Sorcinelli, M. D. (2012). The first meeting with the client. In K. T. Brinko (Ed.), *Practically speaking: A sourcebook for instructional consultants in higher education* (2nd ed.). Stillwater, OK: New Forums Press.

Fabry, D. and Marlaire, C. (2014). Personal interview. June 20.

Fierro, J., & Yankowy, B. (2011, September 19). Using data to effectively evaluate faculty and increase student success. Presentation at the Sloan-C International Conference on Online Learning, Orlando, FL.

Fink, L. D. (2008). Evaluating teaching: A new approach to an old problem. *To Improve the Academy: Resources for Faculty, Instructional, and Organizational Development, 26,* 3–21.

Ford, K. (2012, October 11). Faculty performance assessment using data and dashboards. Presentation at the Sloan-C International Conference on Online Learning, Orlando, FL.

Gaillard, F., Mitchell, S., & Kavota, V. (2006). Students, faculty, and administrators' perception of students' evaluations of faculty in higher education business schools. *Journal of College Teaching and Learning, 3*(8), 77–90.

Gardiner, L. R., Corbitt, G., & Adams, S. J. (2010). Program assessment: Getting to a practical how-to model. *Journal of Education for Business, 85,* 139–144. http:// stepsforassessment.com/uploads/Assessment_How_To_Paper.pdf

Gibbs, G., Habeshaw, S., & Habeshaw, T. (1997). *53 interesting ways to appraise your teaching* (2nd ed.). Bristol, UK: Technical and Educational Services.

Grand Canyon University. (2014). *A faculty evaluation metric* [unpublished white paper]. Phoenix, AZ.

Hanover Research Council. (2009). Best practices in online teaching strategies. www .uwec.edu/AcadAff/resources/edtech/upload/Best-Practices-in-Online-Teaching-Strategies-Membership.pdf

Hanz, P. J., & Nigro, F. (2005). Observing online classes. Academic Senate for California Community Colleges. www.asccc.org/node/176439

Hativa, N. (2013). *Student ratings of instruction: A practical approach to designing, operating, and reporting.* Lexington, KY: Oron Publications.

Hayek, C. (2012). How many faculty discussion posts each week? A simply delicious answer. *Faculty Focus* blog. www.facultyfocus.com/articles/online-education/how-many-faculty-discussion-posts-each-week-a-simply-delicious-answer/

Hutchings, P. (1996). The peer review of teaching: Progress, issues and prospects. *Innovative Higher Education, 20*(4), 221–234.

Ikanow. (2014, February 10). 8 proven steps to starting a big data analytics project. *Brilliant Decisions* blog. www.ikanow.com/8-proven-steps-to-starting-a-big-data-analytics-project/

Illar, T. (2014). Penn State quality assurance e-learning design standards. https:// weblearning.psu.edu/resources/penn-state-online-resources/qualityassurance/

Illinois Online Network and the Board of Trustees of the University of Illinois. (1998). QOCI rubric: A tool to assist in the design, redesign, and/or evaluation of online courses. www.ion.uillinois.edu/initiatives/qoci/docs/QOCIRubric.rtf

John A. Dutton e-Education Institute, College of Earth and Mineral Sciences, the Pennsylvania State University. (2013). Student rating of teaching effectiveness [SRTE] item choices. Penn State University. www.srte.psu.edu/SRTE_Items/

Johnson, G. J., Rosenberger, J. L., & Chow, M. (2014). The importance of "setting the stage": Maximizing the benefits of peer review of teaching. *eLearn Magazine*. http://elearnmag.acm.org/archive.cfm?aid=2673801.

Johnson, L., Adams, S., & Cummins, M. (2012). *NMC horizon report: 2012 higher education edition*. Austin, TX: The New Media Consortium.

Johnson, T. (2002, April 3). Online student ratings: Will students respond? Paper presented at the annual meeting of the American Educational Research Association, New Orleans. www.armstrong.edu/images/institutional_research/onlinesurvey_will_students_respond.pdf

Kamin, B. (2014, May 11). Exhibit features bright lights, "big data." *Chicago Tribune*, p. A8.

Keeley, J. W. (2012). Choosing an instrument for student evaluation of instruction. In M. E. Kite (Ed.), *Effective evaluation of teaching: A guide for faculty and administrators* (pp. 13–21). Washington, DC: Society for the Teaching of Psychology.

Kelly, R. (2012, April 19). Reducing ambiguity, awkwardness in evaluating faculty. *Academic Leader. POD Listserv.* https://listserv.nd.edu/cgi-bin/wa?A2=ind1204andL=PODandF=andS=andP=96860

Langen, J. M. (2011). Evaluation of adjunct faculty in higher education institutions. *Assessment and Evaluation in Higher Education, 36*(2), 185–196.

Lattuca, L. R., & Domagal-Goldman, J. M. (2007). Using qualitative methods to assess teaching effectiveness. *New Directions for Institutional Research, 1*(136), 81–93.

Lavrakas, P. J. (2008). *Encyclopedia of survey research methods*. Los Angeles: SAGE Publications.

Linse, A. (2012, May 1). Re: Improving teaching eval response rates. *POD Listserv.* https://listserv.nd.edu/cgi-bin/wa?A2=ind1205andL=PODandF=andS=andP=51

Lyons, R. E. (2007). *Best practices for supporting adjunct faculty*. Boston: Anker Publishing.

Mandernach, B. J., Donnelli, E., Dailey, A., & Schulte, M. (2005). A faculty evaluation model for online instructors: Mentoring and evaluation in the online classroom. *Online Journal of Distance Learning Administration, 8*(3). www.westga.edu/~distance/ojdla/fall83/mandernach83.htm

Marble, T., & Case, P. (2013). Turbo-boost your onboarding of new online adjunct faculty. *Academic Leader, 29*(9), 6–7.

Marsh, H. W. (1982). SEEQ: A reliable, valid, and useful instrument for collecting students' evaluations of university teaching. *British Journal of Educational Psychology, 52*(1), 77–95.

MarylandOnline. (2004). Quality Matters rubric standards. www.qualitymatters.org/files/Matrix of Research Standards FY0506_0.pdf

MarylandOnline. (2009). Underlying principles of Quality Matters. www.qualitymatters.org/research-grants/fipse/principles

MarylandOnline. (2013). Quality Matters program: Rubric. www.qualitymatters.org/rubric

MarylandOnline. (2014). Quality Matters rubric standards fifth edition, 2014, with assigned point values. http://www.QMprogram.org

McCarthy, S., & Samors, R. (2009). *Online learning as a strategic asset* (*2* vols.). APLU-Sloan National Commission on Online Learning. http://sloanconsortium.org/publications/survey/APLU_Reports

McCullom, D. (2010). Best practices for online teaching. *Best Online Instructional Practices Study*. Batimore, MD: University of Maryland University College (UMUC) Institute for Research and Assessment in Higher Education (IRAHE). www.umuc.edu/facultydevelopment/upload/bestpractices.pdf

McGahan, S., Jackson, C., & Premer, K. (2014a). Gaining buy-in for the evaluation of online teaching: Unionized campus considerations. [unpublished white paper]. University of Nebraska at Kearney.

McGahan, S., Jackson, C., & Premer, K. (2014b). The process of adopting an evaluation of online teaching. [unpublished white paper]. University of Nebraska at Kearney.

McInnis, C. (2002). The impact of technology on faculty performance and its evaluation. *New Directions for Institutional Research, 1*(114), 53–61.

Mueller, B., Mandernach, B. J., & Sanderson, K. (2013). Adjunct versus fulltime faculty: Comparison of student outcomes in the online classroom. *Journal of Online Learning and Teaching, 9*(3), 341–352.

Mueller, L. (2014). Re: Issues concerning mid-semester administration of end-of-semester student surveys? *POD Listserv*. https://listserv.nd.edu/cgi-bin/wa?A2=ind1408&L=POD&F=&S=&P=53068

New Leadership Alliance for Student Learning and Accountability. (2012). Committing to quality guidelines for assessment and accountability in higher education. www.chea.org/alliance_publications/committing to quality-3rd edition.pdf

Norris, J., & Conn, C. (2005). Investigating strategies for increasing student response rates to online-delivered course evaluations. *Quarterly Review of Distance Education, 6*, 13–29.

Nulty, D. D. (2008). The adequacy of response rates to online and paper surveys: What can be done? *Assessment and Evaluation in Higher Education, 33*(3), 301–314.

Office of the Registrar, University of Oregon. (2014). Response rates and accuracy of online course evaluations. http://registrar.uoregon.edu/course_evaluations/accuracy_and_validity

Palese-Sanderson, K. & Mandernach, B. J. (2015). Data analytics and predictive modeling: The future of evaluating online teaching. *eLearn Magazine*. http://elearnmag.acm.org/archive.cfm?aid=2696534.

Palloff, R. M., & Pratt, K. (2011). *The excellent online instructor: Strategies for professional development*. San Francisco: Jossey-Bass.

Patrick, F. (2010). The third question: How to make change happen? *Focused Performance* blog. www.focusedperformance.com/how-to.html

Peltier, J. W., Schibrowski, J. A., & Drago, W. (2007). The interdependence of the factors influencing the perceived quality of the online learning experience: A causal model. *Journal of Marketing Education, 29*(2), 140–153.

Penn State Online Faculty Engagement Subcommittee. (2011). Guidelines for selecting an instructor for an online course. www.e-education.psu.edu/files/sites/file/taylor/HiringGuidelines_OnlineInstructor.pdf

The Pennsylvania State University. (1985). Statement of practices for the evaluation of teaching effectiveness for promotion and tenure. www.psu.edu/dept/vprov/pdfs/srte_statement.pdf

The Pennsylvania State University. (2004). Guidelines for use and administration of the student rating of teaching effectiveness (SRTE) forms. www.psu.edu/dept/vprov/pdfs/srte_guidelines.pdf

The Pennsylvania State University. (2007). *Innovation insights: How to use focus groups to solicit ideas and feedback*. University Park, PA: Office of Planning and Institutional Assessment, The Pennsylvania State University.

The Pennsylvania State University. (2014). Web learning @ Penn State: The official web presence of the Penn State online initiative. https://weblearning.psu.edu/

Pettifor, L. (2012). Self-evaluation. Warwick University Learning and Development Centre. www2.warwick.ac.uk/services/ldc/resource/evaluation/tools/self/

Picciano, A. G. (2012). The evolution of big data and learning analytics in American higher education. *Journal of Asynchronous Learning Networks, 16*(3), 9–20.

Piña, A., & Bohn, L. (2013, December 7). Quality online teaching is critical to student success: How do we evaluate it? Southern Association of Colleges and Schools Commission on Colleges annual conference, Atlanta, GA. www.sacscoc.org/annmtg/2013/annmtgcd/Sunday/CS-35Pina.pdf

Piña, A., & Bohn, L. (2014). Assessing online faculty: More than student surveys and design rubrics. *Quarterly Review of Distance Education, 15*(3), 25–34.

Rosenbloom, S. (2014, August 24). Dealing with digital cruelty. *New York Times*, p. SR1. www.nytimes.com/2014/08/24/sunday-review/dealing-with-digital-cruelty.html

Rothman, T., Romeo, L., Brennan, M., & Mitchell, D. (2011). Criteria for assessing student satisfaction with online courses. *International Journal for e-Learning Security, 1*(1–2), 27–32. www.infonomics-society.org/IJeLS/Criteria for Assessing Student Satisfaction with Online Courses.pdf

Russell, T. L. (2001). *The no significant difference phenomenon* (5th ed.). Montgomery, AL: The International Distance Education Certification Center. www.nosignificantdifference.org/

Savery, J. (2005). Be VOCAL: Characteristics of successful online instructors. *Journal of Interactive Online Learning, 4*(2), 141–152. www.ncolr.org/jiol/issues/pdf/4.2.6.pdf

Schaffhauser, D. (2014, August). 12 essentials of prescriptive analytics. *Campus Technology Magazine, 27*(12), 11–14. http://campustechnology.realviewdigital.com/?i=August%202014#folio=11

Schulz, K. (2014, April 7). Final forms. *New Yorker*, pp. 32–37.

Seldin, P. (1980). *Successful faculty evaluation programs: A practical guide to improve faculty performance and promotion/tenure*. Crugers, NY: Coventry Press.

Seymour, E., Carroll, S., & Weston, T. (2007). *Student assessment of their learning gains (SALG)*. www.salgsite.org/

Shelton, K. (2011). A review of paradigms for evaluating the quality of online education programs. *Online Journal of Distance Learning Administration, 14*(1). www.westga.edu/~distance/ojdla/spring141/shelton141.html

Shreckengost, J. (2013, October 10). Proactively guiding instructor performance through the use of a performance dashboard and real-time data. Presentation at the Sloan-C International Conference on Online Learning, Orlando, FL.

Southern Association of Colleges and Schools Commission on Colleges (SACS COC). (2012). Credit hours: Policy statement. www.sacscoc.org/subchg/policy/CreditHours.pdf

Stewart, I., Hong, E., & Strudler, N. (2004). Development and validation of an instrument for student evaluation of the quality of web-based instruction. *American Journal of Distance Education, 18*(3), 131–150.

Sunal, D. W., & Sunal, C. S. (2002). Checklist for online interactive learning (COIL). MacEwan University. https://facultycommons.macewan.ca/wp-content/plugins/download-monitor/download.php?id=Checklist-for-Online-Interactive-Learning1.doc

Taylor, A. H. (2010). A peer review guide for online courses at Penn State. http://facdev.e-education.psu.edu/evaluate-revise/peerreviewonline

Taylor, A. H. (2011). Faculty competencies for online teaching. Penn State Online. Faculty Engagement Subcommittee. www.e-education.psu.edu/files/OnlineTeachingCompetencies_FacEngagementSubcommittee.pdf

Taylor-Powell, E. (1996). Questionnaire design: Asking questions with a purpose. *Program Development and Evaluation* series. University of Wisconsin-Extension. Madison, WI: Cooperative Extension Publications.

Theall, M. (2012a, September 18). Re: Student evaluations of instructors sample. *POD Listserv.* https://listserv.nd.edu/cgi-bin/wa?A2=ind1209andL=PODandF=andS=andP=104678

Theall, M. (2012b, October 31). Re: Observing online courses. *POD Listserv.* https://listserv.nd.edu/cgi-bin/wa?A2=ind1210andL=PODandF=andS=andP=199558

Tobin, T. J. (2004). Best practices for administrative evaluation of online faculty. *Online Journal of Distance Learning Administration, 7*(2). www.westga.edu/~distance/ojdla/summer72/tobin72.html

University Professionals of Illinois Local 4100 and Northeastern Illinois University Board of Trustees. (2009). Collective bargaining agreement. www.neiu.edu/DOCUMENTS/Faculty_Staff/Faculty_Resources/Policies/CBA.pdf

Varvel, V. (2007). Master online teacher competencies. *Online Journal of Distance Learning Administration, 10*(1). www.westga.edu/~distance/ojdla/spring101/varvel101.htm

Wagner, E. (2014, August 28). 3 questions to ask before implementing predictive analytics for online student success [audio podcast]. *Academic Impressions Higher Ed Impact* blog. www.academicimpressions.com/news/3-questions-ask-implementing-predictive-analytics-online-student-success

Walvoord, B. E. (2004). *Assessment clear and simple.* San Francisco: Jossey-Bass.

Weaver, R. R., & Qi, J. (2005). Classroom organization and participation: College students' perceptions. *Journal of Higher Education, 76*(5), 570–601.

West, E. (2010). Managing adjunct professors: Strategies for improved performance. *Academy of Educational Leadership Journal, 14*(4), 21–36.

Wilkerson, L., & Karron, G. L. (2002). Classroom observation: The observer as collaborator. In K. H. Gillespie (Ed.), *A guide to faculty development* (pp. 74–81). Bolton, MA: Anker Publishing.

Wlodkowski, R. J. (2003). Accelerated learning in colleges and universities. *New Directions for Adult and Continuing Education, 97,* 5–15.

INDEX

D

E